Literature
Study
in the
High Schools

Literature
Study
in the
High Schools

REVISED EDITION

Dwight L. Burton

FLORIDA STATE UNIVERSITY

Holt, Rinehart and Winston, Inc.

New York • *Chicago* • *San Francisco* • *Toronto* • *London*

37239

Preface 1965

The study of literature must remain at the heart of the English curriculum in the secondary schools, for it is only through a literature-centered program that the course in English retains its identity as a humanistic experience. Since the publication of the original edition of this book, much of the activity in the teaching of English has been directed, on the national scene, to written composition and English language structure. As important as these components are, a de-emphasis on literature may reduce the English course to a mere utilitarian status and deprive millions of young people of real contact with the humanistic tradition.

When one speaks of teaching literature in the secondary school, he is making a very broad statement, for the difference in ways and means of teaching literature in an average seventh-grade class and in an honors twelfth-grade class, for example, is dramatic. The literary education—including not only "reading skills," "fun with books," "leisure reading," or even "acquaintance with the literary tradition," but all of these and more—represents a wide continuum across the secondary school years, and the prospective teacher must be ready to play a role at any point on this continuum. Too often, serious study of literature is postponed until the senior high school years without the vital transitional preparation in the junior high school.

The prospective teacher of English needs a more detailed treatment of the problems of teaching literature in the secondary school than is feasible in the comprehensive books—and there are several excellent ones—on the teaching of secondary school English. This book is designed first, then, as a resource for students in courses in the teaching of English in the secondary school. Second, it is designed as a textbook for courses in literature for adolescents or for young adults. A significant amount of space in the book is given to analysis and survey of literature written expressly for adolescents, literature that has an important function as a means to an end in the earlier years of the secondary school. The book attempts to develop the structure of a literature program from the beginnings in the junior high school to the advanced level in the senior high school.

A book devoted to the full range of the literary experiences among adolescents in America could not fail to pay tribute to the work of Dr. Dora V. Smith, even if this great educator had not been the personal inspiration for the author's attention to literature study for adolescents. In addition, the original edition and the present revision were created in part from suggestions and comments from the author's colleagues on his own campus and across the country, including Lois Arnold, Robert Bennett, Samuel Blount, Stephen Dunning, Barbara Goleman, Stanley Kegler, Otis McBride, Joseph Mersand, Paul Jacobs, Helen Rosenblum, John Simmons, James Squire, David Stryker, and Elizabeth White. Especially is the author indebted to John A. Myers, Jr., and Gladys Veidemanis, who contributed the revised chapters on the teaching of poetry and of drama.

D. L. B.

Tallahassee, Florida
December 1963

Contents

WHAT SHOULD LITERATURE DO FOR ADOLESCENTS?

LITERATURE STUDY should result in an enriched life. A successful high school program in literature need accept nothing less as its major outcome. Yet progress toward this outcome involves a complex educational undertaking. Complex but not at all impossible —though "impossible" sometimes occurs to teachers as a proper description. At times all teachers have felt that esthetic values and the restless class of tenth-graders, seemingly preoccupied with football games and party dresses, were startlingly out of harmony. Contemplation of man's condition, which literature can afford, or the search for identity, in which literature can be a crucial vehicle, may seem completely unconnected with the fifth-period class on a warm May (or cold December) afternoon. Gangling Freddy may appear only concerned with the condition of his hot rod, and the bored brunette with the svelte hairdo may appear quite positive about *her* identity.

Such surface realities account for the penchant of some teachers to intone the familiar jeremiad concerning the "decline of the humanities." This is one form of giving up. Its defense mechanism is the teacher's self-picture of himself as a knight-errant standing guard at the gate of culture. Grimly he proceeds with a junior version of the seminar he took at graduate school.

There is another form of giving up: the teacher interprets too loosely the basically sound but hackneyed educational dictum "start where the students are." He organizes units on "Modern Transportation" for the Freddys and on "Grooming and Home Decoration" for the brunettes, no matter whether the units have anything to do with literature, and devotes Fridays to "free reading" in which Freddy can remain with *Popular Mechanics* and the brunette with *Vogue*.

This book assumes, however, that most teachers of literature in junior and senior high schools fit somewhere between these extremes. In these teachers lies great hope for society as well as for the millions of adolescents who each year study something called "literature."

The teacher of literature needs to remain forever practical and idealistic at the same time. His practicality will enable him to understand Freddy and the brunette and to deal with them realistically. His idealism will keep his attention centered on what literature, the principal skein of the humanities in the secondary school, can do for adolescents, even Freddy and the brunette. Obviously, the teacher must know both adolescents and literature, and his admixture of practicality and idealism will enable him to bring the two into consonance. What can literature do for adolescents? How can the realities of the classroom be so manipulated that literature will have the best chance of doing these things? These are the constant—and interlocking—questions.

Immediately a problem arises: teachers' motives and students' motives may come into conflict. The principal motive of the adolescent (and of most adults) in reading literature is to gain enjoyment —now. The teacher's major motive, too, may be that the student enjoy literature, but he may place the stress on the student's *coming* to enjoy it. And it may or may not pain him that, at the moment, Freddy does not associate enjoyment with his study of literature, for, if the important things are to be accomplished, teaching and learning must go on in the literature class. Enjoyment per se does not necessarily indicate the kind of heightening experience that most teachers want to bring about.

Yet it seems wise to consider the rewards that literature can bring to the student *now,* as well as the delayed ones, and to make these count in the gradual process that is the literary education.

Since publication of Bruner's book, *The Process of Education*,[1] there has been much discussion of the "structure" of disciplines and school subjects. Literary scholars seem to agree that the structure of literature is to be found in its recurrent themes and modes and in its various forms or genres. Perhaps no two lists of recurrent themes would agree precisely, but literature of all time is concerned with four basic humanistic relationships—man and deity, man and other men, man and nature, and man and his inner self. These might be considered the basic themes that give structure to literature.

Four basic modes have also been identified: romantic, comic, tragic, and ironic.[2] Aspects of the four basic themes may be dealt with in any of these modes. Finally, any of the literary genres may be cast in any of the four modes or deal with any of the four basic themes. Perhaps, then, the basic structure of literature might be diagramed in this way:

MAN AND DEITY (or MAN AND OTHER MEN,
MAN AND NATURE, MAN AND HIS INNER SELF)

ROMANTIC MODE (or COMIC MODE, TRAGIC MODE,
IRONIC MODE)

LYRIC POEM (or SHORT STORY, NOVEL,
DRAMA, . . .)

SPECIFIC SELECTION

The structure of literature, along with the immediate and long-range rewards that literature study can bring to the student, provides the touchstone for the planning of programs at any school level. Three dimensions define a full program: the developmental dimension, which concerns the role of literature in providing personal delight and insight into human experience; the humanistic dimension, which concerns the role of literature in bringing youth into contact with a cultural tradition; and the dimension of form, which concerns the understanding of genres and development of skill in reading them.

[1] Jerome Bruner, *The Process of Education* (Cambridge, Mass.: Harvard University Press, 1960).

[2] Northrop Frye (Ed.), *Design for Learning* (Toronto: University of Toronto Press, 1962).

Developmental Dimension

Vicarious Experience

At any age, people have a basic need to live life more fully than the boundaries of direct experience make possible. Vicarious experience is a basis for escape, universally necessary as an antidote to routine living, and although reading is only one avenue of escape, it has always been one of the most important. The escape function of literature is not, of course, the one with which the teacher is most concerned. This escape function is not only a legitimate one in itself; it also is linked importantly with more significant functions of literature.

Even in so-called "escape" reading, we are coming to terms with experience at the same time that we are escaping from it. There is particular significance, for example, in the adolescent boy's zest for stories of outdoor adventure, whether laid in the northern forest, in the deep jungle, in the old West, or on the sea. All these locales represent freedom from the complexities of social machinery. Men, or perhaps animals, survive here by individual strength and wit. Through projection into these stories the young reader tries himself out vicariously, as he must inevitably in reality. And his ultimate test will be a lonely one—even though he is surrounded by people—in company with Beowulf, Macbeth, Sir Lancelot, Huckleberry Finn, and Santiago in Hemingway's *The Old Man and the Sea*.

Literature is immediately rewarding to most readers, too, in its power to extend actual experience. Within one's literal little world there simply is not enough of the kind of experience he craves, especially in adolescence. In its function of extending experience, literature offers the chance for adolescents to play roles, to try themselves out. G. Robert Carlsen writes that young people "come to a semi-integrated picture of themselves as human beings. They want to test this picture of themselves in many kinds of roles that it is possible for a human being to play. . . . He [the adolescent] wants to know what it would feel like to be a murderer, even though he is not planning to be one. He wants to know what it feels like to give one's life to religion, to be corrupt in politics."[3] In a sense,

[3] G. Robert Carlsen, "Behind Reading Interests," *English Journal*, XLIII (January 1954), 10.

then, literature functions as preparation for experience. Thus, a fourteen-year-old girl may enjoy reading of a seventeen-year-old girl's experiences in going steady more than may the seventeen-year-old reader. Intense experiences with immature books such as junior novels are valuable in themselves, but they also furnish links with more significant literary experiences later.

Only as the pupil's study of literature progresses is he able to make the abstract identifications that may be required in reading mature works of literature, and to identify himself actively with a person of a different age, sex, race, or nationality, who may live in a time far past. For this reason, teachers have found that use of literature written expressly for adolescents, a considerable body of which has been built up in the last thirty years, is important in the literary education of the adolescent. Some critics have deplored juvenile books as a "subliterary" species and have bewailed "lowering of standards" in the school program when pupils are encouraged to read anything but "classics." But juvenile literature, like adult literature in general, has its quota of memorable as well as of trashy selections, and use of the better juvenile titles in the literature program does not indicate "lowering of standards" unless the teacher is content to make the juvenile selection the standard fare throughout the high school years.

The early adolescent, the junior high school student, thirsts for action, and the vicarious experience he seeks—whether as a viewer of motion picture or television, as a spectator in the bleachers, or as a reader—is action-packed. His thirst for action is often not satisfied by the prescribed reading in his classes. He is addicted at this time to hero worship of the man (or woman) of action; and Dick Tracy and Marshal Dillon may represent a kind of wish fulfillment that can easily mellow into zest for the quality westerns, outdoor adventures, sea tales, mysteries. The boys, especially, are interested in stories of sports action; many of them in junior high are still confidently planning to pitch for the Yankees or play halfback for the state university. Sports stories, such as those by John Tunis, C. Paul Jackson, and Philip Harkins, are popular. And again, the interest in these "subliterary" materials may be important steppingstones to the appreciation of more enduring works. For it is an easy step from the sports novels of Tunis to biographies of men of action in other fields—for example, Mildred Pace's *Clara Barton,* James

Daugherty's *Daniel Boone,* Geoffrey Trease's *Sir Walter Raleigh.* In the senior high school, the step may be to excellent nonfiction about more mature arenas of adventure: the mountain climbing of *Annapurna,* the sea adventure of *Kon-Tiki,* the underwater exploration of Jacques-Yves Cousteau, Frédéric Dumas, and Philippe Diolé —all of these illustrating man's age-old obligation to live dangerously, an obligation that reduces the distance between King Arthur's knights and Freddy, the hot-rodder in the tenth-grade class.

Then, too, man—and the adolescent species thereof—is fundamentally a curious creature. Vicarious experience, especially that obtained through reading, helps him to satisfy his curiosity. This dramatic age of mechanical and scientific advance, of speed and the conquering of distance, poses daring questions and daring answers. Not only is there the ever-enlarging realm of science fiction but the body of nonfiction dealing with man's efforts to reduce the limits of his universe. Our junior high school student (and perhaps senior high school student and adult!) is keenly aware that he may well live to travel to the moon.

The early adolescent, especially, tends to be completely audacious in his beliefs. His fascination with the bizarre is the steppingstone from child fantasy to the eternal adult awe of the unknown and occult. The slimy, crypt-dwelling monster of the comic book, which has aroused so much adult censure, is simply the creature of this intermediate stage of development and is presented at a higher level of artistry by Edgar Allan Poe, one of the favorite storytellers of adolescents. The channel of interest can lead from the Black Lagoon type of creature to Stevenson's *Dr. Jekyll and Mr. Hyde,* Coleridge's "Christabel," and James's "The Turn of the Screw." Inherent in the human being are depths of curiosity that cannot be satisfied by newspaper headlines or television broadcasts. But these depths must be plumbed, else this curiosity will be lost to the television or motion-picture screen, where the ordering of experience seldom reaches that on the printed page.

In its function as vicarious experience, then, literature can do much to meet the need for escape from the confines of the moment and to satisfy the adolescent's thirst for action and his inherent curiosity. Perhaps, in a sense, all the functions of literature could be subsumed under "vicarious experience." But because literature is an *ordering* and *synthesizing* of experience, it can give a dimension essential to maturity of mind and "the flexible but penetrating awareness of the human situation, sometimes gay, sometimes grave, that we call wisdom."[4]

Insight into Human Experience

Few adolescent readers would admit, however, that they were reading or studying literature in order to gain wisdom. But whether they admit it or not, adolescents are engaged in the cradle-to-grave search for identity, the quest for the "I," and their greatest need is for the resources of mind and spirit necessary for coming to terms with life. Inchoate aspiration for these resources marks adolescence, and to the extent that the study of literature relates to this aspiration will it be important to the adolescent.

Literature has a unique capacity for revealing the truth of human experience. A book or a story or a play or a poem may help to ease what James Street called "just the damn hurt of youth, which I contend is not a happy time, but a rather terrifying time of doubts." In the struggle to grow up, inherent in adolescence, literature can play a major role.

AWARENESS OF THE COMPLEXITY OF HUMAN CHARACTER. Growing up involves fundamentally a developing understanding of human nature. A principal touchstone of maturity is the awareness of the complexity of human nature. Characters in good literature, whether real people in nonfiction or people artistically created in fiction, exemplify the complexity of human motivation. The mysteries of personality are explored in literature—as in life—beginning with the child's first exposure to it. Even the characters of the nursery rhymes, for the most part, are people of fault as well as of virtue. Commentaries on the human species, its nobility and its foibles, come early in the reading experience of some children who may read, in the elementary school years, something like Kenneth Grahame's memorable *Wind in the Willows*.

---

[4] Robert B. Heilman, "Literature and Growing Up," *English Journal*, XLV (September 1956), 309.

It is no wonder that *Huckleberry Finn* has been translated into virtually every language known to man. For Huck represents universal adolescence as he discovers the complexity of his own motivations in his battle of conscience about whether to turn Jim over to the authorities. His tortured conclusion, "All right, I'll go to hell!" echoes every adolescent's painful conviction regarding his own dark and lonely thoughts.

Certainly, even the junior high school is not too early for the pupil to come to grips with the most pervasive of all themes in human experience—the struggle between good and evil. In *Tom Sawyer,* Mark Twain was concerned with this struggle and with the rendezvous with evil which is the inevitable destiny of the person growing up. Tom's rendezvous is traumatic—the stabbing scene in the graveyard—as was Mark Twain's own, since he had witnessed a real stabbing near his home in Hannibal, Missouri, an event that caused him nightmares for many weeks. This rendezvous with evil is dramatized impressively, too, in contemporary novels for adolescents. For example, in Paul Annixter's *Swiftwater,* a boy fights and finally kills a wolverine he encounters on his father's trapline. The wolverine here symbolizes evil, and it waits inescapably along the boy's path of responsibility.

In a real sense, a book like *Swiftwater,* read well in the eighth grade, is good preparation for later reading of, say, Thomas Hardy, who "writes on the dark side," as Virginia Woolf put it, frequently leaving his characters on twilight moors to look alone on the gaunt face of destiny. The student needs to be introduced early to the necessity of reading simultaneously at literal and abstract or allegorical levels in order to realize that one of the major functions of literature is to turn events into ideas.

Awareness of the complexity of human personality is gained partly, too, through reflecting on the factors of greatest moment in the human drama, no matter what the individual's station in life. Courage, for example, is one of these factors. It is of great concern to the adolescent who realizes that he must test and try the depths of his own courage in coming to terms with himself, his environment, his fellows, his universe, his god. This inward reaching is exhibited by the hero of Armstrong Sperry's *Call It Courage,* who has to prove his courage to himself and others; by the protagonist who has to make his separate peace with life in John Knowles's *A Separate Peace;* by Anne Frank, who had to accept a martyr's role she never wanted.

AWARENESS OF THE CLASH OF VALUES. Adolescents are becoming aware, sometimes bewilderingly, of the spirit that impels men. Literature, as a humanistic study, is necessarily concerned with human values. Underlying its study are such eternal questions as these: What is the good life? What do men do with their lives? What do men live by and for?

Selections of literature, from Chaucer's *Canterbury Tales* to James Michener's *The Bridges at Toko-Ri* and Archibald MacLeish's *J.B.,* dramatize what men live, and perhaps die, for. Biography plays an important part here. Careers as diverse as those of Albert Schweitzer, Jane Addams, Lord Nelson, Mary of Scotland, and Louis Armstrong illustrate what real people have made of life under varying conditions.

Literature reveals the revolt of men against some of the values of their culture. In his monograph *Freud and the Crisis of Our Culture,* Lionel Trilling says: "The function of literature, through all its mutations, has been to make us aware of the particularity of selves, and the high authority of the self in its quarrel with its society and its culture." Twelfth-graders studying a unit on "Man in Revolt," in which selections as varied as Shelley's "Ode to the West Wind" and Lewis' *Babbitt* might be read, are made aware of the relation of their own time to the tradition of protest against conditions that diminish man and his spirit.

With regard to revolt, traditionally associated with youth, the adolescent is in a paradoxical position. On the one hand, he is a rebel against adult authority and certain adult values; on the other, he is a slavish conformist within his own peer culture. In truth, the timeless conflict between conformity and individuality is a genuine concern of his. This conflict furnishes the theme for many selections of literature, past and present.

AWARENESS OF THE COMMONNESS OF THE HUMAN DRAMA. Another awareness, too, is important in the struggle to come to terms with life. Major problems, whether of an individual or a society, lie in the reaches that stretch between man and man. Our comfort is prey to John Donne's seventeenth-century admonition, "No man is an island." Literature plays an important part in developing awareness of the commonness of the human drama. What an impact a novel has when the reader finds in it a fellow sufferer, one who obviously knows "what it is like"!

Of course no one, least of all the adolescent, seeks to be depressed. Yet a feeling for the tragic elements in experience provides a needed tempering of the spirit, an attuning to the "still, sad music of humanity" that Wordsworth heard, and it is all to the good for adolescents to feel, for example, the slash of the sleety New England wind in *Ethan Frome*. Tragedy, after all, makes suffering bearable by making it understandable, and understanding of tragedy should be an aim of the senior high school literature program. Students may often finish their reading of *Macbeth* without really understanding why it is a tragedy when good triumphs at the end. Certainly, an understanding can be developed of the difference between tragic and "sad" in the Hollywood connotation. Students can learn rather quickly that the "weepy" story is not necessarily the tragic one.

AWARENESS OF THE SIGNIFICANCE AND BEAUTY OF THE EVERYDAY. A criterion of the mature mind is the ability to perceive significance and beauty in the humdrum. Overwhelmingly, the television and movie screens, the radio, the popular magazines, and immature fiction feature one limited kind of experience—the exotic, melodramatic aspects in which few people can share directly. Prose and poetry that treat of everyday sights and sounds and people, and through which everyday experience can be evaluated, are the leavener in all this. A novel such as James Street's *Goodbye, My Lady* can do for the eighth-grader what all literature can do—illuminate beauty. And the junior high school student is more likely to associate beauty with a dog and the natural sounds of the swamp than with, say, a field of daffodils, but the beauty of the daffodils or a Grecian urn or a stand of birch trees or a brickyard by moonlight may become real later, through the alchemy of experience and verbal symbol, as the pupil develops that power of the "inward eye which is the bliss of solitude."

Incisive teaching is at a premium here. Most teachers have worked with students to get them to describe as exactly as possible what some commonplace thing feels like, smells like, looks like, without relying on empty general words or clichés. This is good training for reading, too, for students are likely to shrug off small details in selections of literature. One aim of literature study is to convince students of the truth of the statement that "anything significantly looked at is significant. And that is significant which teaches us something about our own life-capabilities. The function of detail when ordered by a human imagination is to illustrate the universe."[5]

The Humanistic Dimension

The humanistic dimension, in which students are brought into contact with a literary tradition, is in no conflict with the developmental dimension. The concerns of youth and the literary tradition come together at more joinings than the literature program has time for.

Contact with the literary tradition has been rather widely confused with exposure to certain anthologies or to certain lists of books. Yet the literary background presents so many possibilities that it is professional obtuseness to limit students to a narrow list of so-called "classics" or to introduce selections known to be deadly with students merely on the basis that exposure per se is beneficial. The chronological surveys of American and British literature prevalent in the eleventh and the twelfth grades are justified frequently on the basis of acquaintance with the tradition. The survey, of course, was inherited from the colleges in an earlier time, and there has been a trend in both colleges and high schools away from such "Cook's tours" in which undue emphasis may be placed on learning *about* literature at the expense of experience *with* literature. Certainly, high school students should have experience with superior examples of the various literary genres and modes drawn from American, British, *and* world literature. But contact with a

[5] John Ciardi, "The Morality of Poetry," *Saturday Review* (March 30, 1957), p. 14.

literary tradition cannot be defined in terms only of acquaintance with authors and titles. What is most important is contact with ideas that have engrossed man over the centuries: man versus nature; power versus intelligence; individuality versus conformity, for example. A literature program that introduces students to the ways in which these eternal problems are approached in literature of the past *and* present is bringing students into contact with a literary tradition.

The Dimension of Form

The various genres of literature are art forms, and the study of literature must necessarily involve study of these art forms. Form and idea, of course, never can be divorced. As teachers work with the modes, ideas, concepts, and effects in fiction, poetry, and drama, they must at the same time work with the means through which these modes, ideas, and concepts are expressed and these effects achieved. Awareness of the function of form in literature will come gradually from the time that the seventh-grader practices following a plot in fiction until the honors twelfth-grader works with symbolism in modern poetry.

It is important that concern with the dimension of form begin early on a realistic plane. The eighth-grader, for example, must learn to deal with such concrete symbolism as that of the coffee drinking related to growing up in James Street's *Goodbye, My Lady* if he is to be expected to understand, as an eleventh-grader, the color symbolism in Crane's *The Red Badge of Courage*.

This introductory chapter has been concerned with setting our goals in the literature programs for junior and senior high school students. If the rewards outlined in this chapter are to be grasped by the student, a gradual process of growth is necessary for him. This growth involves an increasing maturity in his response to literature. But it is necessary to see the forest *and* the trees. Where, then, do we start?

SELECTED REFERENCES

Alm, Richard S., "The Glitter and the Gold," *English Journal,* XLIV (September 1955), 315–322.
Identifies criteria for judging junior novels that treat personal problems.

Burton, Dwight L., "Reading Experiences to Help Adolescents in Their Search for the 'I'," *Improving Reading in the Junior High School* (Washington, D.C.: U.S. Office of Education, Bulletin 1957, No. 10), pp. 60–67.
Discusses "wellsprings" of reading interests in the junior high school.

———, "Teaching Literature to Our Youth Today," *English Journal,* XLIV (May 1955), 274–279.
Shows the vital relationship of reading skills to broad outcomes in the study of literature.

Carlsen, G. Robert, "Deep Down Beneath, Where I Live," *English Journal,* XLIII (May 1954), 235–239.
Discusses the role of literature in helping the adolescent to develop.

———, "The Dimensions of Literature," *English Journal,* XLI (April 1952), 179–186.
Discusses the various aspects, or dimensions, of literature that must be considered in the high school program.

Heilman, Robert B., "Literature and Growing Up," *English Journal,* XLV (September 1956), 303–313.
Analyzes the relationship of literary experience to the achievement of maturity of mind.

Loban, Walter, Margaret Ryan, and James Squire, "Discovery of Values," in *Teaching Language and Literature* (New York: Harcourt, 1961), pp. 600–630.
A remarkable discussion of the relationship of the development of values to literature and other aspects of the English curriculum.

Pollock, Thomas C., "Transmitting Our Literary Heritage," *English Journal,* XXXI (March 1942), 200–210.
A famous statement of the connection between teaching and the literary heritage and of the fallacies that beset teaching of literature.

"Report of the Literature Committee of the School and College Conference on English, April 1942," in G. W. Stone (Ed.), *Issues, Problems, and Approaches in the Teaching of English* (New York: Holt, Rinehart and Winston, 1961), pp. 41–66.
A thoughtful, thorough discussion of issues and problems in the teaching of literature.

Tovatt, Anthony L., "Two Basic Convictions about Teaching Literature," *English Journal,* XLIX (November 1960), 528–535.
A statement of the need to gear literary experiences to stages in the growth patterns of students.

WHERE
DO
WE START?

"START WHERE THEY ARE," though an educational cliché, is perhaps the best answer to the question posed in the title of this chapter. But where *is* the pupil in his potential for experience with literature when he begins the junior high school? The answer to this might vary greatly for individual pupils. But some important generalizations can be drawn about these young human beings who flock noisily into our seventh- and eighth-grade classrooms.

Most important, he is not averse to reading and he is eager for vicarious experience. In fact, voluntary reading may be more important to the seventh-grader than it ever was before or ever will be again, although, in general, he has not yet *studied* literature. Much of this reading, though, may be of material that sends chills down the spine of his English teacher—comic books, for example. Just before television became widespread—around 1949—one billion comic books were being sold each year, and the comic book topped the list in many studies of students' reading interests, especially of pupils in grades four to eight. The phenomenal appeal of the comic book in the years following the end of World War II stirred much public concern across the country. In one widely read book, *Seduction of the Innocent,* Fredric Wertham, a New York psychiatrist, contended that comic books promoted illiteracy, unwholesome states of mind, and delinquent behavior. The *Journal* of the National Education Association, in its November 1954 issue, designated Wertham's book as "the most important book of 1954," and admonished local education associations and parent-teacher groups to see that their communities took steps "to protect children from the menace it describes." Between 1945 and 1952, more than 250 essays and articles on the comics appeared in American periodicals, including *Saturday Review, Atlantic Monthly, New Yorker,* and the *American Scholar.* Even a Congressional committee dealt with the matter.

Nonetheless, publication of books for children and adolescents has been increasing constantly. Circulation of comic books has declined somewhat, partly because of attempts to suppress objectionable ones and partly because of the increasing influence of television. Today the junior high school pupil's principal source of vicarious experience is the television screen. According to a study in 1956,[1] elementary school pupils spent an average of twenty-one hours a week in televiewing, and high school pupils spent twelve. (Their parents, seventeen!) The time spent in televiewing had changed little in the years since television had become widespread, according to the study.

Basic Appeals of Popular Screen and Page

The vicarious experiences popular with the junior high school pupil—whether of television or motion-picture screen, comic book, or fiction—have certain common patterns of appeal. Some examination of these patterns is important for the teacher of literature. One obvious appeal of the comic book, the television program, and the popular magazine is that they require little effort, much less than the printed page of the ordinary book requires. Although the vocabulary in many comic books is not particularly easy, the actual text need not be read at all. Looking at the pictures and reading a few words here and there are enough. Capable readers may read as many comic books as poor readers, but the less able reader may be especially attracted to the comics if the required reading in class is continually beyond him. Little imaginative effort is needed in

[1] Paul Witty, "A Seventh Report on TV," *Elementary English,* XXXIII (December 1956), 523–528.

televiewing or reading comic books. There is no need to conjure up images in the mind's eye. The situations and characters, complete with bulging biceps and golden tresses or with obviously evil visages, are there already. These media may be a deterrent to real play of the imagination.

Though comic books apparently are losing popularity among early adolescents, certain other types of magazines that give no more comfort to the teacher may be gaining favor. One study showed that of the preferred magazines for leisure-time reading among ninth-graders in a suburban Los Angeles community, *Dig, Mad, Horror,* and *Seventeen* led the list.[2] *Seventeen* often contains excellent fiction and nonfiction and there is nothing objectionable about *Mad,* but *Playboy* and *Escapade* tied for twelfth place. Somewhat different—and perhaps more reassuring—results came from a survey of the preferred magazines of the eighth-graders in one Tallahassee, Florida, school. Two or more of the boys in the group read regularly the following magazines, which are listed in order of popularity: *Mad, Boys' Life, Life,* boating magazines, sports magazines, *Outdoor Life, Saturday Evening Post, Field and Stream, True, Popular Science.* Two or more of the girls regularly read the following, in order of popularity: *Mad, Calling All Girls, Seventeen,* movie magazines, family magazines, *Look, Saturday Evening Post, Life, Boys' Life, Teen,* love magazines.

The content of popular television programs, comic books, and magazines is highly compatible with the nature of early adolescents. The major types of comic books, television programs, and magazines popular with junior high school pupils feature themes of horror and crime, western adventure, the fantastic, animal adventure, physical disaster, and for girls, love. Common to all of them are the magic ingredients of action—suspense, mystery, and adventure—adding up to "punch" in the mind of the young reader. The zest for the fantastic or bizarre, cited in the first chapter, is capitalized on. Also, the main television-program or comic-book characters tend to be either supermen, who represent a kind of ideal fulfillment, or simpletons to whom the reader can feel superior. Al Capp, the creator of the famous Li'l Abner, once remarked, "When Yokum speaks, he speaks for millions of morons."

[2] John Q. Adams, "A Study of the Leisure-Time Reading of Ninth-Grade Students," *High School Journal,* XLVI (November 1962), 67–72.

The appeal of the comic-book popular-television level of experi-ence is rooted, too, in the fact that its picture of life and the as-sumptions underlying it are naturally acceptable to the immature mind of the reader or viewer. Life is an exciting physical adventure or should be; heroism and courage are measured in physical daring —this is one assumption. Another is that people are either good or bad. Often one can tell the difference by physical appearance alone. It is obvious that clean-cut Marshal Dillon is a "good guy," while his unshaven adversary is a crook. The outlaws in the Dick Tracy strip usually have revolting physical characteristics and man-nerisms.

Another assumption underpinning this type of representation of experience is that romantic love and money lie at the heart of life's problems; a familiar twist ranges the affluent on the side of evil. Romantic campaigning is waged pretty much on the "cave-man" level. Another assumption is that the end justifies the means. It matters not that the hero kills a few people and destroys countless dollars' worth of property so long as ostensibly he is on the side of righteousness.

A familiar assumption, too, is that people in authority—police-men, mayors, teachers, corporation presidents, and often parents— are stupid, pompous, or sadistic, and inevitably they are humili-ated. This is very appealing to the early adolescent who is much under the thumb of adult authority and beginning to chafe from it. The rebellion against established authority, whether of the Bugs Bunny or "private eye" variety, furnishes a very real lure. Sheer availability is an obvious advantage of the television and comic-book experience. A large percentage of American families now own television sets, and comic books and other popular magazines are on sale at any drugstore or supermarket.

Ladders Upward: Transition Literature

Generalizations such as those just made about dominant patterns in the voluntary reading and viewing of early adolescents always need qualification. Though these patterns fit a great number of young people, it is true that individuals exhibit widely varying tastes. Some pupils, for example, enter the seventh grade already well beyond *Horror* (perhaps they never stopped there in the first place), "Lassie," or "Wagon Train." There are those, too, who never develop the interests of the majority. For many, however, the early junior high school may be a crucial period of transition from the enthusiasm for comic books, horror or movie magazines, and certain sensational television programs to the liking for reading and viewing fare in which human experience is reconstructed in more mature modes. It is important for the literature program in the seventh and eighth grades to make available selections that can facilitate this transition. The nature of the basic appeals of popular reading and viewing fare furnishes the key to characteristics of such transition selections, which have similar basic appeals but which provide them in more artful form.

TRANSITION LITERATURE WILL BE EASY TO READ. Much work-reading must be done at any level of school, and a rigorous concern with reading skills is much in order in the junior or senior high school. However, a student's difficulty in recognizing more than one word in a hundred will quickly kill his pleasure in reading, and pleasure is basic to appreciation of literature. Mature readers may keenly enjoy the struggle with a profound and difficult selection, but the junior high school student, just embarking on his literary education, is often far from this point. Of course, though the difficulty level is low, a selection may be artful and esthetically satisfying, as writers such as Eleanor Estes, Doris Gates, and Stephen Meader have demonstrated.

TRANSITION LITERATURE WILL REFLECT EXPERIENCE COMPATIBLE WITH THE NATURE OF THE READER. Identification with characters and situations in a selection is a keystone of appreciation. Many of the selections in the junior high school literature program should feature adolescent characters and exciting or familiar kinds of experiences with which the early adolescent wants to identify.

TRANSITION LITERATURE WILL NOT GROSSLY DISTORT EXPERIENCE. As teachers we may be willing that the experience represented be simplified, since life for most early adolescents is still relatively uncomplicated. Action still may occur mostly on the physical plane, but the plots will avoid the wild coincidence and improbability of the comic-book level of story. Often in these transition selections, it is true, the young protagonists may do surpassing things in a world curiously detached from adult control. This, too, may be acceptable at this stage of the pupil's literary education. Traumatic experiences involving macabre violence and the sordid should not be featured.

TRANSITION LITERATURE WILL HAVE ACTION, SUSPENSE, DANGER, RO- MANCE. Pupils should not get the idea that the required or recom- mended selections are more likely to be dull than interesting.

SUCH SELECTIONS WILL BE EASILY AVAILABLE. Classroom libraries, book exhibits and bazaars, and bulletin board displays of book jackets will help. PTA's and other groups that are disturbed by the nature of some popular television programs and with the comic book "menace" might concern themselves with making other materials more plentiful and available.

Types of Transition Literature

With what types of selections will the ladder upward be fash- ioned in the early junior high school? What kinds of books fit the characteristics identified above? The area of folklore offers rich possibilities as an antidote for comic books. Each region of the country has its folklore, which can be appreciated at various levels of awareness, but which has much in common with the comics and with popular TV fare: the lusty, sometimes slapstick, humor; the action; the quality of the unusual and amazing; the super- heroes. The myths, with their assortment of superheroes and sur- passing deeds, also have much to offer. Many of the newer litera- ture anthologies for junior high school have good selections of both folklore and myths.

A number of publishing houses have made available series of true adventure stories and biographies that are excellent for the early junior high school years. Among these are the Landmark Books of Random House, with the stories of General Custer, the pirate Lafitte, and others; and the Real People Series of Harper & Row.

A number of writers have concerned themselves with the type of fiction that fits excellently the transition need in the junior high school. Among them are James Kjelgaard, Montgomery Atwater, Howard Pease, Kenneth Gilbert, Stephen Meader, Doris Gates, Robert Du Soe, and Eilis Dillon. All of them write stories of lusty adventure, often including mystery. Each features characters of adolescent age, usually boys (it is an old truth that junior high school girls will read "boys' books" but that boys will not read "girls' books"). The youthful protagonists usually are placed more or less on their own in precarious situations. Although adults play important parts, parents usually are conveniently absent for one reason or another. Almost never is there a love plot.

James Kjelgaard and Montgomery Atwater write highly masculine stories of adventure in the woods. Atwater is best known for his youthful forest ranger, Hank Winton, and Winton's associates in the forest service. Kjelgaard's characters are inveterate hunters, and he usually injects a mystery involving violation of the game laws. Both authors are skillful in constructing credible, straightforward plots. The style of neither is distinguished and neither makes any attempt at real characterization.

Though Howard Pease has written few books for adolescents in recent years, many of his popular novels are on shelves of school libraries. Pease is at his best in the modern sea mysteries, such as *Wind in the Rigging* or *The Tattooed Man,* in which the veteran seaman Jarvis and the younger Tod Moran are usually the major characters. Robert Du Soe also writes often of the sea, and his slender novels are based on the early days of the American Navy. In *Your Orders, Sir,* for example, a very young officer pilots a mystery-enshrouded ship through the British blockade. Like Pease and Du Soe, Kenneth Gilbert writes fast-paced adventure mysteries, his against the background of the lumbering and salmon fishing industries in the Pacific Northwest.

Stephen Meader and Doris Gates are among the best-known writers for young people. Each has written stories of several widely different types, but each has produced several adventure books. Both are skilled craftsmen, their styles simple but deft. Meader, especially, has combined well-wrought, suspenseful plots with better-than-average characterization in such tales as *Bulldozer* and the mystery, *The Fish-Hawk's Nest.* Doris Gates has dealt tellingly with young people in *River Ranch* and *North Fork,* although the plot in each book is somewhat contrived. Better books by Gates are discussed in later chapters.

One of the most talented members of this particular group is Eilis Dillon, an Irish writer. Into her thoroughly romantic adventure mysteries she has injected an effect of mood and a sensitivity of style rare in writers for adolescents. The Irish background partly explains this. Though basically realistic, her stories are shot through with Irish legend, folklore, and superstition, and there is a fullness of characterization lacking in most of the other writers of this group.

Books such as these have a special importance in the junior high school literature program, but they may serve a useful function in the senior high school as well. Adolescents develop at widely different rates, of course, both in reading skill and in general ability to respond to literature. In the senior high school it is difficult to provide for the poorer, less imaginative reader. For him, books of the type just discussed—in which the characters are likely to be young adults and the adventures mature, but which are simple and generally lacking in subtlety—may be important.

Two Pervasive Interests: Animal Books and Sports Books

The teacher of literature in the junior high school can capitalize on two pervasive and keen interests—animals and sports. The interest in animals, held by many boys and girls equally, has largely evaporated for most of them by the time they reach senior high school. The preoccupation with sports, involving mostly the boys but occasionally girls, lingers through the senior high school. In addition to the many short selections on animals and sports to be found in any anthology for seventh or eighth grade, the teacher can bring into the classroom and recommend many full-length selections valuable not only in satisfying these two strong interests but also in building the understandings and discriminations

plot of Farley's *The Black Stallion* can be contrasted with the down-to-earth, yet suspenseful sequence of events in Gipson's splendid *Old Yeller*. Foreshadowing is definitely evident in this book, and in, say, Street's *Goodbye, My Lady,* but is obviously lacking in the Farley story.

AWARENESS OF THEME. Even the juvenile animal story can say something significant about human experience, and the pupil must develop an awareness of theme at this level if he is to deal with it in more mature books. Most junior high school pupils will be able to recognize the theme, the boy's growing up, so sensitively handled in *Goodbye, My Lady*. And they will be able to see by contrast that Lippincott's *The Wahoo Bobcat,* for example, though it is excellent in some ways, has no recognizable theme to give the book unity.

A very common theme in animal fiction is that of faith justified, the faith, perhaps, of the young master that the animal will become a successful hunting dog or racing horse, despite the doubts of others. Of course, this theme can be handled skillfully, or clumsily and sentimentally. For example, James Kjelgaard develops this theme well in the popular *Big Red,* the story of a boy and his Irish setter; so, too, at a more mature level, does Enid Bagnold in *National Velvet,* which is about a girl and a race horse. Oversentimentality is one of the most common faults of animal fiction, and junior high school pupils are sensitive to "mushiness" in anything. On this point alone, it is possible for them to recognize the adequacy of Thomas Hinkle and the excellence of *Old Yeller* and *Goodbye, My Lady*.

CHARACTERIZATION. The young people in animal fiction are monotonously similar from author to author. Often, there is no real attempt to bring them truly alive. As pupils discuss books they have read, describing and contrasting main characters, it may become apparent which authors have developed multidimensioned characters, such as those Eric Knight creates in *Lassie Come-Home*.

DIFFERENCES IN QUALITIES OF STYLE. The best authors can communicate unobtrusively the wonder of wild places and the amazing rhythm of nature in locales where man does not usually penetrate, the deep swamps and thickets and high peaks. Joseph Lippincott, for example, succeeds in this in *The Wahoo Bobcat,* set in the Florida swamp land. Reading aloud by the students and teacher will be helpful in illustrating this point. Few pupils fail to respond to a passage like the following:

Uncle Jesse slouched in his chair and puffed his pipe and took in the beauty of the words he did not understand, the words about marvels that only his fancy could picture; the prairies so different from the swamp and so far away. The hard dry gulches, the brave men, the brave land—the never-felt land of his own boyhood dreams.

Out there the winds sang high and free. Thus the words said. Here in his world the winds hummed and sobbed, crying for something that had no answer—like something never seen but only felt and this something touching the strings to the heart of an unlettered old man who could not speak the things he felt and who felt them all the more because he could not speak them: the aching hurt of being old and the happy sorrow of watching a boy grow up and knowing that he, too, must wear a symbol around his neck, that he, like all men, must carry some foul thing forever, some weakness—and also knowing that some day the swamp winds, the home sounds so long remembered, would feel for the strings to the boy's heart and bring forth only the echo of the melody of what used to be—the beauty of the sprouting years, the hope of longing, then the misery of loving something that must grow old; all this the mystery that the old man felt and could not say, this miracle of man's life on God's earth.[3]

"READING BETWEEN THE LINES." *Goodbye, My Lady,* again an example, is rich in symbolism. In this book, the obvious but satisfying symbolism of the coffee and its value in the theme of growing up is worth discussing. For this and other reasons already implied, Street's book is excellent for group reading in the seventh or eighth grade.

One of the well-known Scholastic Literature Units, entitled *Animals,*[4] represents a skillfully built unit for seventh-graders. The interest generated in reading from the unit anthology a series of short selections of fiction and nonfiction about animals leads

---

[3] James Street, *Goodbye, My Lady* (Philadelphia: J. B. Lippincott Company, 1954), pp. 137–138. By permission of the publishers.

[4] Stanley B. Kegler, *Animals,* a Scholastic Literature Unit (New York: Scholastic Book Services, 1962).

into work in oral and written composition and small-group and individual reading of full-length books.

Of course, not all fiction involving animals has been written for the juvenile audience. There are adult pieces appropriate for reading in the senior high school; among them are Bagnold's *National Velvet;* Mary O'Hara's trilogy, *My Friend Flicka, Thunderhead,* and *Green Grass of Wyoming;* David Stephen's *Six-Pointer Buck;* and MacKinlay Kantor's *The Voice of Bugle Ann.*

Books about Sports

The interest in sports fiction grows naturally out of the preoccupation with athletics in most junior and senior high schools. The thrill of the clash on gridiron or diamond or court is a part of the experience of almost every student, whether as participant or spectator. Adolescents in the junior high school, especially boys, are likely to admire physical prowess more than almost anything else, and of course sports heroes are legion. A continuing spate of sports fiction is directed at this interest. These books, whether wretched or excellent, are guaranteed an audience. The minority of good ones present credible, well-knit plots, solid characterization, authentic play-by-play action, and occasionally a theme of some significance. Some of these better titles are listed at the end of this chapter.

Learnings through Class Discussion

Like animal stories, sports fiction can fill an important niche in the junior high school literature program, exciting the interest of some pupils who are likely to be classified as naturally "unliterary." From the soil of sports fiction can sprout some discriminating reactions to literature. In a seventh- or eighth-grade unit on "Sports and Sportsmanship" or "Heroes, Past and Present," for example, the class, or a group within the class, may consider sports fiction. The following questions discussed in class may lead the students in the direction of appreciating some of the elements of good writing.

DO THE ATHLETES AND THE COACHES IN YOUR BOOKS SEEM REAL? Does their conversation sound natural? The boys who are athletes themselves and who are working with coaches are in a good position to discuss these questions. Use of stereotypes or creation of real characters is a literary matter worth discussing here. In sports fiction, coaches, for instance, are likely to fall into two stock categories: dark villains who exploit their players or impossible bundles of omniscience who are concerned much more with building character than with winning games. In these books, dialogue is often badly handled. Scenes are common in which coaches deliver pompous orations in locker rooms between halves and thus send forth rejuvenated teams that sweep all opposition away before them. Pupils quickly catch the falseness of this. And they can recognize the ridiculousness in this statement by the gangling seventeen-year-old southpaw who has just been offered an athletic scholarship: "I appreciate the offer more than I can tell you, sir. But it isn't a real business proposition. I mean you are offering to lend us considerably more money than we can offer security for, are you not?" They can see the superiority of characterization in, say, John Tunis' *Keystone Kids,* in which the main characters chew tobacco and talk as many major league baseball players really do.

HOW DO THE SPORTS HEROES IN YOUR BOOKS GAIN SUCCESS, SOLVE THEIR PROBLEMS? What sorts of obstacles do they encounter? In the better sports fiction, success is not won easily; sacrifice and dedication, involving training and learning, are usually featured. The southpaw does not often move from the sandlot to the big league and strike out the "murderers' row" in his first appearance on the mound. And the junior high school boy, yearning for the athletic peak himself, is able to recognize the truth of experience. The most common theme in sports fiction is that of an individual coming to terms with himself, finding confidence or throwing off some immature pattern of reaction. Such themes are valid in sports stories—they can be mawkishly handled, featuring perhaps a sudden "coming to realize" twist; or well handled, in which the gridiron or the diamond becomes the proving ground that it can be for certain traits of character. Some writers have even injected social themes into sports fiction. One of John Tunis' books, for

"Transition" Adventure Stories

*Atwater, Montgomery, *Hank Winton: Smokechaser,* Random House.
A young forest ranger's adventures, underlain by a message on forest conservation.

Ball, Zachary, *Bar Pilot,* Holiday.
The story of a young bar pilot on the Mississippi Delta in the days of the sailing ships.

Dietz, Lew, *Full Fathom Five,* Little, Brown.
Three college boys become involved in a summer vacation mystery.

Dillon, Eilis, *The Lost Island,* Funk & Wagnalls.
An Irish boy finds his long-shipwrecked father and a strange treasure on a lost island.

————, *The San Sebastian,* Funk & Wagnalls.
The mystery of an abandoned vessel on the Irish coast.

*Du Soe, Robert, *Your Orders, Sir,* McKay.

*Gates, Doris, *North Fork,* Viking.
A summer in a logging camp toughens an aristocratic tenderfoot.

————, *River Ranch,* Viking.
Two adolescents become involved in an exciting mystery when their rancher parents are away on a vacation.

Gilbert, Kenneth, *Arctic Adventure,* Holt, Rinehart and Winston.
An Eskimo and an American youth share hazardous adventures in the far north.

————, *Triple-Threat Patrol,* Holt, Rinehart and Winston.
Adolescent boys solve a summer vacation mystery involving timber thieves in Puget Sound.

Haig-Brown, Roderick, *Mounted Police Patrol,* Morrow.
An exciting story of the Canadian Mounted Police.

Janes, Edward C., *Wilderness Warden,* McKay.
A young game warden's battle against poachers in northern Maine.

Kjelgaard, James, *Hidden Trail,* Holiday.
Outdoor winter fiction involving a young conservation department cameraman who solves the mystery of a lost elk herd.

Kjelgaard, James, *A Nose for Trouble*, Holiday.
Exciting forest adventure and mystery.

Lathrop, West, *Northern Trail Adventure*, Random House.
More Canadian Mounted Police adventure in the far North.

Meader, Stephen, *The Fish-Hawk's Nest*, Harcourt.
A mystery involving smugglers on the New Jersey coast in the 1820's.

———, *Bulldozer*, Harcourt.
Against formidable odds, a boy just out of high school carries on a business with a salvaged bulldozer.

*Pease, Howard, *The Tattooed Man*, Doubleday.

———, *Wind in the Rigging*, Doubleday.

Stanford, Don, *Crash Landing*, Funk & Wagnalls.
The son of a policeman is involved in a well-written adventure and mystery involving airplanes.

Ullman, James R., *Banner in the Sky*, Lippincott.
A remarkable mountain climbing story involving a big decision a Swiss boy must make.

Wood, Kerry, *Wild Winter*, Houghton Mifflin.
A young writer spends an excruciating winter in a log cabin in northern Canada.

Animal Stories

(A—adult level;   E—especially easy.)

Appell, David, *Comanche*, Harcourt.
The horse which survived the Custer massacre tells the story. (E)

*Bagnold, Enid, *National Velvet*, Morrow.
A fourteen-year-old English girl wins a horse in a lottery and takes it through the Grand National race.   (A)

Ball, Zachary, *Bristleface*, Holiday.
The growing up a little of a boy and his dog some decades ago. (E)

Balch, Glenn, *The Midnight Colt*, Crowell.
Two young people and a spoiled, temperamental race horse.

Chipperfield, Joseph, *Storm of Dancerwood*, McKay.
The theme of the part-wolf dog who returns to the world of man.

Corbin, William, *Golden Mare*, Coward-McCann.
A ranch boy has to part with a wonderful horse. (E)

Gipson, Fred, *Old Yeller*, Harper & Row.
A boy and an incorrigible yellow dog in the Texas hill country of the 1860's. (Also *Savage Sam*, featuring the son of Old Yeller.)

Grew, David, *Beyond Rope and Fence*, Grosset & Dunlap.
The career of Queen, a buckskin horse.

Henry, Marguerite, *King of the Wind*, Rand McNally.
An Arabian boy and the ancestor of the great race horse, Man o' War. (E)

*Kantor, MacKinlay, *The Voice of Bugle Ann*, Coward-McCann.
A strange story of a man and a fox hound in the Missouri woods. (A)

*Kjelgaard, James, *Big Red*, Cadmus Books. (E)

———, *Haunt Fox*, Holiday.
An unusual fox and the boy who hunted him. (E)

———, *Stormy*, Holiday.
Unusual story of a boy left alone with his dog in a lake cabin when his father is sent to prison. (E)

*Knight, Eric, *Lassie Come-Home*, Holt, Rinehart and Winston.
The moving story of the great collie and her long trek back to her real home.

*Lippincott, Joseph, *The Wahoo Bobcat*, Lippincott.
A boy and a magnificent bobcat in the Florida swamp country.

*London, Jack, *The Call of the Wild*, Macmillan.
A great dog succumbs to the lure of the Klondike wild.

Lyons, Dorothy, *Dark Sunshine*, Harcourt.
A teen-aged girl, a polio victim, finds new life in training a horse.

Montgomery, Rutherford, *The Golden Stallion and the Wolf Dog*, Little, Brown.
A mystery and a great white stallion that challenges the golden stallion—a series book.

Mowat, Farley, *The Dog Who Wouldn't Be*, Little, Brown.
The story of the author's remarkable and eccentric dog Mutt. (A)

O'Hara, Mary, *My Friend Flicka*, Lippincott.
A young ranch boy gets a colt of his own. (A) (In the trilogy with *Thunderhead* and *Green Grass of Wyoming*.)

Powell, Miriam, *Jareb*, Crowell.
A Georgia pine country boy and his "no account" hound dog.

Rawlings, Marjorie Kinnan, *The Yearling*, Scribner.
A pet deer figures in a boy's growing up in the Florida scrub country. (A)

Sports Fiction

Bowen, Robert, *The Big Inning*, Lothrop.
A big league baseball player overcomes an injury that forces him to give up baseball.

Carse, Robert, *The Winner*, Scribner.
From high school competition to professional tennis.

Decker, Duane, *Long Ball to Left Field*, Morrow.
A hard-hitting young pitcher is reluctant to switch to the outfield.

Douglas, Gilbert, *Hard to Tackle*, Crowell.
An exciting football story with a racial theme. (Also, *The Bulldog Attitude*, basketball.)

Flood, Richard T., *Penalty Shot*, Houghton Mifflin.
Another Radford Academy story. Hockey action from page 1 to the end.

Friendlich, Dick, *Baron of the Bull Pen*, Westminster.
A relief pitcher and a feud between two young players—the self-confidence theme.

Jackson, C. Paul, *Rose Bowl All-American*, Crowell.
Exciting football with the "finding confidence" theme. (Also *All-Conference Tackle* and *Tournament Forward*.)

Jackson, C. Paul, and O. B. Jackson, *Puck Grabber*, Whittlesey.
Unattenuated hockey excitement—high school competition.

Meader, Stephen, *Sparkplug of the Hornets*, Harcourt.
A "shorty" makes the grade in high school basketball.

Tunis, John, *All-American*, Harcourt.
A high school football story with a well-handled racial theme.

*———, *Keystone Kids*, Harcourt.
A brother combination in major league baseball.

Tunis, John, *Schoolboy Johnson*, Morrow.
A temperamental rookie pitcher becomes a winner and a man.
*———, *Yea! Wildcats!* Harcourt.
A basketball story with political overtones.
Waldman, Frank, *The Challenger*, Harcourt.
A hard-working athlete wins the heavyweight boxing title.

LITERATURE
OF
ADVENTURE

3 ❧

ALTHOUGH CERTAIN TYPES of adventure stories are important as a starting point of literature study in the junior high school, it is obvious that the literature of adventure belongs to no particular age group: people do not outgrow the zest for adventure. For, as Whit Burnett wrote, adventure is "a climate of the mind." In the introduction to his excellent anthology, he says: "Adventure is an atmosphere and essence. . . . It is the man plus the place and the event; a man out of the ordinary in daring, endurance, and vision, and a place out of our common ken, even perhaps out of this world."[1]

Everyone likes to imagine that if circumstance demanded, he would prove to be out of the ordinary in daring, endurance, and resourcefulness. During the pall of routine, one keeps an inner vision of himself, and occasionally he must hold this up to comparison with those who have met peril surpassingly. This is especially true of the adolescent, who feels a pressing need for private opportunities to test himself, vicariously as well as actually.

Hazardous undertakings, out-of-the-ordinary characters, and places "out of our common ken" have been the essentials of the traditional adventure story. The recent popularity of science fiction attests to increasing taste for the "out of this world." The presence

[1] Whit Burnett, *The Spirit of Adventure* (New York: Holt, Rinehart and Winston, 1955), pp. xii–xiii.

of these characteristics accounts for the entrenched position of certain "classics" in the school curriculum—for example, *Treasure Island, Ivanhoe,* and *A Tale of Two Cities.* The fact that these books were once chosen for school study because they are good stories has become obscured through the decades, and teachers today often search for a more profound rationale for traditional practice. The three selections cited, as well as other commonly taught "classics," may be no more indispensable for class study than a number of other books. Serious critics have never cited any of the three as outstanding examples of the art of the novel. One recent writer concludes that *Ivanhoe* "is always interesting as spectacle but only sometimes interesting and revealing as a serious work of fiction."[2] Although widely praised, *A Tale of Two Cities* is never cited as the best work of Dickens; its technical weaknesses are obvious. The fact remains, however, that all three novels are compelling stories. Of course, *A Tale of Two Cities* is more than just an "adventure" story. And the adventure story, in general, has a more significant function than merely providing escape reading. When the story of perilous undertakings and surpassing deeds presents a hero whose understandings are enlarged and whose attitudes are changed through his experiences, it has a special importance in the high school program. To select such books from the plethora of adventure fiction and nonfiction is the teacher's responsibility.

The Sea in Fiction

The seas, covering a large proportion of the earth, have been a prominent setting for adventure fiction, from the blood and thunder of tales of piracy to the profound allegory of *Moby Dick.* Byron's famous lines beginning, "Roll on, thou deep and dark blue ocean, roll!" express the eternal fascination with the power and vastness and inscrutability of the sea.

Though it has lost some of its appeal in recent years, the search-for-treasure theme has been one of the most common in fiction of

[2] Herbert Goldstone, "The Question of Scott," *English Journal,* XLVI (April 1957), 195.

the sea. *Treasure Island* remains among the finest adventure
stories for young adolescents, although appealing contemporary
stories of treasure hunting have been written by Harry Rieseberg
and Frank Crisp, and the more modern counterpart of treasure
hunting, deep-sea salvaging, has furnished the basis for popular
books by Edward Ellsberg. *Ocean Gold,* the sequel to the well-
known *Thirty Fathoms Deep,* presents the practical details of salvage operations as well as the excitement.

Of course, pirates, modern or traditional, appear in most of the
books of treasure hunting, and the flashing cutlass is one of the
symbols of adventure fiction. Pirates, like other types of outlaws in
romantic fiction, may be noble as well as evil. Rafael Sabatini's
Captain Blood, for example, is a sort of Robin Hood of the sea.
The pirate story is still popular with high school boys, although in
popular entertainment the pirate has been largely replaced by the
cloak-and-dagger figure of international intrigue.

The man-against-nature theme, so common in literature of adventure generally, is prominent in fiction of the sea. Symbolic is
Nicholas Monsarrat's title—*The Cruel Sea*—for his long, well-
written book about a British ship on convoy duty during World
War II. Definitely the best of Monsarrat's books, it is excellent
for senior high school boys, and a long excerpt from it appears
in the twelfth-grade anthology of one publisher. Alistair McLean's
HMS Ulysses, another story of British naval experience in World
War II, is also an admirable treatment of the struggle against a
formidable sea. Of course, Nordhoff and Hall's earlier *Men
against the Sea* is memorable. At a much less mature level, suitable for the early junior high school, is Armstrong Sperry's *Call
It Courage,* the story of a South Sea island boy's struggle to overcome his fear of the sea.

A recurring variation of the man-against-nature theme is found
in the tales of shipwreck, beginning with Defoe's celebrated
Robinson Crusoe; perhaps most prominent among them is Johann
Wyss's *Swiss Family Robinson,* an extraordinary story of courage
and ingenuity. Recently, two excellent books based on actual
events involving shipwreck have appeared. One of them, written
expressly for younger readers, is Richard Armstrong's *Cold
Hazard,* in which a collision with an iceberg causes a small group

to be set adrift; the other, Kenneth Roberts' *Boon Island,* is based on a shipwreck off the Maine coast.

Kipling's *Captains Courageous* epitomizes another use of the sea in fiction—as a leveler and tester of men. In the Kipling story a wealthy mollycoddle is rescued from drowning by a fishing boat, and its harsh and exacting routine "makes a man" of him. Jack London, like many other writers, views the sea as an escape from the falseness and artificiality of social position and privilege, against which he protested in most of his works. The plot of *The Sea Wolf,* perhaps London's best novel, resembles that of *Captains Courageous.* A wealthy and prominent young man is rescued by a seal-hunting ship under the command of the ruthless and barbaric Wolf Larsen. The young man survives the voyage in complete ignominy, thoroughly beaten and cowed by Larsen. The plot, featuring a "shanghaiing" and the subsequent experiences of the novice on the sea, is generally popular. One such competent story among recent books for adolescents is Victor Mays's *Fast Iron,* about the tribulations of a farm boy shanghaied aboard a nineteenth-century whaler.

With the outbreak of World War II, the sea story turned to the theme of heroism and leadership in naval combat. Before this, however, C. S. Forester had written his exciting, satisfying stories of Horatio Hornblower, an officer in the British navy that kept England safe from Napoleon. Hornblower, a full-dimensioned character with his quota of faults, represents the British navy's proud traditions of courage and discipline. Though the Hornblower books were written for the general audience, they have been highly popular with high school boys. Forester, too, has produced one of the more interesting books of World War II naval combat, *The Good Shepherd,* with another indefatigable captain as the main character. A less admirable, but more complex, captain is found in the best-known sea story of World War II, Herman Wouk's *The Caine Mutiny.* Though marred by a somewhat maudlin ending, emphasizing Wouk's defense of authority, the novel is a fascinating study in divergent character, and the gripping plot is beautifully wrought. Strong, too, in characterization are Monsarrat's *The Cruel Sea* and Kenneth Dodson's *Away All Boats,* which traces the career of an American transport in the Pacific war.

With the sea as background, a few books, treating man's moral condition and his relationship with his universe, rise far above those so far mentioned. Perhaps the greatest is Melville's *Moby Dick,* which a few high school students may read with profit. Excerpts from the book, in some of the high school anthologies, may be useful. Splendid for reading in high school is Ernest Hemingway's Nobel Prize winner, *The Old Man and the Sea,* the moving and tragic struggle of an old Cuban fisherman and a magnificent fish. The novel, most appropriate of Hemingway's books for high school use, will appeal to some students as a tale of action; more able students will be able to discern the symbolic and allegorical value so ably discussed in an essay by Leo Gurko.[3]

The sea as background for the examination of man's personality is most readily associated with Joseph Conrad. Though many of his books are too subtle for the majority of adolescents, *The Secret Sharer,* classed by critics as both short story and novel, seems especially appropriate for reading in high school and is included in several anthologies for the twelfth grade. Though the story is slow in starting, it builds into a compelling narrative that, like *The Old Man and the Sea,* can be read with profit at both a literal and symbolic level of awareness. At the literal level, it is a suspenseful tale of a fugitive helped to escape by a young sea captain who finds self-confidence. At the symbolic level, it is an exploration of Conrad's theme of the bond of the great human family and of the good and evil mixed in the human personality. The technical perfection of *The Secret Sharer* adds to its importance for class study.

The Western Story

The western story, long a staple of popular entertainment, has been traditionally associated with the pulp magazine and the Saturday evening double feature at the movies. However, the

---

[3] Leo Gurko, "The Heroic Impulse in *The Old Man and the Sea,*" *English Journal,* XLIV (October 1955), 377–382.

Old West background has been lifted to higher levels by some writers in the last few decades. These writers are not Zane Grey and Harold Bell Wright, who, with a few others, set the pattern for stereotyped western fiction. Most of their books have been relegated to the trash heap by serious readers.

Other less widely read authors, beginning perhaps with Owen Wister, whose popular *The Virginian* was published at the turn of the century, have relied upon familiar patterns but have invested them with sound characterization, an authentic atmosphere, and distinctive style. Some of these authors who demand more serious attention have addressed themselves to adolescents, some to the adult public.

Jack Schaefer's *Shane* probably is as revealingly battered as any novel in the school library. Its plot is traditional horse opera: a lean, mysterious stranger appears at the Starrett farm, takes part in a war between the ranchers and the small farmers, and disappears, much to the chagrin of Bob Starrett, the young adolescent who tells the story. But the characterization of Shane comes through, even though that of the adolescent does not. Fortunately, the incipient love triangle involving Shane and Bob's mother and father never really develops, and there is no other love angle. A sense of values, unusual in western fiction, pervades the story.

A fifteen-year-old boy, son of an Army officer at Fort Dodge, is the principal character in Val Gendron's *Powder and Hides,* suitable for reading in the junior or senior high school. Accompanying two veterans, the boy goes on the last great buffalo hunt in 1873. Gendron's characterization is adequate and her style terse. A strong feeling for the passing of an epoch is threaded through the unmelodramatic story. Buffalo hunting as well as herd riding is featured, too, in Ross Santee's competent *Rusty,* the story of a cowboy in the early West. Definitely one of the better adult westerns is Conrad Richter's short, lyrical *The Sea of Grass* with its theme of the breakdown of the great cattle empires.

Much of the better western fiction has ignored the hackneyed cattle-rustling intrigues and sundown gun duels and has concentrated on the historically significant conflict with the Indians inherent in the westward movement. Elliott Arnold, for example, has been preoccupied with the relations between the Army and the Apaches. In writing a simplified version of his long *Blood Brother,* he has produced a worthy book for adolescents, *Broken Arrow,* dealing with the last stand of Cochise and his strange friendship with the white man, Tom Jeffords.

The Cheyenne Indians, whom she presents with insight, are the interest of Mari Sandoz. Though her style is in general undistinguished, she has a flair for detail in charactization and description and creates an admirable unity of plot. *The Horsecatcher* sensitively traces a Cheyenne boy's struggle for acceptance and prestige in his family and tribe. Younger adolescents may find much to discuss in the Indian boy's rejection of the role of warrior for the more pedestrian one of horsecatcher. For more mature readers, Oliver La Farge's *Laughing Boy* presents, without the excitement of the Sandoz book, the theme of a Navajo boy's growing up.

A few westerns may appeal especially to girls. Sandoz's *Miss Morissa* features a woman doctor on the Nebraska frontier of the 1870's. General Custer, Calamity Jane, and Buffalo Bill all appear in the book. Rose Wilder Lane's *Let the Hurricane Roar,* about a young couple on a Dakota homestead and the young wife's excruciatingly difficult winter, is popular with older girls. Somewhat similar, though more involved, is Loula Grace Erdman's *The Edge of Time,* about a young couple homesteading in Texas in 1885.

Undoubtedly the most important writer to use a western background is Walter Van Tilburg Clark. In its surface events a rather traditional western, his best novel, *The Ox-Bow Incident,* is a moving tragedy involving the psychology of mob action. Three men are lynched for a murder and then discovered to have been innocent; the leader of the lynching posse and his son commit suicide. Critics have lauded the technical perfection of this novel.[4] *The Ox-Bow Incident* and another excellent novel by Clark, *The Track of the Cat,* are appropriate for reading in the upper high school years. *The Track of the Cat,* too, is a psychological novel, about a Nevada family in the early 1900's. The plot is simple: three brothers, all different in personality, track a moun-

4 Frederic I. Carpenter, "The West of Walter Van Tilburg Clark," *English Journal,* XLI (February 1952), 64–69.

tain lion that has killed some of their cattle. Two of the brothers are killed, one by the cat and one by his own fear. The plot is exciting on the physical level, and on the allegorical level it is clearly the struggle between good and evil. The black mountain lion, of course, represents evil.

Men at War

The theme of man in battle runs through the legends and myths and epics—through all literature—of all countries. Unfortunately, the war experience has loomed large in the human drama, and each of the great wars has harvested its crop of fiction, much of it ephemeral.

Battle, of course, presents one of the great testing grounds of human courage and stamina, and exploring the depths of human courage is one of the major themes in all literature of adventure. It seems ironic, perhaps, to classify war fiction as "adventure." Yet action and peril, which furnish the lure of adventure fiction, are inherent in the war story, which is popular with high school boys because of this.

The older tales of war tended to stress its romance rather than its tragedy. Sometimes war was the pathway to escape from a tragic or distasteful civilian life. The French Foreign Legion, about which so many popular tales centered, became the symbol of the soldier fleeing from his past. One notable foreign legion story, Percival Wren's *Beau Geste,* remains popular with adolescents. Recent war fiction emphasizes the nightmare qualities of terror and hardship, in inescapably hair-raising narrative— and it is this, of course, that the adolescent is most responsive to. Yet many modern war novels present the terrible hardship of war as they also portray the exalted heroism of men who rise to the near impossible. James Michener's excellent story of aerial warfare in the Korean War, *The Bridges at Toko-Ri,* with its smashing ending, is a kind of memorial to the heroism that combat exacts, and Alistair McLean's *The Guns of Navarone* recounts the near-impossible mission of a small patrol in World

War II. Among the most suspenseful novels of World War II is Pierre Boulle's *The Bridge over the River Kwai,* a tale of British soldiers forced to construct a railroad bridge for their Japanese captors. This novel is notable, too, for the quality of its writing and for its irony.

If these books, despite the authenticity of the events, come near to romanticism, there are others that are rock-ribbed in their realism, although they present occasional flashes of humor and even of sentimentality. Perhaps most unrelenting is Elleston Trevor's *The Big Pick-Up,* which deals with a squad of British soldiers at Dunkirk. In fact, in Trevor's spare novels is some of the most distinguished writing about World War II. His *The Killing Ground,* based on the terrible Falaise campaign (in Normandy), contains one of the most gripping passages in war fiction. Its hero, a Corporal Pike, in his heroism of resourcefulness as well as of necessity, represents the best of soldiers who went to war unwillingly.

Few war novels have equaled Erich Maria Remarque's story of German soldiers in the trench warfare of World War I, *All Quiet on the Western Front,* with its blend of heroic, comic, and tragic events. In addition to books such as these, ones with light touches of humor and satire also have been produced by most wars. From World War I came Jaroslav Hasek's *The Good Soldier Schweik,* presenting the "sad sack" of the German Army, and from World War II the hilarious *No Time for Sergeants* by Mac Hyman.

The love element is not absent, of course, from war fiction. The theme of warrior and the lover who waits and fears is eternal and has been no more neglected in modern than in ancient tales. A tender, mature, and basically wholesome love story, told against the background of the planning and launching of the great invasion of Normandy in World War II, is the basis of Lionel Shapiro's *The Sixth of June.* Nevil Shute's love stories of World War II, *The Legacy* and *Pastoral,* are appealing to older girls.

Naturally, many of the most mature war novels are essentially protests. Horrified at barbaric events involving civilized peoples, authors have sought causes for these events. Norman Mailer's long, angry *The Naked and the Dead* places the blame on the capitalistic system. Irwin Shaw probes some of the neuroses of society through individual characters in *The Young Lions*. Such books as these suggest one of the major problems of teaching war fiction to classes of adolescents—the language used and the type of experience frequently portrayed. In *The Naked and the Dead, From Here to Eternity,* and some other war novels the language is extremely profane and gross. Occasionally there are detailed scenes involving sex. Even in James Gould Cozzens' Pulitzer Prize winning *Guard of Honor,* lauded by many critics as structurally the finest novel of World War II, there is a hotel bedroom scene that would make many high school teachers and librarians loath to recommend it.

Such books must be recommended and included in literature units with care. Teachers and librarians frequently have been overprotective; it is as easy to underestimate the background and sophistication of adolescents as to overestimate it, and teachers have sometimes predicted shock at elements that did not bring even a lifted eyebrow from their students. Two criteria may guide selection: (1) Is the work excellent as an example of the art of fiction? (2) Is the theme likely to be comprehensible to adolescents? Certainly meeting the first test are such hard-hitting novels as *The Naked and the Dead, The Young Lions,* Heggen's *Mister Roberts,* Hemingway's *A Farewell to Arms,* along with a number of others with little objectionable material, such as *The Bridges at Toko-Ri* and Hersey's *A Bell for Adano.* Using the second criterion, however, Mailer's book and perhaps Hemingway's might be eliminated. Still, the presence of "dirty" language or erotic scenes in a book is not reason alone for eliminating it.

For adolescents must learn to judge details, sordid or not, in terms of their relevance to theme and purpose. In the spate of war fiction, the truly unified novel stands out because it interrelates events and characters in a significant whole, in the manner of the masterpiece *War and Peace.* Many of the ephemeral novels of World War II merely recount amazing events as their authors experienced them; of these the better-written ones are skillful journalistic pieces. But the battle arena affords a canvas for fascinating character portraits. Tom Heggen's young naval officer,

Mr. Roberts, is one. He represents the effects of a certain aspect of war on sensitive, intelligent men, brought up in an atmosphere of culture, and when the reader identifies this theme, he recognizes the Rabelaisian touches in the book not as spicy sidelights but as essential details.

Though war remains a major reading interest of adolescent boys, little has been done with the topic in fiction written expressly for adolescents. John Tunis' *Silence over Dunkerque* features a British sergeant akin to Elleston Trevor's Corporal Pike. Isolated from his unit, the sergeant tries to get back into action. Frank Bonham, in *War Beneath the Sea,* a novel concerning the submarine USS "Mako," produces a supple story of a young sailor's involvement in the war of action and nerves that was submarine warfare.

It is well for adolescent readers to perceive that the real heroes of war fiction (or nonfiction), past and present, are not the swashbuckling killers, but men of compassion for whom it is a tragedy, which we all share, that they must do what they do. The nature of the hero is a good point of departure for discussion of war fiction.

War literature is not only an interest of adolescent boys, of course, but represents a general vein of interest as any rack of paperback books reveals, and World War II has produced a spate of nonfiction as well as of fiction. Two remarkable titles among these books are Cornelius Ryan's *The Longest Day* and Walter Lord's *Day of Infamy*. The Ryan book is an engrossing narrative of the twenty-four hours of D Day in Europe, told from the viewpoints of various Allied and German officers and soldiers; *Day of Infamy* concerns the Japanese attack on Pearl Harbor.

Science Fiction

The teacher of adolescents is keenly aware of the modern vogue of science fiction, which is likely to envelop boys in about the ninth or tenth grade. Developing rapidly since the mid-1920's, science fiction was given tremendous impetus, as was science nonfiction, by the exploding of the atomic bomb—which ushered in an era possibly more fantastic than the science fiction writers had ever imagined. In his illuminating book, *Inquiry into Science Fiction*, Basil Davenport identifies the basic appeal of science fiction: "That man is a creature with awesome potentialities for achievement and for self-destruction, and that the inhabitants of Earth are not the only powers in the universe—these are truths that men have never been able to forget for more than a generation or two. It is science fiction which is telling them to us now."[5]

Science fiction reflects man's eternal curiosity about the unknown and his fascination with predicting the future. The fantastic imaginings of one day, the prophecies of science fiction, become the commonplace realities of another. The reader of science fiction asks himself, "How long before this will come true?" In March 1944, slightly a year before the dropping of the first atomic bomb, *Astounding Science Fiction* magazine carried a story entitled "Deadline," about atomic weapons and how they were made. The story prompted an FBI investigation because the government was convinced there was a "leak" from the research laboratories!

Though, as Basil Davenport points out, science fiction in its present form dates from the founding of *Amazing Stories* in 1926, it has forerunners that extend back across centuries. Francis Bacon's *The New Atlantis* in 1627, for example, predicted submarines, airplanes, refrigeration, and the conveying of sound over long distances. Of course, a specially important ancestor of science fiction is Jules Verne's *Twenty Thousand Leagues under the Sea,* still relatively popular with adolescents. In the early twentieth century H. G. Wells's fiction predicted atomic energy, rockets, and helicopters, among other things.

Like the western story and other popular forms of fiction, space adventure is widely associated with the comic book and the juvenile movie and television programs. Yet science fiction covers a broad range of subjects other than space travel, from radioactive mosquitoes to extrasensory perception, and some of its writers have risen to a rank of respectability in contemporary literature. Significantly, selections of science fiction have begun to appear in junior and senior high school literature anthologies.

[5] Basil Davenport, *Inquiry into Science Fiction* (New York: McKay, 1955), p. 81.

Basil Davenport and other critics have identified several kinds of science fiction: the "space opera," the story based on scientific hypotheses, the gadget piece, the speculative story, and the fantasy. The space opera is that story in which the wild profusion of events just happens to occur in outer space instead of in the jungle, on the cattle range, or in the New York City underworld. It is the typical pulp-magazine adventure story in which the only requirement is action.

The gadget story, apparently in decline now, and the story based on scientific hypotheses both utilize scientific material. Based usually on some curious scientific fact, the gadget story, of course, is focused on a device. Some writers of science fiction, like Isaac Asimov who is a scientist himself, have utilized known information to develop and extend a hypothesis through a process of logical reasoning. Excellence or the lack of it in this type of story, dear to the original science fiction fan, who was at least an amateur scientist, may be lost on the present reader—who may not be able to tell a ridiculous "scientific" hypothesis from a sound one. For example, as Davenport points out, many stories have included man fighting insects as large as man himself. The impossibility of this is not evident to the person who does not realize that because of the difference in circulation between mammal and insect, an insect cannot be much bigger than a tarantula (a large venomous spider) or a mammal much smaller than a shrewmouse.

All science fiction is based essentially on the projection into the future of present trends or tendencies. The speculative story, however, is likely to be based on trends outside the natural sciences. From the nineteenth century, Edward Bellamy's *Looking Backward,* uncannily accurate at points, is still fascinating. It is interesting that contemporary authors of the speculative story usually foresee a grim future in which man, through his own distorted values, is again living in caves or in abject slavery. In this category of fiction, George Orwell's *1984* is feasible for senior high school students, a few of whom also might profit from reading Aldous Huxley's *Brave New World.*

Discussion of science fiction in class might lead into a writing assignment to which adolescents usually respond with interest— projecting into the future a trend they discern in the present. Or, conversely, the writing assignment may lead into discussion of science fiction. The main value of science fiction in the high school literature program lies not in any back door to scientific information that it might open nor in any light it might throw on eternal themes in human experience—though it may possibly have both these values. For some students, science fiction will provide another type of vicarious adventure, helping to satisfy the appetite for the unusual. Perhaps for even more students, science fiction is a respectable form of fantasy, the usual varieties of which are not popular in the adolescent culture, where the need for occasional fantasy is kept well camouflaged. "Fairy" tales, magic carpets, and jinn are not for the adolescent. But their counterparts, space ships and time machines and otherworld creatures, may be because they are tied, implausibly or not, to something called science. The main value of science fiction in the high school literature program lies in the fact that interest in the better-level science fiction (see list at the end of the chapter) may lead to a taste for other explorations of the unknown and unworldly in prose and poetry.

True Adventure

The period following World War II may well be cited in future literary history for the flowering of nonfiction then current. Certainly, the personal narrative of adventure, firmly rooted in the age-old longing to live dangerously, represents some of the finest in contemporary writing. The books of true adventure furnish a rich resource for the high school program in literature.

The true adventure narrative finds its earlier origins not only in the many adventure tales involving man against nature, but also in works like those by Izaak Walton and especially in *Walden* by Thoreau, works that explore the role of nature in the good life and its effects upon the personality of man.

Conquest of the sea, of the mountains, of the sky, of remote and inaccessible places in general is the subject of a group of important true adventure books, beginning with Thor Heyerdahl's *Kon-Tiki* in 1950. Heyerdahl, a Danish anthropologist, and his associates made an amazing ocean voyage in a primitive craft to test a theory, and their exploit caught the public fancy. It is the underwater world, however, that has most challenged men's imaginations and ingenuity in recent years, and a number of books on undersea exploration have appeared. Jacques-Yves Cousteau and Frédéric Dumas, the authors of one of the finest of these, *The Silent World,* point out that since ancient times men have tried to penetrate the mysterious depths of the sea; even Leonardo da Vinci designed impractical diving lungs. Superb books of undersea adventure, too, are Philippe Diole's *The Undersea Adventure* and Hans Hass's *Diving to Adventure.*

The towering mountain peaks, long inaccessible to man, have always posed a challenge. Within very recent years the highest have finally been conquered. Probably the finest story of mountain climbing is Maurice Herzog's *Annapurna,* which describes the scaling of Annapurna, at the time the highest peak ever climbed, a feat that permanently disabled Herzog. The feat, though not the book, was surpassed by an expedition commanded by Sir John Hunt, whose *The Conquest of Everest* records the ultimate victory in mountain climbing.

Among the recent narratives of flight, William Bridgeman and Jacqueline Hazard's *The Lonely Sky,* in part about one author's adventures in flying the "Skyrocket," at that time the world's fastest airplane, is outstanding. Adventure in remote places also has produced a long series of books. Of particular stature is Heinrich Harrer's *Seven Years in Tibet,* years in which the adventurer-writer became a sort of right-hand man to the fabulous Dalai Lama. Comparable is the account of a year spent among the Eskimos, *Kabloona* by Gontran de Poncias.

Superior books of personal adventure have certain elements in common with good fiction—exciting events, suspense, revelation of character, quality of style. Yet, as Gorham Munson points out,[6] the fact that they are based on true experience gives them a stronger impact in disclosing man's great reserves of courage and resourcefulness, affording a catharsis to the reader even though the narra-

---

[6] Gorham Munson, "High Up and Deep Down," *English Journal,* XLIII (December 1954), 481–487.

tives of true adventure—unlike those of war—are romantic rather than tragic.

What gives the true adventure narrative significance and what distinguishes the superior from the run of the mill? Why, in the first place, would a mature person want to climb a mountain when there is nothing but ice at the top, or plunge to the bottom of the ocean? Perhaps Maurice Herzog gives one of the most effective answers:

Rocked in my stretcher, I meditated on our adventure now drawing to a close, and on our unexpected victory. One always talks of the ideal as a goal towards which one strives but which one never reaches. For every one of us, Annapurna was an ideal that had been realized. In our youth we had not been misled by fantasies, nor by the bloody battles of modern warfare which feed the imagination of the young. For us the mountains had been a natural field of activity where, playing on the frontiers of life and death, we had found the freedom for which we were blindly groping and which was as necessary to us as bread. The mountains had bestowed on us their beauties, and we adored them with a child's simplicity and revered them with a monk's veneration of the divine.

Annapurna, to which we had gone emptyhanded, was a treasure on which we should live the rest of our days. With this realization we turn the page: a new life begins.

There are other Annapurnas in the lives of men.[7]

In the books by Herzog and Cousteau and Diole, for example, there is a nobility of motive, a symbolic value to their physical feats that invests them with significance, not just the thrill to be found, for instance, in the big-game hunting tales of Robert Ruark or Jim Corbett. The superior narrative of adventure makes clear the point of the experiences recounted, leading the reader to realize, with Herzog, that "events that seem to make no sense may sometimes have a deep significance of their own."

A maturity and sensitivity of style also distinguish the excellent adventure narratives. Again, Herzog, Diole, and Cousteau

<hr>

[7] Maurice Herzog, *Annapurna* (New York: Dutton, 1952), p. 311.

may be cited along with others such as Antoine de Saint-Exupèry and William O. Douglas. The following passage is an example:

> Like the sea, [the desert] reveals the depths of being within us. Through it, there is every chance of our arriving at a certain secret door within ourselves. From this threshold other inner landscapes appear before our eyes. When consciousness makes its way beyond this wall, it achieves the greatest of all transitions: the transplanting of the inner man.
>
> It is here that the sea and the desert have an equal value, are one in their human significance. It is here that the spell of the Sahara and the spell of the ocean depths bring a richness and satisfaction to certain spirits that the charm of cities, the smiles of women, the sweetness of home cannot bestow. Is this the arrogance of choosing a bleak and naked destiny? The vanity of the hermit? I am not so sure of that. In these retreats into sparseness and solitude, these voluntary divestments of all that is extraneous, the same psychological alchemy is at work. There is always the question of a spiritual gain. The stake is the appropriation of the world by irrational means: a stake à la Rimbaud.
>
> I have found again in the desert—or rather, I have brought to perfection there—the magic process by which, in the water, a diver is able to loose the ordinary bonds of time and space and bring life into consonance with an obscure inner poem: to bypass habit, language, memory. . . .[8]

Books of true adventure, then, can figure importantly in the high school program. The increasing prominence of nonfiction in contemporary literature makes it especially desirable to teach students to recognize excellence in this genre as well as in fiction. Selections of true adventure may be used along with fiction in units exploring men's motives. Or the teacher may organize a unit on the nonfiction of adventure by requesting permission from publishers to duplicate excerpts from such books, listed at the end of this chapter. Another possibility is for all the students to read one of the true adventures, together, using a paperback edition, and to read others from the library individually.

[8] Reprinted by permission of Julian Messner, Inc., from *Sahara Adventure* by Philippe Diole. Copyright September 27, 1956, by Julian Messner, Inc.

POSSIBILITIES FOR STUDENT READING

(Books mentioned in the preceding chapter are marked with an asterisk [*]. They are annotated only if the nature of their content was not indicated in the chapter. A indicates an adult book; E, one that is especially easy.)

The Sea

*Armstrong, Richard, *Cold Hazard*, Houghton Mifflin.

Conrad, Joseph, *Typhoon*, various publishers. (A)
Captain McWhirr takes his ship through a furious storm. (Also *The Secret Sharer*, various publishers.) (A)

Crisp, Frank, *The Treasure of Barby Swin*. Coward-McCann. (E)
Life in a whaler and a strange treasure story with a well-wrought villain.

*Defoe, Daniel, *Robinson Crusoe*, various publishers. (A)

*Dodson, Kenneth, *Away All Boats*, Little, Brown. (A)

*Ellsberg, Edward, *Ocean Gold*, Dodd, Mead.
Story centering on deep-sea salvage operations.

*Forester, C. S., *The Good Shepherd*, Little, Brown. (A)

———, *Mr. Midshipman Hornblower*, various publishers. (A)
The young British officer takes command of a ship in the war against Napoleon. (Also, other Hornblower stories.)

Hammond-Innes, Ralph, *The Wreck of the Mary Deare*, Knopf. (A)
A mystery concerning a deserted ship in the English Channel.

*Hemingway, Ernest, *The Old Man and the Sea*, Scribner. (A)

*Kipling, Rudyard, *Captains Courageous*. Doubleday, and Grosset & Dunlap.

*London, Jack, *The Sea Wolf*, various publishers. (A)

*McLean, Alistair, *HMS Ulysses*, Doubleday. (A)

*Mays, Victor, *Fast Iron*, Houghton Mifflin. (E)
(Also *Action Starboard*.)

*Melville, Herman, *Moby Dick*, various publishers. (A)

*Monsarrat, Nicholas, *The Cruel Sea*, Knopf. (A)

*Nordhoff, Charles, and James Hall, *Men against the Sea*, various publishers. (A)

The miraculous voyage of Captain Bligh and the men who were set adrift with him after the Bounty mutiny.

Rieseberg, Harry, *My Compass Points to Treasure*, Holt, Rinehart and Winston. (E)
Searching for lost treasure ships in the Caribbean.

*Roberts, Kenneth, *Boon Island*. Doubleday. (A)

Sabatini, Rafael, *Captain Blood*, Houghton Mifflin. (A)
The career of the fabulous English privateer.

*Sperry, Armstrong, *Call It Courage*, Macmillan. (E)

*Stevenson, Robert Louis, *Treasure Island*, Dodd, Mead.
The famous treasure hunting story with young Jim Hawkins and the immortal pirate, Long John Silver.

*Wouk, Herman, *The Caine Mutiny*, Doubleday. (A)

*Wyss, Johann, *Swiss Family Robinson*, various publishers.

Western Stories

*Arnold, Elliott, *Broken Arrow*, Little, Brown.

*Clark, Walter Van Tilburg, *The Ox-Bow Incident*, various publishers. (A)

*———, *The Track of the Cat*, Random House. (A)

*Erdman, Loula G., *The Edge of Time*, Dodd, Mead. (A)

*Gendron, Val, *Powder and Hides*, McKay. (E)

*LaFarge, Oliver, *Laughing Boy*, Houghton Mifflin. (A)

*Lane, Rose W., *Let the Hurricane Roar*, McKay. (E)

Norton, André, *Stand to Horse*, Harcourt. (E)
A young cavalry recruit fights the Apaches in 1859.

*Richter, Conrad, *Sea of Grass*, Knopf. (A)

*Sandoz, Mari, *The Horsecatcher*, Westminster. (E)

*———, *Miss Morissa*, McGraw-Hill. (A)

*Santee, Ross, *Rusty*, Scribner. (A)

Scarborough, Dorothy, *The Wind*, Harper & Row. (A)
A woman of the East and her battle with the West.

*Schaefer, Jack, *Shane*, Houghton Mifflin.

*Wister, Owen, *The Virginian*, Grosset & Dunlap. (A)
A gallant Virginian goes West and sets the classic pattern of the cowboy.

War Fiction

(All titles are adult pieces except those by Bonham and Tunis.)

*Bonham, Frank, *War Beneath the Sea*, Crowell.   (E)

*Boulle, Pierre, *The Bridge over the River Kwai*, Vanguard.

Brown, Harry, *A Walk in the Sun*, Knopf.
An American infantry platoon in the invasion of Italy, World War II.

Crane, Stephen, *Red Badge of Courage*, Appleton.
A young soldier proves his courage to himself in his first Civil War battle.

*Hasek, Jaroslav, *The Good Soldier Schweik*, New American Library.

*Heggen, Tom, *Mister Roberts*, Houghton Mifflin.

*Hersey, John, *A Bell for Adano*, Modern Library.
An American military government officer administers a small Italian town after the Italian surrender in World War II.

————, *The War Lover*, Knopf.
An Air Force story of World War II. The psychological disintegration of a loud-mouthed pilot and the renewal of the self-esteem of a member of his crew.

*Hyman, Mac, *No Time for Sergeants*, Random House.
A Georgia hillbilly's escapades in the Army.

*McLean, Alistair, *The Guns of Navarone*, Doubleday.

*Michener, James, *The Bridges at Toko-Ri*, Random House.

*Remarque, Erich Maria, *All Quiet on the Western Front*, Little, Brown.

*Shapiro, Lionel, *The Sixth of June*, Doubleday.

*Shaw, Irwin, *The Young Lions*, Random House.
Three soldiers, two Americans and one German, in World War II.

Shute, Nevil, *Pastoral*, Morrow.
A love story, in which the background is an RAF base in World War II. (Also *The Legacy*.)

*Trevor, Elleston, *The Killing Ground*, Macmillan.
(Also *The Big Pick-Up*)

*Tunis, John R., *Silence over Dunkerque*, Morrow.

*Wren, Percival, *Beau Geste*, Lippincott.
The suspicion cast by the disappearance of a jewel sends three
brothers into the French Foreign Legion.

Science Fiction

Asimov, Isaac, *Caves of Steel*, Doubleday.
A robot teams with a human detective in solving a mystery in
the New York City of the future.

Bradbury, Ray, *The Martian Chronicles*, Doubleday.   (A)
An earth group visits Mars in the twenty-first century.

Brown, Fredric, *Martians, Go Home*, Dutton.
The funniest science fiction episode results when the Martians—
two and a half feet tall, green, and with very unpleasant personalities—invade Earth.

Heinlein, Robert, *Citizen of the Galaxy*, Scribner.   (E)
A young businessman's problems with his family's interplanetary
interests. (Also *Tunnel in the Sky, The Red Planet, Rocket Ship
Galileo, Space Cadet.*)

*Huxley, Aldous, *Brave New World*, various publishers.   (A)

Leinster, Murray, *The Last Space Ship*, Frederick Fell.
A strong social theme underlies this prophecy of future des-
potism; "matter transmitters" are featured.

Norton, André, *Star Rangers*, Harcourt.
Adventures of a space patrol in A.D. 8054. "Mind control" plays
a dominant part.

*Orwell, George, *1984*. Harcourt.   (A)
A picture of what a totalitarian future might be like with
thought control.

Shute, Nevil, *On the Beach*, Morrow.   (A)
The few survivors of a cobalt war find they are doomed from
radiation.

Stevenson, Robert Louis, *The Strange Case of Dr. Jekyll and Mr.
Hyde*, various publishers.   (A)
A doctor discovers a drug that changes him into a creature of
evil.

Stewart, George, *Earth Abides*, Random House.   (A)
A strange disease nearly wipes out human life, but two young
survivors begin a new community.

*Verne, Jules, *Twenty Thousand Leagues under the Sea,* various publishers.
   The famous nineteenth-century story of Captain Nemo and his submarine *Nautilus.*

True Adventure

(All titles are of adult books.)

*Bridgeman, William, and Jacqueline Hazard, *The Lonely Sky,* Holt, Rinehart and Winston.

Corbett, Jim, *Man-eaters of Kumaon,* Oxford.
   Hunting man-eating tigers in India.

*Cousteau, Jacques-Yves, and Frédéric Dumas, *The Silent World,* Harper & Row.
   Undersea exploration and salvage in the Mediterranean.

*De Poncias, Gontran, *Kabloona,* Reynal.

*Diole, Philippe, *Sahara Adventure,* Messner.
   Exploration by camel in the Sahara Desert. Poetic style.

*————, *The Undersea Adventure,* Messner.
   A classic of skin diving.

*Harrer, Heinrich, *Seven Years in Tibet,* Dutton.

*Hass, Hans, *Diving to Adventure,* Doubleday.

*Herzog, Maurice, *Annapurna,* Dutton.

*Heyerdahl, Thor, *Kon-Tiki,* Rand McNally.

*Hunt, John, *The Conquest of Everest,* Dutton.

Saint-Exupéry, Antoine de, *Wind, Sand and Stars,* Harcourt.
   Adventures of an aviator on three continents. Poetic and philosophical.

Scott, Robert, *Between the Elephant's Eyes,* Dodd, Mead.
   A hunting story with a strange ending.

Tenzing, Norgay, and James Ramsey Ullman, *Tiger of the Snows,* Putnam.
   The career of the Sherpa, Tenzing, who, with Edmund Hillary, reached the summit of Everest.

Wilkinson, Doug, *Land of the Long Day,* Holt, Rinehart and Winston.
   Describes a year of living as an Eskimo.

LITERATURE
OF THE
ADOLESCENT
CULTURE

4 ✖

Personal problems, inherent in the lifelong struggle toward self-realization and in the search for identity, are not unique to adolescents. But the in-between period that is adolescence is a particular time of stress—a no man's land of questioning and doubting and fearing and aspiring. The happy vagueness of the "when I grow up" in the childhood period has given way to the sharp realization that the growing up is nearly complete and that, in the senior high school period at least, there must be a coming to terms with personal shortcomings and a facing of the question, How do I measure up to a role in the adult world? The high school period is frequently marked by conflicts between adolescents and parents, as the teen-ager strives to advance toward independence and adult status faster than his parents think he should. And yet, despite his striving, the fact is—psychologically if not physiologically—that the adolescent is *not* adult. The adolescent culture has its own unique and rigid code, in which a type of conformity is at a premium, and the teen-ager who would have reasonably satisfactory status with his peers (and which one would not!) can only pretend to be adult within the boundaries of the peer culture and the rules enforced by adults. Around the stresses of the adolescent period a large body of fiction has developed. Titles from this body of writing are among the most popular in the voluntary reading of adolescents, making this category of fiction worthy of serious analysis by teachers and librarians.

Categories of Problems

A number of studies over a period of years have established a rather definite pattern of personal problems in adolescence. One exhaustive study, for example, of 1244 students from fourteen to eighteen years of age, in schools in New York, Pennsylvania, and Ohio, found the following ten categories of problems to be most crucial.[1] The categories are listed in the order of their importance.

School problems—grades, relations with teachers, and so on
Personal problems—shyness, anxieties, fears, nervousness
Family problems—late hours, dating, and so on
Money—part-time jobs, inadequate allowances, and so on
Boy-girl relations—dates, going steady, popularity
Concern about the future—career, success or failure, and so on
Recreation problems—use of leisure, success in sports, need for car, and so on
Problems of personal appearance
Danger from world tensions—draft, army, war
Moral issues and ideals—smoking, drinking, lying, and so on

Other studies invariably identify similar categories of adolescent problems. A synthesis of the findings of these investigations indicates that most of the personal problems of adolescents cluster in the following five categories.

COMING TO TERMS WITH SELF. Most adolescents are actively taking stock of themselves, even though for some the process may be carried on under a veneer of irresponsibility and devil may care. The student who has been struggling to maintain a "C" average realizes that MIT and a career in engineering are not for him. The plain girl with the unenticing figure faces the fact that the coming

[1] Don M. Wolfe, "Students' Problems," *English Journal*, XLIV (April 1955), 218–225

years probably will bring no increase in glamour. And the introverted, retiring boy decides, reluctantly or otherwise, that he will never be the center of "the gang."

PROBLEMS OF RELATIONS WITH PEERS. Popularity, which may be tempered ultimately to acceptance, is a major goal of adolescents. The pull to live up to peer-set or gang-set standards, to conform, may involve the teen-ager in conflicts with his parents, his teachers, and his own convictions. For example, the intellectually gifted student may have to play down his ability in order to avoid being labeled "a brain." Of course, the whole web of boy-girl relations presents major issues of social know-how, of going steady, and of sexual morality. Senior high school students are much more serious about love than their parents or teachers frequently realize. A few students marry before completing high school, and many think seriously about marriage and their future roles as homemakers. The problem of dating is more serious to the girl, who is an outcast if she doesn't date, than to the boy, who merely may be labeled a "woman-hater."

FAMILY PROBLEMS. Although the adolescent tends to pull away from domination and control by his parents, he greatly needs their advice and guidance. Countless minor tensions are created by the adolescent in the household. Occasionally, his problems may be deep-seated. It is not unusual, for example, for the adolescent to be ashamed of his home or of some member of his family.

PREPARATION FOR THE FUTURE ADULT ROLE. His role as a marriage partner is not the only aspect of his future with which the adolescent is concerned. He has the problem of choosing a career or an occupation, of deciding whether or not to go to college. Boys may be preoccupied with their military obligations.

MORAL AND PHILOSOPHICAL PROBLEMS AND ISSUES. Few adolescents would admit openly to an interest in "philosophy of life." Yet teenagers are keenly concerned with values, with the things that people live for, and with the motives that impel men. The "Omar Khayyam" period has long been associated with the adolescent experience, and *weltschmerz*, sometimes serving as a defense mechanism, is a hallmark of the teen years. Often the adolescent has to carry on a lonely tussle with concepts of right and wrong. Typically, adolescence is a time of outward cynicism and inward idealism.

Personal Problems and Literature

What significance do the personal problems of adolescents have for the junior and senior high school literature program? Certainly, it is not the burden of the literature program alone to help students solve their personal problems. Reading of books can never be the sole means of solving problems at any stage of life, and to the high school student the entire school curriculum, along with varied out-of-school influences, should offer help. The study of literature has other objectives, among them to contribute to the esthetic life of the individual and to acquaint each person with his cultural heritage.

Yet there are highly important connections between the personal problems of students and their study of literature. For one, the problems that vex students can motivate reading and can provide an opportunity to convince students that literature really is a re-construction of experience, that it is related to things that are important and vital to them, not just something vaguely cultural and worthwhile, in the eyes of adults, upon which to spend leisure time.

The fact that adolescents are seeking insight into their problems through reading is shown in a study carried out by A. Stephen Dunning.[2] The following writers of junior novels were judged most popular by a group of well-known librarians representing different sections of the country: Betty Cavanna, Rosamond Du Jardin, Henry Felsen, Ann Emery, Mary Stolz, Maureen Daly, James Summers, John Tunis, Amelia Walden, Robert Heinlein, Walter Farley, Sally Benson, and Jessica Lyon. Three of these writers were on the list by virtue of only one title: Maureen Daly with the celebrated *Seventeenth Summer,* Sally Benson with *Junior Miss,* and Walter Farley with one of his Black Stallion stories. All the others were represented by four or more titles. John Tunis is popular mainly as a writer of sports stories and Robert Heinlein as a writer of science fiction. But the rest on the list write of con-

[2] A. Stephen Dunning, "A Definition of the Role of the Junior Novel Based on Analyses of Thirty Selected Novels," unpublished Ph.D. dissertation, Florida State University, 1959.

temporary adolescent culture, and they treat three general themes: love, family relationships, and values generally.

It is important for the teacher to keep in mind the key role of identification in the literary experience. When the adolescent locates in fiction a kindred spirit, a fellow sufferer, the identification is acute and moving, and an important step has been taken in esthetic development.

Does this identification, the vicarious attack upon one's problems through identification with a fictional character, help one to solve his real problems? Research can give no definite answer to this, though the school of bibliotherapy has said "Yes" and many readers have vouched for the personal therapy of literature. It is safe, at least, to assume that the literary experience gives the adolescent a chance to approach his problems from the objective role of observer, to gain greater insight because of the creative writer's power to order experience, to identify the vital components, and to clear away the irrelevancies and ambiguities.

It seems important, however, for the teacher to avoid certain pitfalls in dealing with fiction that takes as its theme the personal problems of adolescents. First, one of the major contributions of literature lies in the understanding it gives of human experience. Thus, the major insights into specific problems, whether those of adolescent or adult, will inevitably come through the broader comprehension of human problems that the study of literature affords. It is important for teacher and student to realize that not only the contemporary piece of fiction reflects contemporary problems. Not only the contemporary selection can be vitally related to students' problems. The erosion of time is in itself a criterion of the older book, giving it the power to wash away the irrelevancies and provide a steady view of existence. It is always good in the literature class to link past and present, gaining the rewarding perspective that results. Chaucer's Canterbury pilgrims, for example, live today because their problems are not far different from those of people who ride home on the bus with us each night. And the motivations of Malory's knights are not essentially different from those of the hot rodders in our classes. Finally, it is important that the teacher judge—and teach students to judge—the contemporary novel about the adolescent culture on the basis of literary rather than psychological or social criteria alone.

The Anatomy of the Junior Novel

The term "junior novel" apparently came into use in the 1930's at the outset of the great surge of books written expressly for adolescents. Of course, as other chapters in this book indicate, the junior novel is concerned with a variety of themes, but its major stronghold is the area of personal problems, in which adolescent readers have shown the greatest interest.

Some critics have attacked the quality of the junior novel, dismissing it as a "subliterary" genre, and it is quite true that the majority are slight, mediocre at best, and wanting greatly in literary quality. The same thing can be said of fiction for the general audience: the majority of adult novels also are unworthy of serious attention. Good, mediocre, and wretched work is to be found both in literature for adolescents and in that for adults.

Though the great majority of junior novels are ephemeral, the genre cannot be dismissed lightly. One librarian cites, for example, the increased influence of the junior novel in the high school by pointing out that in 1931, 11.4 percent of the books added to her library were junior novels; in 1951, 73 percent.[3] Of course, this quantitative measure proves nothing by itself. However, studies of reading interests indicate that the junior novel is widely read; apparently it fulfills an important function in the literary education as well as in the personal development of the adolescent. In his literary development it is a steppingstone. The student who can read the junior novel well most probably will develop the ability to read the serious adult novel well. If in the junior high school, for example, the pupil is able to discern the simple symbolic treatment of the theme of good versus evil in something like Annixter's *Swiftwater*—in one exciting scene a boy fights with a wolverine—he is making important preparation for reading later, say, the novels of Thomas Hardy, or of Nathaniel Hawthorne.

As a literary form, the junior novel has established its respectability because of the achievement of some of its writers, and the dividing line between the junior and adult novel may be tenuous.

[3] Emma L. Patterson, "The Junior Novels and How They Grew," *English Journal*, XLV (October 1956), 381–387.

The junior novel is not merely "easier" or less mature than the adult novel, although in the main it is shorter and easier to read than its adult counterpart. Its uniqueness, for better or worse, however, is born of some rather rigid conventions of form and content.

The taboos imposed upon writers of books for adolescents have called forth severe criticism of the overinnocuous quality of junior fiction. One scathing analysis concluded:

The adolescent's world is fraught with change; its charms "are wound up," its horizons are pulsing with expectancies and actualities. His most heartfelt cry is, as Sherwood Anderson warned us long ago, "I want to know why!" The pastel, gum-drop fiction that has been wrought for him avoids both question and answer.[4]

The taboos of the junior novel are the same as those rigorously enforced by publishers of literature anthologies for the junior and senior high school. The "seamy" side of life is generally avoided; erotic drives are ignored; smoking and drinking are seldom alluded to (adolescents, of course, never drink in the books); swearing and bad grammar are avoided—these are some of the most obvious taboos. It can be argued, therefore, that in much junior fiction basic realism is avoided, and that a rounded view of life is not given. Insistence upon a too-narrow concept of "wholesomeness" may tend to cripple the junior novel as a true form of literature, but avoidance or violation of taboos such as those just cited, of course, has little to do with the quality of a work. Good taste as well as verisimilitude is important to adolescent and adult fiction alike. Criticism has centered mainly on the fact that in many junior novels there is slick superficiality, a failure to plunge below the surface into the deeper and more complex human emotions and motivations. In discussing junior novels in which the focus is on the problems of teen-agers, Richard S. Alm writes:

. . . most novelists present a sugar-puff story of what adolescents should do and should believe rather than what adolescents may or

---

[4] Frank G. Jennings, "Literature for Adolescents—Pap or Protein?" *English Journal*, XLV (December 1956), 526–531.

will do and believe. Such stories reveal the novelists' lack of knowledge or insight into adolescent behavior as well as a lack of writing ability. These writers do not penetrate beneath the surface of the situation they create. Their stories are superficial, often distorted, sometimes completely false representations of adolescence.[5]

Superficiality obviously is not a unique shortcoming of fiction for teen-agers. There is patterned, formula writing for both the adult and the adolescent markets, and there is the serious writing for both audiences. Even some talented writers for adolescents, however, apparently feel impelled to "write down," and their failure to probe deeply is intentional. With adolescents, as with adults, the superficial formula story may be popular, but it is important that teachers and librarians stock the fiction shelves and make up book lists from books that represent art rather than artifice.

The junior novel is greatly didactic, frequently obtrusively so, partly because its sale depends largely on the favorable judgments of teachers and librarians who are much interested in the power of fiction to "teach" and to dramatize values. Though didactic, the junior-novelist seldom attempts to be "inspirational" in the venerable success-story tradition; there is little of the Horatio Alger influence. Within the boundaries of its conventions, the junior novel is realistic, pointing toward adjustment and featuring the minor triumphs that are the best most people can hope for. This reflects the writers' awareness of the conservatism of contemporary youth—greater than that of earlier periods—and its concern for security rather than for conquest.

Accordingly, the adolescent reader finds *himself* mirrored, sometimes penetratingly, sometimes only in vague blur with few of his own ideas or feelings. The young super-hero of a few decades ago is uncommon now. The adolescent finds it easy to identify with the characters of the junior novel, but only infrequently has he a desire to change places with them, to drop into the middle of the book, as one girl reading *Little Women* wished to do. He observes the people in the run-of-the-mill story with interest, but it is only

[5] Richard S. Alm, "The Glitter and the Gold," *English Journal*, XLIV (September 1955), 315–322.

in the extraordinary selection that he can identify with protagonists to the point of pain or exhilaration. The junior novel shares with contemporary adult fiction an oft-bewailed failing—memorable characters are hard to find.

In structure, the junior novel tends to be quite rigidly patterned. Its length is standardized at somewhat more than half that of the adult novel. Told almost invariably from an "omniscient" point of view, the plot builds to a climax near the end of the story, leaving only a very brief wrap-up needed. Such subtleties as a change from first to third person in the narrative or use of stream of consciousness are lacking; even the "flashback," a favorite device of the adult novel, is rare. Subplots are uncommon, and the story usually concentrates firmly on one or two major characters.

The Novel That Treats Personal Problems

The teacher in the junior or senior high school can be sure that novels in which the focus is on the personal problems of adolescents, a broad range of good and bad selections, will be widely read. It is important that the teacher continually extend his own knowledge of books that have some real merit and direct pupils to valid evaluation of the selections they read. Class discussions may be directed to the following points:

THE TREATMENT OF THE PROBLEM. Is the problem dealt with significantly? The nature of the problems that the book treats is unimportant. The run-of-the-mill book may deal with a serious problem, the estrangement of father and son, for example, and yet treat it superficially and patly with no real insight into its genesis or the motivations of the people involved. On the other hand, some junior novelists are prone to take a tongue-in-cheek attitude that assures the reader at the outset that the problem is really not important and that if he will but be patient through 240 pages, all will be well.

By what means are problems solved or adjusted to? This is a key question by which the student often will be able to differentiate the valid from the formula piece. In the latter, solutions are often complete and phony, dependent upon external circumstance and coincidence rather than upon any development of the main character. For example, Jim's ambition is to make the football team, but he is woefully inept. His older brother takes him in hand for some private backyard sessions, and Jimmy becomes a shifty tailback. Or Gretchen is the wallflower, aspiring to be part of the round of dates and picnics with "the gang." This comes to pass when a worldly-wise aunt shows her certain tricks of dress and mannerism. The better books often avoid any complete and final solution of a problem, emphasizing rather the inner change of the character as he gains greater maturity and understanding.

THE VIEWPOINT OF ADOLESCENCE. The most competent novels about the adolescent period—and usually the ones most popular with adolescent readers—are fundamentally serious, presenting characters who are complex people with dignity. Many of the personal-problem novels are actually written from the adult's point of view and turn into faintly camouflaged homilies. The formula book usually plays to the adult grandstand. It is easy, of course, for the adolescent reader to recognize the book that consistently presents the adolescent's point of view, and the student's effort to do so is a good exercise in literary discrimination. A certain tradition in writing about the adolescent, dating probably from Booth Tarkington's *Seventeen,* is still evident in the junior novel. In this, adolescence is a kind of madness, a period about which one will laugh later, and adolescent protagonists are caricatured rather than characterized. The tradition has been particularly evident in motion-picture and television treatments of adolescence, about which the real teen-ager can become indignantly vocal.

THE STORYTELLER'S ART. The point has already been made that the novel centering on personal problems—or any other kind of novel —must be judged finally on the basis of literary rather than psychological (or some other) criteria. In the good junior novel, the art of the storyteller is evident—the author's sensitivity to language, his power to build a compelling, suspenseful story from tragic, comic, or heroic events, the aura of verisimilitude with which he is able to surround the narrative. The realistic story, true to human experience, need not be pedestrian in style or plot.

Representative Junior Novelists

Maureen Daly

Since she has written only one junior novel, Maureen Daly is not "representative" in the usual sense. But that one novel, *Seventeenth Summer,* coming before the great flood of fiction for adolescents, can hardly be excluded from any discussion of the art of the junior novel. The book, which has gone through dozens of printings since its publication in 1942, has been hailed as a milestone in the writing of fiction for adolescents. It has stimulated a host of imitations, but few books of the genre have approached it, and it remains one of the most popular books among teen-age girls.

Simple but beautiful in structure and language, the book's almost astonishing verisimilitude may be explained in part by the fact that the author was nineteen when she wrote it. Essentially, the book is the first-person account of seventeen-year-old Angie Morrow's summer-vacation love affair with boy-about-town Jack Duluth in Fond du Lac, Wisconsin. The story is quietly and poignantly told, the unobtrusive introspection given added effect through the first-person technique.

Although the plot is loose, an unusual characteristic in the junior novel, the story progresses well, with no tinge of melodrama, as the summer moves swiftly on to the end when Angie says good-by to Jack and goes away to college. This ending, in which the reader knows with Angie that an important experience has been passed through but that the romance is at an end, is a real triumph:

> The drab edges of the town straggled past, shabby, sad-eyed houses and sagging sheds, trailing bits of worn fence rail around them. Fond du Lac gathered her shoddy outskirts in about her. . . . And slowly, slowly out of the grayness, morning was coming.
>
> And I saw it all glide past me, lopped off by fence posts, and I felt myself ache inside with a quiet sadness. And now I knew suddenly that it could come and could come forever, slipping by in the breath of a moment, and yet never again would there ever be anything quite as wonderful as that seventeenth summer![6]

[6] Reprinted by permission of Dodd, Mead & Company from *Seventeenth Summer* by Maureen Daly. Copyright 1942 by Dodd, Mead & Company, Inc.

As one critic notes: "That the story does not end in a Hollywood manner with Jack and Angie walking off into the sunset together is a credit to Maureen Daly, who does not compromise a characterization in order to make *all* her readers happy."[7]

Angie is an example of skillful characterization. There is no direct statement of her "awareness" from the summer love affair, but it is evident that by the end of the summer she has grown in understanding of herself, the members of her family, and other people. It is a perennial source of surprise to teachers and librarians that sophisticated girls identify so readily with naïve Angie, although it is true that *Seventeenth Summer* is usually read several years before the readers are seventeen. Perhaps the book gives an opportunity for girls to drop their protective shields of sophistication (or pseudosophistication) for some sharing of Angie's introspection. And then, of course, there still are naïve girls!

Angie's family, her home town, even her experiences of the summer are quite ordinary, and on the surface she is ordinary. Yet in her we sense unusual reserves of courage, resourcefulness, and moral stamina. The contrast with her older sister, Lorraine, who is involved in a humiliating (at least, to Angie) affair with the shoddy Martin, is effective.

Seventeenth Summer is one of the few junior novels that has successfully violated certain standard taboos. But the "violations" are subtle and directly related to Angie's development during the summer. For example, in one scene, Angie, at Jack's suggestion, experiments with her first bottle of beer; it leaves her a bit dizzy and she dislikes the taste, but it was something she had to try. In another scene, at a supper club, Angie wonders about the male piano player who has painted fingernails. And near the end of the book, when Angie and Jack are on a picnic with a group, the existence of erotic impulses, at least on Jack's part, is acknowledged.

Anne Emery

Prolific Anne Emery has enjoyed a huge following among adolescent girls. In content and in structure, Emery's books epitomize the average in the junior novel, though her competency in using lan-

[7] Alm, *loc. cit.,* p. 320.

guage is better than average. Scrupulously observing all the standard taboos, Emery presents a world largely purged of unpleasantness, in which the problems of teen-agers are real but highly manageable. "Wholesome" has frequently been applied to Emery's works, but the wholesomeness is rather frequently overwhelming, and "innocuous" probably is more apt.

Her third-person, single-track narratives proceed rapidly with only mild suspense to a very predictable ending, which lays a satisfactory basis for the sequel. There is lavish use of dialogue and little introspection on the part of the teen-age girls who are the main characters. Along the way there is a satisfying—to the girl reader— amount of detail concerning dates and dress and parties.

Probably part of the appeal of Emery's books lies in the fact that they dramatize the upper-middle-class norm—the secure, the average, the comfortable. The fathers in the stories are professional men, and the Burnaby family, on which centers a major series of Emery's books, lives, for example, on Juniper Lane. Hickory Hill is the name of the farm—and of the book that is a sequel to the 4-H story, *County Fair*—and through the farm runs Lazy Creek. Departures from the norm are rare among Emery characters and are rather severely frowned upon. This is evident most clearly in *High Note, Low Note,* one of the books in the Burnaby family series. Jean Burnaby becomes friendly with Kim Ballard, a new girl in school whose family is bohemian. Jean's parents view the friendship, and the Ballard family, with a very troubled eye, exhibiting, in the eyes of an adult reader, a rather amazing lack of sympathy for Kim. Finally, as the elder Burnabys had feared, Kim leads Jean astray, albeit not too seriously.

Characterization in Emery, in general, is limited to categories rather than individuals. There are five categories: fathers, mothers, adolescent girls, adolescent boys, and less-than-adolescent girls and boys. Within each category, characters are very much alike. Fathers are usually rather vague and preoccupied with their work, coming into the story mainly when money becomes an issue. Mothers are youthful, attractive, calmly philosophical, and intelligent. This description from *Campus Melody* is typical: "Mrs. Burnaby looked cool and fresh as she sipped her second cup of coffee while she wrote out 'Things to Be Done Today.' "

The theme of "Mother (and occasionally Father) is right" is the most prevalent one, sometimes irritatingly so, in Emery's books. Early in *Going Steady,* Sally decides: "How could her mother be so wise?" And in *High Note, Low Note:* "But deep down underneath, try as she would to ignore it, Jean could not help wondering if her mother were not right." Perhaps the most irritating play for adult favor occurs at another point in *High Note, Low Note.* The morning after a minor tiff with her father over going to a party with Kim Ballard and some other friends, Jean Burnaby comes down the stairs to find at the bottom a paper on which is written: "X marks the spot where the world came to an end last night." And shortly after, Jean decides: "Oh, well . . . it's just as comfortable not to stay mad—especially when you can't win."

The adolescent boys in Emery's books—with the exception of *Vagabond Summer,* in which there are some rather well-developed characters, and the cad in *Campus Melody*—are almost indistinguishable from each other. Scotty, who appears in several books and epitomizes "the boy who lives next door," is exactly like Jeff, for example, who at one point is described thus: ". . . Jeff returned at 7:30, shining with soap and water." And Jean and Sally Burnaby, who share the major roles in the Burnaby series, are identical.

Though not her most popular book, *Vagabond Summer* may be Anne Emery's best, because of its originality and sounder characterization. The story's teen-age heroine goes on a summer hosteling tour with a group of other young people and makes some tentative decisions about her future. In this book, unlike most of Emery's others, there is an interesting group of well-drawn personalities. Of course, there is a radiantly happy ending with the quite typical final lines: "The world lay before them. All their bright young world."

Despite her shortcomings from a literary point of view, Anne Emery has captured the interest of a large number of adolescent girls, and in so doing she has made a contribution. She presents characters who experience, after all, the mundane kind of problems that are true, although not the whole truth, of adolescence. Identification with her characters furnishes no moving experience nor any depth of insight. But her readers find in her books what they are seeking there—entertainment and, to some extent, wish fulfillment.

James L. Summers

The books that James Summers has so far written, though of mediocre literary value, have helped to fill a long-existing gap—competent stories about teen-age problems for boys. The dearth of such books is partly explained by the fact that boys are less interested in the story that centers on teen-age romance and family problems than are girls, and partly because most of the writers of teen-age problem stories are women who choose to write of girls' problems. Certainly, a masculine counterpart to Anne Emery would have little appeal to adolescent boys, whose tastes run to more virile and exciting fare. Yet a counterpart to *Seventeenth Summer,* which has not been produced, would undoubtedly enjoy vast success.

Essentially, Summers is a humorist. His books are amusing, at points hilarious, and his over-all approach is light, though he evidences good insight into the adolescent culture. His approach is perilously near caricature, however, when his attempts to amuse sometimes get out of hand. Several reviewers of his books have noted that fathers might enjoy some of the passages more than their sons for whom the books are written.

Like Anne Emery's heroines, Summers' heroes are virtually identical from book to book. Rodney Budlong of *Prom Trouble,* Don Morley of *Girl Trouble,* and Roger Holman of *Trouble on the Run* are all slightly-less-than-average boys who aspire, above all else, to be average. These characters are fit subjects for light treatment and provide easy identification for most readers, who can be genuinely amused at the protagonists' foibles.

Summers' plots are very similar: they involve his heroes, who cannot do anything too well, in two types of problems—love and school. The love plot usually involves the hero's pining for the wrong (as the end of the book shows) girl and a failing (until the end) to appreciate the right girl who was there all the time. The school problem involves the hero's being saddled with a responsibility for which he is not quite qualified. In *Prom Trouble,* Rodney Budlong is elected junior class president as a "gag," and has the task of directing plans for the prom. In *Trouble on the Run,* Roger Holman is put in charge of preparing a float. Both muddle through with moderate success. A variation in *Girl Trou-*

ble has Don Morley having to drop football in order to work so that he can pay a traffic fine.

Like Emery, Summers relies largely on categories of characters and general impressions rather than on detailed delineation. His mother and father categories are similar to Emery's except that Summers' fathers are small businessmen. The Morleys in *Girl Trouble* are typical: "Both the elder Morleys were slim and faintly youthful." Perhaps because of his experience as a high school teacher, Summers is at his best in characterizing school administrators and teachers, whom he treats with kind humor and gentle irony. The details of school life in his books are authentic and genuine.

Summers consistently overwrites, as this passage from *Trouble on the Run* reveals:

Glenn Harlan, on the other hand, was little and thin and a pretty fair hurdler who would be a neat guy if he could ever lay off math. His brain was water-logarithmed on the stuff and anything he couldn't find the square root of in one minute he regarded with suspicion and disdain. When Harlan was quiet, a person could almost hear his brain whirring around like Univac, feeding itself data about people, distance, and time, squishing the information around in the right tubes, and coming up with the perfect answer. If he hadn't been so boring with math, he could have been one interesting guy. The way it was, everybody expected him to be blasted off in a Navy rocket in the interests of national defense.[8]

And frequently Summers' dialogue, though usually amusing, is written in a jargon and in patterns of speech that border on the grotesque.

Most of the statements made so far about Summers do not apply to two of his books. One of his most unusual—though not necessarily his best—is *Operation ABC*. Apparently, the author had become interested in the problem of retarded reading ability and had read the work of Fernald or others who have used the "kinesthetic" approach in remedial reading. The book tells an engrossing story

[8] From *Trouble on the Run* by James L. Summers. Copyright 1956, by James L. Summers, the Westminster Press. Used by permission.

of a senior boy who is a retarded reader and very fearful that someone will find out. He faces his problem realistically in an ending
that is hopeful but semitragic. Summers' most impressive novel,
The Limit of Love, develops poignantly a theme highly unusual in
teen-age fiction. The main characters, a boy and girl just out of
high school, face the problem of controlling their passions. Deeply
in love, they realize that immediate marriage is impossible, and
they agree to separate. The love scenes are handled skillfully; in
fact, in this novel Summers' style reaches a level not found in any
of his other books. These last two books are proof that Summers
can treat a serious theme competently.

Mary Stolz

Undoubtedly the most interesting and accomplished writer of
junior novels is Mary Stolz. Though she has produced a surprising
number of novels in a short time, the level of quality has remained
consistently high. Several of her books are definitely within the
conventions of the junior novel; several are iconoclastic.

Essentially, Stolz's books are love stories, though she injects minor social themes in several. Her treatment of love in late adolescence is far different from that of Emery, Summers, or even of
Daly's *Seventeenth Summer.* Love, in the Stolz novels, is fraught
with a tempestuousness and an anguish that is foreign to most
other novels for the adolescent. This is true even of the books in
the familiar junior novel pattern—*To Tell Your Love* and *The
Sea Gulls Woke Me,* for example. Serious, intense Anne Armacost,
of *To Tell Your Love,* suffers a bitter summer of putting on ap-
pearances, hoping, waiting for the telephone to ring, and of final
hurt when her intenseness "scares off" the boy she loves. The ending, highly characteristic of Stolz, features quiet resignation on
Anne's part. Though the members of the Armacost family—father,
mother, younger brother—are akin to those in Anne Emery, they
come to life to a much greater degree, and the portrait of Anne is
a real triumph. As with all the Stolz protagonists, there is a pain
in the identification with Anne; the Stolz novels are designed for
a more mature and sensitive audience than those of Emery and
many other junior novelists. Not at all in the lighthearted manner,
the Stolz stories are overhung with a sense of the sadness of life,

the possibilities of emotional disaster, and the *weltschmerz* that is highly characteristic of late adolescence.

Stolz has explored the problems of family life as it is lived at several economic levels. In *Ready or Not* and *The Day and the Way We Met,* sequel books, the family lives in a semitenement district in New York City and the father is a subway token seller. The first book concerns the problems of an adolescent girl in managing the household after her mother dies. In the second, the younger sister takes over when the elder marries. *The Day and the Way We Met* is a tender story that shows the typical lack of concern for plot and structure in the late Stolz books. Essentially, it is a well-done character study, but many adolescent readers would find the slow-moving narrative boring. The wonderfully conceived ending finds the heroine answering the phone, wondering—with the reader—which of three men is calling!

Characterization is especially splendid in *Pray Love, Remember.* The theme of this hard-hitting novel is prominent in Stolz—the estrangement of the adolescent heroine from her family. The conflict is particularly marked between Dody Jenks, the heroine, and her older brother, who appears even more loutish in her eyes than he really is. The younger sister is the "ugly duckling" and the contrast between her and Dody is effective. Dody is a highly unusual and interesting character, enigmatic even to herself. She is a great social success in her senior year in high school and much envied, though she is almost without friends. Her essential coldness, making her anything but endearing, is in marked contrast to the heroines of most of the other Stolz books. All the Emery-Summers patterns of the father and mother and of the family situation are smashed here. The dialogue in general and the dinner table conversations in particular are superb. Graduating from high school, Dody finally escapes her family and the town by taking a position as governess with a wealthy family. Dody's love affair with a Jewish boy seems a rather artificial and tangential addition, and ends with the boy's death in a car accident and Dody's near collapse. However, the end finds her returning to her job as governess with a new sense of her identity.

The originality of *Rosemary* comes as a mild shock. The book begins in a fashion highly standard in teen-age fiction. Rosemary, who is working in a store rather than attending the college in her town, meets the dashing college boy and a date is set. But the boy, quite understandably misinterpreting Rosemary's rather tawdry behavior at a dance, makes "a pass" at her. This provides the opening trauma in the development of Rosemary's love interests and her relations with several people, including her none-too-appealing father.

Departing completely from the mold of the junior novel is the moving *Two by Two,* the only Stolz story in which a boy is the main character. The plot involves the conflict between Harry Lynch and his father, a wealthy lawyer, and Harry's love affair with Nan Gunning. Sex and the erotic impulses are thoroughly probed in the love plot, which is a far cry from the round of dates, picnics, and cool-lipped kisses of the Emery stories. In fact, Harry and Nan are discovered in her bedroom by her father. And in a scene in which Harry and a friend visit a night club, a waitress "hovered over them, muskily perfumed, in a dress deeply cut at the bodice, confident in a society where mammary worship came second only to mammon worship."

An air of doom hangs over the story; the reader may suspect that Harry will commit suicide. Instead, he kills someone else, a drunkard, accidentally when he drives away from the night club. Actually, the swift ending is happy—the reconciliation of Harry with his own and Nan's father. Like several of the other Stolz books, *Two by Two* is slow moving, full of the introspection, sometimes bordering stream of consciousness, typical of Stolz. The action is mainly psychological and, as in several of her other books, there are rambling lyrical passages at times slightly reminiscent of Thomas Wolfe.

Mary Stolz is a talented and original writer with a deep regard for the dignity of the adolescent. Done in richly subtle shades, rather than in pastels, her work bodes well for the future of the junior novel.

Henry Gregor Felsen[9]

A prolific as well as an extremely versatile author of junior novels is Henry Gregor Felsen. Probably best known for his novels

[9] Commentary by Helen O'Hara Rosenblum, Florida State University.

involving cars, his writings also include such diverse subjects as war, humor, and conflict with society.

In his earlier novels, such as *Navy Diver*, the style is masculine, the plot is exciting, and the characters emerge as real with only a slight "willing suspension of disbelief" on the part of the reader. The total effect is a kind of cross between Howard Pease and Ernest Hemingway. However, there are overtones of meaningful issues. In *Navy Diver*, Jeff's best friend on the farm had been a Japanese. Felsen tersely illustrates his hero's conflict during the World War II crisis.

Contrasted with the dramatic conflict portrayed in *Navy Diver* is the slapstick comedy saturating the Bertie novels. The roly-poly protagonist of the series is Bertie Poddle, an overfed junior edition of Walter Mitty. The difference is that Bertie naïvely attempts to make his dreams materialize. His efforts inevitably backfire in hilariously ludicrous situations.

The chapters in the Bertie novels are rather episodic, unified by Bertie himself and his rather motley assortment of type-cast friends —handsome, intelligent Ted Dale and his equally remarkable sister, Marcia; Wiggins Hackenlooper, Heeble High School's powerful fullback; Wilbur Frost, the caustic agnostic who is finally humanized by Bertie's intensely candid efforts; and the female antithesis of Bertie also providing humor, Hyacinth O'Houlihan. Hyacinth, a wild red-head and as skinny as Bertie is phlegmatic, falls in love with Wiggins only because he can beat her at Indian wrestling. These characters are introduced in the initial book of the series, *Bertie Comes Through*.

Bertie provides more than just entertainment, however. Pervading the comic situations are significant ideas. In *Bertie Takes Care*, the hero is rejected as a camp counselor because of his overweight. Making the best of his misfortunes, Bertie herds together the town rejects, organizes his own camp, and finally triumphs when beating the snobbish and egotistical baseball team from Camp Ijoboko. The Bertie novels are entertaining stories of achievement and good sportsmanship that especially appeal to younger boys.

Felsen's car novels, however, interest boys (and girls) in a range of junior high school through the late teens. There is no absolute upper interest limit for these stories of life adjustment, especially for the very popular *Street Rod* and *Hot Rod*. Both novels deal with boys in their late teens whose interest in cars is portrayed as a means of adjustment, a kind of compensation or escape from an indifferent culture. Bud Crayne in *Hot Rod* is without parents. School and other societal institutions apparently offer little for Bud. In a defiant gesture reminiscent of Holden Caulfield and Huck Finn, Bud wears an old fedora hat with the brim turned up in front and fastened to the crown with a giant safety pin. He makes his own rules until the guidance of Ted O'Day, a patrolman, and Mr. Cole, a shop teacher, demonstrates the real tragedy of an accident in which all but one of Bud's companions are killed. These characters, like Bud, have all sought refuge from a society where adolescents don't "belong." Felsen vividly conveys the problem of the search for identity. The funeral is, perhaps, a dramatic précis of the theme:

> Avondale buried its dead and their dreams.
> Ralph Osler was buried with his dream of a college career in sports. La Verne Shuler was buried with her dream of escape to Hollywood. Walt Thomas was buried with his dream of getting away from the farm. Marge Anderson was buried with her dream of being popular. And the others were buried with their dreams. There was no buying Ralph out of this scrape, no smiling her way out for La Verne, no blustering his way out for Walt.
> The victims of a careless moment were laid to rest.[10]

The "careless moment" is likewise important in *Street Rod*. Sixteen-year-old Ricky Madison attempts to set up the Dellville Timing Association so that the hot rodders may race without breaking speed laws. When the village council refuses to cooperate, Ricky and his friends operate outside the law. With the help of his girl friend Sharon, Ricky enters and wins an auto-design competition. On his way back from the competition, his careless immaturity results in death.

Impulsiveness is dealt with in more profound terms in what may be Felsen's most controversial novel, *Two and the Town*. Buff Cody, the senior football star, has reached his moment of heroic

[10] From Henry Gregor Felsen, *Hot Rod* (New York: E. P. Dutton & Co., Inc., 1950).

glory only to find it sour in the defeat of the big game. Elaine Truro, overly protected, quiet, and scholarly, gives the rejected Buff genuine sympathy, warm and tender feeling. In this moment of intensity, abstract feelings lose their meaning. With deep psychological insight Felsen describes the situation:

. . . She became as furiously unrestrained as Buff himself, made one last, frightened effort to break away, and, in a situation where Carol would have laughed and saved herself, Elaine wept and was lost.

The remainder of the novel deals with the manifest problems inherent in a "forced" marriage. Felsen realistically portrays the problem in a specific setting, but the implications of the theme are more universal in scope. Because he deals with very human problems, Henry Gregor Felsen writes novels for young people that capably meet their needs and interests. His themes are communicated in a professional style that may provide an important step in the development of literary appreciation.

Variations on the Theme of Personal Problems

One of the largest categories of literature for adolescents is comprised of fiction that deals with the particular problems of the early and late teen-age period. Yet many of the books in this category are slight and highly patterned, many of them failing to rise above the level of the typical soap opera script. Good, bad, or indifferent from a literary or psychological point of view, these books are perennially popular, drawing to them a great host of readers, especially among girls in junior and senior high school. Rising above the mainstream of books for girls are those by Madeleine L'Engle, Elizabeth Headley (the pen name of Betty Cavanna), Rosamond Du Jardin, Laura Rendina, Beverly Cleary, Elizabeth Gray Vining, Zoa Sherburne, Jean Nielsen, and Jessica Lyon.

Varied in her subject matter and settings is the impressive Madeleine L'Engle, whose focus is on the awarenesses of her heroines but who does not neglect other characters in her stories. The family of Dr. Austin and his cultured wife—a family including two boys, two girls, a theological grandfather, an artist uncle and his wife, and assorted pets—is the subject of two of L'Engle's books. In the first, *Meet the Austins,* the story concerns the death of Aunt Elena's test-pilot husband, ten-year-old Maggie's stay at the Austins, and the anticipated marriage of Aunt Elena and Uncle Douglas. *The Moon by Night,* the sequel, opens with this wedding and is centered on the Austins' trip to California to visit Elena and Douglas. The camping trip across the country is replete with episodes of rock slides, flash floods, and earthquakes. The real center of interest, however, is Vicky's relationship with two boys —Zachary, a rebellious cynic, and Andy, a sincere and upstanding youth. Superior in style, both novels are narrated by teen-age Vicky. *And Both Were Young* presents the problems of Phillipa (Flip) Hunter, who is sent to an exclusive girls' school in Switzerland. Her problems of adjustment are complicated by her relationship with Paul Laurens, an orphan of World War II whose traumatic experiences have blocked his memory. Like Maureen Daly, Madeleine L'Engle captures an essence of adolescent thinking.

Prolific Betty Cavanna, who is nearly as popular as Anne Emery, especially with younger girls, has dealt more convincingly with the adult culture than has Emery, and is more sensitive to the pain as well as the enchantment of the teen-age period. She has a particular gift for handling the scenes in which adolescents are together, and her most notable book probably is *Going On Sixteen,* in which shy Julie Ferguson, who grows more confident in the course of the story, is the main character. Her more recent *The Boy Next Door,* a competently written story, represents the typical admixture of school, love, and family problems in her novels. Though her books are uneven and, on the whole, undistinguished, Betty Cavanna maintains a consistently realistic point of view toward the adolescent period. Her humorous, plotless, and episodic books, written under the name Elizabeth Headley, feature Diane Graham, and have been very popular. Though shallow in characterization, these books present effectively the jealousies and rivalries of middle-adolescent girls, and a few of the episodes are memorable—for example, the one in *A Date for Diane,* in which Diane, cringingly sensitive about the new braces on her teeth, discovers that the boy of her dreams has worn braces for months.

Very much in the mold of Anne Emery, and equally popular, in writing of the problems of boy friends and the light side of middle-class family life, is Rosamond Du Jardin. In *Class Ring,* Tobey Heydon, who is the main character in *Practically Seventeen* also, struggles with the problem of going steady and decides, in good didactic fashion, that one should not become too serious too soon. Written competently in the first person, *Class Ring* is light, frequently humorous, and deals with the typical round of boys, dates, and school affairs and with minor family conflicts, such as a crisis involving the length of Tobey's fingernails.

More original than most books of this genre are those by Laura Rendina. Her best book is *My Love for One,* a moving story of a girl's efforts—and her family's—to adjust to a new way of life after the death of the mother. Debbie Jones's quest for fulfillment has an adult depth, and her final satisfaction in love is far from the usual girl-gets-boy pattern. A more recent book, *Lolly Touchberry,* though undistinguished in style, is a better-than-average story of a fifteen-year-old Florida girl, her school, family, and dating affairs. A minor social theme, which finds Lolly thinking faintly that racial segregation is not right, is gingerly presented.

Though long established as a writer for children, a newcomer to the field of junior fiction, Beverly Cleary has made an auspicious beginning in her first two novels for adolescents. *Fifteen,* the first one, handles with unusual skill the theme of the adolescent girl's emergence from the awkward stage, the transition period in which she is learning to suffer in a girdle and turning ankles in high heels. Characterization of the adolescent girls and portrayal of their relations with parents are realistically done, though the dialogue is somewhat unrealistic. The woes of baby-sitting, so much a part of the modern adolescent's culture, are cleverly and convincingly portrayed. The second book, *The Luckiest Girl,* is somewhat less successful because of a strained setting—a sixteen-year-old girl rather unbelievably visits friends for a year. Yet the story has the aura of real modern high school experience, in which grades *are* important, and of the moods of adolescent life.

One of the earlier writers of junior novels, Elizabeth Gray Vining, has produced two books that stand with the better novels for girls—*The Fair Adventure* and *Sandy. The Fair Adventure* presents family relationships extremely well, as the heroine experiences the disappointment of not winning the scholarship that seemed her only hope of attending college. The familiar high school activities in the book have a fine verisimilitude. In the other book, *Sandy,* there is the usual summer vacation interlude in which the seventeen-year-old heroine comes to realize a number of things. However, the author's style lifts this book, as well as the other, above the run of the mill.

Among the better writers for older girls is Zoa Sherburne, author of *Almost April* and *The High White Wall.* Both books, though marred by a pedestrian style, flash occasionally to the dark side of life and possess a fairly unusual originality. *Almost April* is the story of a girl's adjustment to her stepmother, an attractive young woman, and her friendship with a boy figuratively from the "other side of the tracks." *The High White Wall* features an older girl's break with family ties and her romance with a young poet, who is the most interesting character in the story. The mother in this story is well drawn, too. It is unfortunate that the heroine remains a vague character. Both books plunge more deeply into human feelings than do most junior novels, and in both, Mrs. Sherburne's sympathy with the adolescent character is apparent. There is no moralizing in either book.

Distinguished for their substance, their greater "heart" than that in the usual novel about the adolescent culture, are the books of Jean Nielsen. Her best story is *Green Eyes,* which recounts the senior year of Jan Morgan, editor of the high school newspaper. The book centers on Jan's problems as editor and on her family problems, which are excellently handled, rather than on the usual round of dates and parties. In this book and also in *Look to the New Moon,* the adolescent characters are highly serious and very believable.

Less expert in style, but popular, is Jessica Lyon (pen name for Cateau de Leeuw), who presents young adults in the out-of-school world. The principal value of *This My Desire,* a love story that ends happily, lies in the interesting, though far from admirable, main character, a girl subject to "crushes." *The Proud Air,* a story of two snobs engaged at first sight, is highly contrived but manages to produce suspense.

The teen-age boy and his problems have received scant attention in the fiction for adolescents. Of course, boys figure actively in many of the books that have girls as main characters, but there are very few junior novels in which the adolescent boy is treated seriously and perceptively. One of the best is the poignant *Swiftwater,* by Paul Annixter, in which lonely fifteen-year-old Bucky Calloway strives to establish a game refuge for wild geese. The excellence of the book lies in the fine characterization of Bucky and his family and in the author's amazing facility in conveying the atmosphere of wild places.

The books by Don Stanford are better than average. His most successful one, *The Red Car,* presents an exciting, uncomplicated plot in which sixteen-year-old Hap Adams acquires a wrecked sports car, rebuilds it, and enters a race that furnishes the climax. The abundant detail of car lore in this book appeals to many boys.

Versatile Marguerite Harmon Bro has produced one of the most original, if not popular, books for adolescents in *Stub, a College Romance.* Stub Larsen, in his freshman year at a college patterned after Shimer College, which the author knew well, has problems of love and human relations. Stub's friends, a group of varied and unusual young people, are well drawn and, unlike most college stories, their intellectual life furnishes the main fabric of the narrative.

Adolescent Problems in Adult Fiction

The problems of adolescence, of course, have appeared not only in junior fiction. In fact, one critic remarks that "a few American novels about adolescence have embodied some of the most adult wisdom that America has produced."[11] The classic example, naturally, is *Huckleberry Finn,* which represents universal adolescence through Huck's struggle to come to terms with adult ways and to fathom the complexities of motivation.

Of course, there is the tradition, stemming from Booth Tarking-

[11] Frederic I. Carpenter, "The Adolescent in American Fiction," *English Journal,* XLVI (September 1957), 314.

ton's *Seventeen,* in which adolescence is viewed as a temporary kind of insanity, the problems of which will dissolve in the stability and serenity of adulthood. In this type of book the adolescent is caricatured. But, as Frederic Carpenter points out, "at his best the modern American novelist of adolescence describes the problems of his protagonists so that they become also the problems of our adolescent civilization, with both its mixed-up confusion and its splendid potentiality."[12]

Probably the clearest illustration of the truth of Carpenter's observation is Thomas Wolfe, whose long, impassioned novels can be read with profit by a minority of senior high school students but whose books arouse a tremendous response in some of these students, who find in Wolfe an echo of their own inner shouts. The most notable treatment of adolescent character in recent fiction is J. D. Salinger's *The Catcher in the Rye,* which, with seeming artlessness, touches the most tender and sensitive spots in the adolescent make-up. In the story, mixed-up Holden Caulfield views his world as "phony" and "crummy," searches for values, and suffers a nervous breakdown. Because of the language and some of the scenes, the teacher should be chary of recommending it except to mature adolescents. The book would be very difficult to discuss in a class.

Strikingly similar to *The Catcher in the Rye* in accomplishment, though notably more positive in effect, is John Knowles's splendid *A Separate Peace,* set in a boys' preparatory school in New England during the early years of World War II. Gene Forrester, the protagonist, misunderstands the friendship of his roommate, Phineas. Torn between love and hate, he pushes Phineas from a tree and causes an injury that ultimately leads to Phineas's death. Through his relationship with Phineas and the events of his last year at school, Gene makes his "separate peace," in existential fashion, before he ever gets into the war. *A Separate Peace* is already fairly commonly taught—and deserves to be—in high school classes.

Quite a different type of book, but one full of insight, is *Cress Delahanty* by Jessamyn West. Cress's adolescence is "normal" and usually happy. The book has its hilarious scenes as well as its poignant ones. Highly appropriate for reading by adolescents them-

[12] *Ibid.,* p. 319.

selves, the book stands as one of the most valid treatments of adolescence in American fiction.

Continuing in popularity among older girls is Mildred Walker's competent and tender novel, *Winter Wheat*. The essential theme of the story is the heroine's developing understanding of love, particularly that between her parents, an understanding furthered through her own tragic love affair with a young man she meets at college. For high school girls, *Winter Wheat* is in a line of natural progression from, say, *Seventeenth Summer* or *To Tell Your Love* to *Jane Eyre* and *Wuthering Heights*.

For mature students Ruth Moore's *The Fire Balloon* also deals interestingly and significantly with adolescent characters. Basically a regional story, the plot centers on the members of a Maine-coast family, particularly the nineteen-year-old girl and her younger brother. The girl is involved in a melodramatic imbroglio, which is given significance through its effect on her and on the unity of the family.

The Vocational Novel

Concern with his future role as an adult is a major preoccupation of the adolescent, especially when he reaches the senior high school. From this concern has come the "vocational story," which presents in fictional form information about professions and occupations. These books, though rather widely read, have little significance for the literature program. Most of them could quite fairly be called "subliterary," and many of them have doubtful value as sources of information. The senior high school student who is seriously considering a vocation is inclined—and should be urged—to consult authentic sources of information that lie outside the area of literature.

The vocational novel for adolescents probably had its beginning with the publication of Helen D. Boylston's first Sue Barton story in 1936. The subsequent series that takes Sue Barton through the various stages of her training and professional life has been extremely popular with girls in their mid-adolescence. For some reason—probably the romantic tradition surrounding the profession—stories of nursing have been a staple in this genre of writing for young people. Another popular series about nursing, somewhat better in quality than Boylston's, are those by Dorothy Deming. Mary Stolz, however, has contributed the best stories of nursing in her *Organdy Cupcakes* and *Hospital Zone*. Though these books lack the introspection and lyricism of other Stolz novels, and the "writing down" in them is evident, they are definitely a cut above most others in this genre.

The better vocational novels, of course, are able to present authentic, unglamorized information in the context of a well-told story. Adele de Leeuw has accomplished this in some of her many vocational stories, the best known of which is probably *With a High Heart*, dealing with rural library work. Also unusually well done is Phyllis Whitney's *A Window for Julie*, in which the heroine starts as a salesgirl in a department store and finally becomes a window-display designer.

Another unusual book that fits loosely into the vocational category is Nancy Hartwell's *Dusty Cloak*, in which the tribulations of getting a start in the professional world of acting are delineated. The heroine experiences disappointment without disillusionment, and a deftly handled love plot is woven skillfully into the well-written story.

POSSIBILITIES FOR STUDENT READING

(Books discussed in the preceding chapter are marked with an asterisk [*]. They are annotated only when the nature of their content was not made clear in the chapter. A indicates adult books; E, especially easy ones.)

Alcott, Louisa May, *Little Women*, various publishers.
　　Family life as four sisters grow up.

*Annixter, Paul, *Swiftwater*, Wyn.

Austen, Jane, *Pride and Prejudice*, various publishers.　(A)
　　Five marriageable daughters and a matchmaking mother.

Benson, Sally, *Junior Miss*, Doubleday.　(E)
　　A thirteen-year-old girl and her family in New York City.

*Bro, Marguerite H., *Stub, a College Romance*, Doubleday.
(Also *Sarah*.)

Brontë, Charlotte, *Jane Eyre*, various publishers. (A)
An English girl's life as a governess and her romance with a mysterious man.

Caudill, Rebecca, *The House of the Fifers*, McKay. (E)
A New York girl spends an illuminating summer on the farm of her relatives.

*Cavanna, Betty, *Going on Sixteen*, Westminster. (E)
(Also *Paintbox Summer, A Girl Can Dream, 6 on Easy Street*.)

*Cleary, Beverly, *Fifteen*, Morrow. (E)

Dahl, Borghild, *Under This Roof*, Dutton.
After her mother's death, a sixteen-year-old girl takes on unusual family responsibilities.

*Daly, Maureen, *Seventeenth Summer*, Dodd, Mead.

*Dickens, Charles, *Great Expectations*, various publishers. (A)
A young man changes his life when he loses his anticipated fortune. (Also *David Copperfield*.)

*Du Jardin, Rosamond, *Class Ring*, Lippincott.
(Also *Practically Seventeen*.)

*Emery, Anne, *Going Steady*, Westminster.
Two high school seniors plan to be married but change their minds after thinking it through. (Also *Campus Melody, *High Note, Low Note, *Vagabond Summer*.)

*Felsen, Henry Gregor, *Bertie Comes Through*, Dutton (E)
Bertie, the fat boy, tries everything in school activities, but never quite makes the grade in anything but the affections of his classmates. (Also *Bertie Makes a Break* and *Bertie Takes Care*.)

*———, *Street Rod*, Dutton.
(Also *Hot Rod*.)

Gorsline, Douglas, *Farm Boy*, Viking. (E)
A rebellious teen-age boy is sent to work on his uncle's farm and gains a new point of view.

Harkins, Philip, *Road Race*, Crowell.
A hot-rodder builds a jalopy into a hot-rod club winner.

Hartwell, Nancy, *My Little Sister*, Holt, Rinehart and Winston.
Two teen-age sisters find serious conflicts between their parents' ideas and those of their social crowd. (Also *Dusty Cloak*.)

*Headley, Elizabeth, *A Date for Diane.* Macrae.   (E)

*Knowles, John, *A Separate Peace,* Macmillan.   (A)

*L'Engle, Madeleine, *The Moon by Night,* Farrar, Straus.
    (Also *Meet the Austins* and *And Both Were Young.*)

*Lyon, Jessica, *This My Desire,* Macrae.

*Moore, Ruth, *The Fire Balloon,* Morrow.   (A)

*Nielsen, Jean, *Green Eyes,* Funk & Wagnalls.
    (Also *Look to the New Moon.*)

*Rendina, Laura, *My Love for One,* Little, Brown.
    (Also *Lolly Touchberry.*)

*Sherburne, Zoa, *Almost April,* Morrow.
    (Also *The High White Wall* and *Princess in Denim.*)

Stanford, Don, *Ski Town,* Funk & Wagnalls.
    Skiing in a Colorado resort town furnishes the unity for the
    story of several interesting people with varied motivations.
    (Also *The Red Car.*)

*Stolz, Mary, *Ready or Not,* Harper & Row.
    (Also *The Day and the Way We Met,* virtually a sequel.)

*————, *To Tell Your Love,* Harper & Row.
    (Also *Two by Two, *Pray Love, Remember* and *Rosemary.*)

*Summers, James L., *The Limit of Love,* Westminster.
    (Also *Prom Trouble, *Girl Trouble, *Trouble on the Run* and
    Operation ABC.)

Twain, Mark, *The Adventures of Tom Sawyer,* various publishers.
    (Also *Huckleberry Finn.*)

*Vining, Elizabeth Gray, *The Fair Adventure,* Viking.
    (Also *Sandy.*)

*Walker, Mildred, *Winter Wheat,* Harcourt.   (A)

*West, Jessamyn, *Cress Delahanty.* Harcourt.   (A)

*Wolfe, Thomas, *Look Homeward, Angel,* Scribner.   (A)
    Eugene Gant's boyhood and adolescence, based on Wolfe's ex-
    periences in North Carolina.

SOCIAL PROBLEMS
AND THE
LITERATURE
PROGRAM

THOUGH THE PERSONAL PROBLEMS of the adolescent and the mores of the adolescent culture furnish the major raw material for fiction written specifically for adolescents, the traditions and functions of literature relate social or group problems importantly to the literature program at any level of the school. Because, unlike social problems, certain personal problems are unique to the adolescent period, the teen-ager is more concerned with them in his daily life, and writers who address themselves to the teen-age audience have been less inclined to treat social themes.

But the tradition of social significance and of social protest has been a major one in the literature of the world. In 1956 the New American Library published a paperbound edition of the book by Robert B. Downs entitled *Books That Changed the World*. On the cover is a reference to the fact that the books discussed "caused people to revolt against oppression, started wars, and revolutionized man's ideas about the universe and himself." Many of the books discussed in this particular volume do not belong in the sphere of imaginative literature; yet the novel, for example, has been a powerful shaper and inciter of public opinion on social issues and conditions. In the nineteenth century, Victor Hugo, with *Les Misérables,* and Charles Dickens, with books like *Oliver*

Twist, centered attention on social injustice in France and England. One of the most incendiary books in American history is Harriet Beecher Stowe's novel, *Uncle Tom's Cabin.* It is generally conceded that Upton Sinclair's powerful novel, *The Jungle,* which revealed conditions in the Chicago stockyards at the turn of the century, was influential in bringing the passage of the pure food and drug laws. Sinclair Lewis' widely read novels savagely attacked America's small-town business culture. More recently, John Steinbeck dramatized the plight of the migrant worker in *The Grapes of Wrath;* Richard Wright, in his *Native Son,* protested angrily against the condition of the Negro; Laura Hobson attacked anti-Semitism in *Gentlemen's Agreement;* Willard Motley pointed to the relationship between delinquency and living conditions in *Knock on Any Door;* Irwin Shaw etched the dilemma of the American liberal, caught between communism and extreme reaction, in *The Troubled Air.* The fundamental protest against conditions that diminish man and his spirit is reflected in the literature of all periods.

Teachers have realized for a long time, apparently, that literature which deals with social or group problems can aid in improving human relations and in developing a rational approach to social problems, an approach based upon an awareness of alternatives in our group life. One of the most widely circulated book lists arranges titles under such headings as: "Community Contrasts," "Economic Differences," "Belonging to Groups," "Experiences of Acceptance and Rejection."[1] In his foreword to the volume, Arthur S. Adams, then president of the American Council on Education, states: "The technique embodied in this volume grew from the experience of classroom teachers who, knowing the importance of stories and books to children, believed that the printed page could be used to teach attitudes as well as facts—and to teach in the process of entertaining."

The National Council of Teachers of English has published a book list, the purposes of which are stated as follows:

---

[1] Margaret M. Heaton and Helen B. Lewis (Eds.), *Reading Ladders for Human Relations* (Washington, D.C.: American Council on Education, 1955). [A new edition, edited by Muriel Crosby, will be available by spring 1964.]

. . . to present the underlying principles in guiding teachers and librarians in choosing books for young people and, second, to list many books now available that depict Negro life honestly and accurately and to annotate some which should be balanced by others that round out the portrait of Negro life as it is lived in America today.[2]

The National Council for the Social Studies has published a bibliography for secondary schools.[3] In their preface the editors state: "This bulletin has been prepared to meet the need of social studies and core teachers for imaginative literature and biography that illuminate the issues about which modern problems courses are built."

The teachers of Denver outline a unit for the ninth grade entitled "Who Are Americans?" about the contributions and problems of various minority groups.[4] The introduction states the belief that "students whose reading is carefully guided may well become increasingly sensitive to their own responsibility for improving human relations." One of the suggested units for grade eleven in Minnesota is entitled "Diversity of Cultures in America."[5] The purpose of this unit is "to help students realize, through the language arts, that America has achieved greatness because of the traditions, beliefs, and ideals of many races and nationalities."

Units such as these for teaching literature can help accomplish two important purposes in the field of human relations. First, they can help to relieve group tensions by stressing the universals, the basic similarities in life as it is lived at many different levels and under many different conditions in our American society and in our world. Although we have in our society a number of economic levels, people in these varying groups are faced with the

<hr>

[2] Charlemae Rollins (Ed.), *We Build Together* (Champaign, Ill.: National Council of Teachers of English, 1948).

[3] G. Robert Carlsen and Richard S. Alm (Eds.), *Social Understanding through Literature* (Washington, D.C.: National Council for the Social Studies, 1954).

[4] *Guide for Teaching the Language Arts* (Denver: Department of Instruction, Denver Public Schools, 1953).

[5] *A Guide for Instruction in the Language Arts* (St. Paul: Minnesota Department of Education, 1956).

same basic need for finding some measure of success and happiness.

The basic problem of finding his or her place, of harmonizing the various forces playing upon him or her, is the same for the Seminole Indian boy in Zachary Ball's *Swamp Chief,* the young teen-age boy in Douglas Gorsline's *Farm Boy,* the older adolescent girl in Margot Benary-Isbert's *The Ark,* although the three are of different nationalities and races, live in different parts of the world, and are the products of vastly different cultures and environments. The dramatization of what different people have made of life under different conditions helps to make literature the integrating force it always has been in men's lives.

This integrating function can be applied, too, to literature dealing with the various minority groups. Books about Negro life and problems, for instance, not only portray the unique problems of people of the Negro race, although these are important, but also serve the function of helping Negro children to find satisfaction in life, its beauty and humor as well as its squalor and pathos—as Langston Hughes suggests in his title, *Not Without Laughter,* the story of a Negro boy's struggle to get an education. Books such as Florence Means's *Shuttered Windows,* Doris Gates's *Little Vic,* and Bill Roeder's biography of Jackie Robinson present not only the problems but also positive approaches to them.

The second of these dual purposes of literature in human relations is to develop a sensitivity to the problems of people living under conditions different from one's own and to reveal the stake each of us has in the plight of other groups. Most readers come away from Richard Wright's *Native Son,* for example, not only with a depressed feeling about the tragic and sordid net of circumstances in which Bigger Thomas is entrapped but also with an awareness of the importance for all of us of Bigger's experience. Wright's novel is meant to pose a problem, stir action. The same is true of, say, Motley's *Knock on Any Door* or Steinbeck's *The Grapes of Wrath.*

Closely allied to the function of literature in improving human relations is that of aiding students to become aware of alternative approaches to group problems. Such awareness is the touchstone of the informed, individual conscience for which we can never substitute the censorship of constituted authority.

The vicarious participation in different ways of life may have a . . . broadly social liberating influence. The image of past civilizations or of past periods within our western civilization, as well as images of life in other countries today, can help the youth to realize that our American society is only one of a great variety of possible social structures. When this insight has been attained, the individual is able to look at the society about him more rationally. He is better able to evaluate it, to judge what elements should be perpetuated and what elements should be modified or rejected.[6]

This "broadly social liberating influence" of which Dr. Rosenblatt speaks will not be manifest so much in terms of changed attitudes as in this awareness that alternative solutions to problems often exist. The whole matter of the relationship of a person's reading to his attitudes is a complex and controversial one, but research tends to indicate, for example, that the person who considers the Negro race anthropologically inferior to the white will not necessarily change his attitudes after reading Arna Bontemps' *We Have Tomorrow,* and may only deepen his prejudice by reading *Native Son.* The hater of labor unions will not necessarily take a more sympathetic view after reading Jean Gould's *Sidney Hillman, Great American,* although people with less entrenched predispositions may modify their attitudes considerably.

Yet intelligent reading in controversial literature makes for the informed conscience, the awareness of alternatives, which remains our best hope for finding solutions to group problems. One forte of literature is that it can translate the intangibles of experience— great abstractions such as equality, justice, freedom, and security —into the specific feelings and actions of human beings like ourselves.

[6] Louise Rosenblatt, *Literature as Exploration* (New York: Appleton, 1938), p. 221.

Criteria for Judging Fiction Dealing
with Group Problems

In judging and evaluating fiction that deals with a social problem, the reader has the formidable task of distinguishing his criticism of the selection as a piece of literature, a work of art, from his opinion of the importance of its theme or message. An ideology may favorably prejudice the reader's estimate of the literary worth of a selection, for when a book deals with values in which we believe deeply, which are interrelated with our security and by which we live, the matter of mere literary technique may become a minor one. On the other hand, a selection, wretched as an example of literary art, may receive serious attention because of the importance of the problem with which it deals. Most literary scholars agree that the importance of *Uncle Tom's Cabin* is historical rather than literary. *Gentleman's Agreement,* a well-known book in recent decades, can scarcely be defended as an example of mature technique in fiction, though the problem it emphasizes is vital.

It is important that teachers and librarians select fiction—and teach students to judge it—as fiction rather than as sociology, economics, political science, psychology, though fiction may have some elements in common with all these disciplines. Steinbeck's *The Grapes of Wrath,* or any other socially significant novel, must stand or fall on its merits as a novel and not on its importance sociologically. This is equally true of books written specifically for adolescents.

How do we distinguish between literary art and propaganda? What are some criteria that will help students to tell when the socially significant selection is literary art and when it is propaganda, either of the "good" or "bad" variety?

DOES THE SELECTION PLACE THE MAIN STRESS ON THE TIMELESS RATHER THAN THE TIMELY? Because we can say "Yes" to this question about *Anna Karenina,* for example, the novel stands as one of the greatest of the world, though all the artifacts of life in nineteenth-century tsarist Russia have changed. The human problem of Anna and her decision remains timeless. Timeless elements are human emotions and problems and characteristics, though timely events and problems may have inspired many a timeless story. It is relatively unimportant that Dickens' *A Tale of Two Cities* has as its background the French Revolution; its memorable characters make the book live.

IS THE READER GIVEN ALTERNATIVES IN EMOTION OR ARE HIS FEELINGS RIGIDLY CHANNELED? This question, like any other that might be posed in making a judgment of literature, brings different answers from readers of the same selection. A principal characteristic of propaganda, whether in fiction or in some other form, is the attempt to direct the emotions into a narrow channel. Objectivity, in the sense of impartiality, is not important. Little socially significant fiction is objective; much of it is impassioned. The essential difference again can be defined in terms of characterization: Does the author make us feel *with* the characters or only *about* them? When we feel *with* characters we become concerned with the "why" rather than the "what" of human acts; we are concerned with the basis of motivation. Thus, we are offered alternatives in feeling.

Richard Wright's *Native Son* illustrates the point clearly. Though it is an angry protest, the book offers the reader grounds for different ways of feeling about the final result. Bigger Thomas, a teen-age Negro, is the semihoodlum product of the Negro district in a large northern city. He gets an unusual "break," a job as chauffeur for a wealthy family. One evening the daughter of the family, whose parents think she is attending a concert, persuades Bigger to drive her and the man with whom she is having an affair on a round of night clubs. When they arrive home, the daughter, who has gotten drunk, makes advances to Bigger, who is terrified that the whole matter may be discovered. He gets her to her room, but in a desperate attempt to keep her quiet, accidentally suffocates her. Then in panic he takes the body to the basement and puts it into the furnace, finding it necessary to sever the head from the body. The rest of the story concerns the flight and capture of Bigger, his trial and execution.

Most readers feel sympathy with Bigger, though few would excuse his crime, made purposely horrible, and few would deny the justice of his execution. On the surface, the reader has every right to believe that Bigger got what he deserved. The propagandist melodrama would probably have had Bigger "framed" by a white man. Considering the "why" of Bigger's act, the thoughtful reader is led to a condemnation of certain elements in the social system. And, of course, this was Richard Wright's purpose. In short, the novel has a message but it rises above the level of propaganda. The same thing could be said, for example, of *Oliver Twist* or *Les Misérables*. The reader tends to hate Fagin in *Oliver Twist* and Javert, the relentless pursuer of Jean Valjean in *Les Misérables,* but he understands why they are as they are, how they "got that way." Novelist Jessamyn West makes this point in a memorable article:

Openness, persisted in, destroys hate. The novelist may begin his writing with every intention of destroying what he hates. And since a novelist writes of persons, this means the destruction (through revelation) of an evil person. But in openness the writer becomes the evil person, does what the evil person does for his reasons and with his justifications. As this takes place, as the novelist opens himself to evil, a self-righteous hatred of evil is no longer possible. The evil which now exists is within; and one is self-righteous in relation to others, not to oneself. When the writer has himself assumed the aspect of evil and does not magisterially condemn from the outside, he can bring to his readers understanding and elicit from them compassion. This is why we do not, as readers, hate the great villains of literature. Milton does not hate Satan; nor Thackeray, Becky; nor Shakespeare, Macbeth. For a time Milton *was* Satan; Thackeray, Becky; Shakespeare, Macbeth. And the openness of the novelist (together with his talent and his skill) permits us, his readers, though we know that Satan must be cast down and that Macbeth must die, to respond to them without narrowness—with compassion instead of hatred.[7]

WHATEVER PROBLEM IS DEALT WITH, DOES THE STORY REPRESENT THE TRUE ART OF THE STORYTELLER? The nature of the social problem on which the story centers, no matter how pressing it may be in contemporary society, has nothing to do with the worth of the

---

[7] Jessamyn West, "Secret of the Masters," *Saturday Review* (September 21, 1957), pp. 13–14 ff.

selection as literature. The appeal of the original, well-constructed story must be there. Social significance cannot compensate for the absence of heroic or tragic or comic heroes and deeds, and of disciplined structure and artistic use of language.

These three are criteria that the high school student can learn to apply to all fiction, junior and adult.

The Social Problem Theme in Literature for Teen-Agers

Relations among Religious and Racial Groups

Race relations, especially Negro-white relations, have been a major preoccupation of writers of recent adult fiction. Primarily responsible for this, of course, is the famous Supreme Court decision declaring segregation in the public schools unconstitutional. Adult fiction, however, has not been concerned with the school problem but rather with the psychology of individuals, Negroes and whites in the Deep South, and occasionally with the sensational matter of Negro-white love affairs. It is interesting that the best-known Negro writers have chosen settings outside the Deep South; one of them, Willard Motley, does not even introduce Negro characters. Richard Wright's autobiographical *Black Boy* is set in the South, but *Native Son* takes place in Chicago. One of the most highly praised novels by Negro writers is Ann Petry's tragic *The Street,* the story of a young Negro widow and her son in Harlem. Miss Petry's *The Narrows* deals with a Negro-white love affair in a New England town. Perhaps the best-known Negro novelist is Frank Yerby, who writes historical romance in which race relations have only an incidental and minor place. Langston Hughes' probably autobiographical *Not Without Laughter,* featuring a Negro boy's struggle to get an education, has Kansas for its locale. Undoubtedly the most celebrated adult book dealing with Negro-white relations, Alan Paton's *Cry, the Beloved Country,* takes place in South Africa, where the problem has been as acute as in the southern United States. Notable for its beauty of style, Paton's novel has been widely read by high school students.

Junior fiction dealing with Negro-white relations has been sparse. No doubt the problem of school desegregation, still at the merest beginnings in the South, will be exploited in this fiction eventually. Up to the present, however, the few junior novels featuring Negro-white relationships have been set mostly outside the Deep South and have been concerned with dramatizing, often superficially, various attitudes held by Negroes and whites. Probably the best use of the theme in fiction is to be found in two slender novels by Jesse Jackson, a Negro writer: *Call Me Charley* and *Anchor Man*. In *Call Me Charley,* Charley Moss, a thirteen-year-old Negro, moves into a formerly white neighborhood, where he has a paper route, and becomes the first Negro to attend the junior high school in the area. Charley is subjected to some hazing, and he encounters prejudice on the part of both age mates and adults, but he finds that the majority of his acquaintances come to judge him as a person. The story is lively and supple, free of sentimentalism, with a social thesis made clear—that the hope of the Negro lies in *some* white people, provided the Negro is willing to make the best of himself under the existing conditions. *Anchor Man,* the sequel, finds Charley a senior, a member of the track team, and still the only Negro in the school. When other Negro students are transferred to the school Charley is caught in an emotional no man's land, becoming the pivotal figure in the tense situation that develops. Jackson's books have a depth of characterization rare in the junior novel, particularly in that which is preoccupied with a social problem. Charley and his acquaintances are well-drawn adolescents, and the scenes of adolescent boys together are among the most skillful in junior fiction.

Florence Means, whose books invariably stress some aspect of intercultural relations, has produced in *Shuttered Windows* one of the best junior novels having a Negro as the main character. Harriet Freeman, who had lived all her life in Minneapolis, goes to South Carolina to spend a year with her ailing grandmother and to attend a school for Negro girls. Of course, she finds the adjustment hard to make, and in the beginning counts the days until she can return North. At the end, she decides to stay and work among her people. Told with quiet feeling, the story is neither sentimental nor angry, stressing the problems of the Negroes as a group but still emphasizing the similarity of the problems of young people, white or colored. The success of the book lies mainly in the author's ability to tell a lively, exciting tale.

One of the best-known books on the racial theme and frequently included on recommended book lists for adolescents is Phyllis Whitney's *Willow Hill*. However, the book's only virtue lies in the social material rather than in the story, which is completely lacking in real characterization and pedestrian in style. A government housing project for Negroes brings on a crisis in the small town of Willow Hill. Eighteen-year-old Val Coleman, whose father and mother have highly different views on the matter, is in doubt at the beginning, particularly when she loses the coveted editorship of the school newspaper to a Negro girl. But she makes up her mind, and is instrumental in helping to resolve the tense situation at school. The book, really a treatise with characters, is skillful in describing prejudice and in identifying types of attitudes but is highly inadequate from a literary point of view. Dialogue and details are carelessly handled.

A more skillful story is Catherine Blanton's *Hold Fast to Your Dreams*. Emmy Lou Jefferson, whose main interest is ballet dancing, goes to Arizona to live with an aunt and to avoid the handicap of race prejudice in her Alabama town. However, she encounters prejudice in Arizona, too: her dancing teacher is forced to take a lead part in the school ballet away from Emmy, and there is an attempt to keep her out of the civic ballet in the town. However, Emmy Lou wins recognition and the book ends on a note of hope. Although the style is terse and the story well paced, again there is no introspection or depth of character portrayal.

Occasionally, in the junior novel, the racial theme has been treated incidentally, notably in John Tunis' *All-American*, Laura Rendina's *Lolly Touchberry*, and Marjorie Allee's *The Great Tradition*. The Tunis novel is obviously protest—the main character and his teammates on the football team refuse an invitation to play a postseason, intersectional game with a southern team because a Negro teammate is unable to play. In the Rendina novel, Lolly, a Florida high school girl, thinks disconcertingly about the inequities of Jim Crow, but there is no resolution of the problem for her. Obviously, however, Lolly is a symbol of "new" youthful thinking in the South. Allee's rather slow-moving *The Great Tradition,* which appears on many recommended book lists, tells the story of four girls who are graduate students at the University of Chicago. The problem of the Negro student and her various adjustments is a minor skein in the plot.

In treating Jewish-Gentile relations in fiction, the few attempts of the junior novelists have been even less successful than those attempts to deal with Negro-white relations. For girls in the early junior high school, Lorraine Beim produced a fine story in her *Carol's Side of the Street.* The main character is a twelve-year-old Jewish girl who encounters prejudice in the new neighborhood into which her family moves. The ending is, not surprisingly, happy and the book stresses story, involving the normal interests of early adolescent girls, as well as social message. Again in the context of sports, John Tunis treats the problem in *The Catcher from Triple A,* the story of a Jewish catcher who makes good on a major league baseball team. Solid characterization distinguishes this book. A fairly well-known novel for adolescents is *The New Broome Experiment* by Samuel and Beryl Epstein (writing under the pseudonym of Adam Allen). In this, two city boys, one of them Jewish, come to work on the Broome dairy farm for the summer. For teen-age Nick Broome it is a turbulent period of changing his attitudes toward Jews. The book makes a comprehensive attack on the stereotypes of Jews, although a great deal of dairy farming lore is also worked in. Essentially, however, it is a clumsy story, lacking literary value.

In the field of the adult novel that treats Jewish-Gentile relationships, Laura Hobson's *Gentlemen's Agreement* excited a flurry of public interest some years ago. The central character, a newspaperman, pretends to be a Jew in order to learn the nature of anti-Semitism in ordinary human affairs. A far better novel, and one that has continued to interest adolescents, is Gwethalyn Graham's *Earth and High Heaven.* The marriage plans of Mark Reiser, a Jew, and Ericka Drake, the daughter of an aristocratic Montreal family, are vigorously opposed by both families. The resolution of the conflict, in which the young couple decide to lead their own lives, is highly appealing to older adolescent readers.

A powerful novel which received little attention is Jo Sinclair's *Wasteland,* in which the main character is a young Jew who is pathologically afraid that his associates will discover he is Jewish. The book is built on flashbacks as the protagonist visits a psychiatrist. A somewhat similar theme is the basis of Myron Kaufmann's long first novel, *Remember Me to God,* which traces Richard Amsterdam's revolt against his Jewish background and traditions, during his four years at Harvard, and his parents' attempt to suppress it. The length of the book, as well as the nature of some of the scenes and conversations, makes it suitable for only the mature adolescent reader. The protest against anti-Semitism has been prominent in the fiction of Irwin Shaw, especially in his splendid short story, "An Act of Faith," and his long novel of World War II, *The Young Lions.* One of the three major plots in the novel involves the Army experiences of a Jewish soldier whose wife is a Gentile.

A few junior novelists have dealt interestingly with American Indian groups. Two simple, brief stories by Zachary Ball, *Joe Panther* and *Swamp Chief,* feature, in the context of exciting stories, the problems of a young teen-age Seminole Indian boy in the Florida Everglades country who has one foot in the primitive culture of his people and another in the cosmopolitan life of Miami. This same theme of pride in the past but desire for a normal American future is found in Don Wilcox's *Joe Sunpool.* Joe, from a Navajo reservation, attends the Haskell Institute in Kansas, where he hopes to learn the printing trade. His doubts and hopes and ambitions, as well as his exploits in boxing and horsemanship, are the stuff of the book, which is distinguished by a more sophisticated style than that of many junior novels. It is notable that both Ball and Wilcox are never diverted from their roles as storytellers, and their stories are essentially about young people and their problems, rather than about the problems or plight of the Navajos or the Seminoles, though these are reflected in their books.

Relations among Economic Groups

The problem of relations among people from various economic levels of society has been of much less concern to writers of fiction for adolescents than have other major social problems. Though this is no condemnation, it is a fact somewhat difficult to understand. The adolescent has emerged from the "classless" peer culture of childhood and preadolescence into the teen-age culture of cliques and crowds in which class consciousness sometimes takes the form of extreme snobbishness, and sometimes that of an idealistic, even romantic, equalitarianism.

The school may be the only place in many communities in which there is a mixing of the various groups within the population. Differences in such groups within the community may be accentuated or minimized within the school, depending upon school policies, the attitude of the faculty, and the atmosphere in the community. The problem of high school sororities, vexatious in some schools, has involved, in the main, the problem of relationships among socioeconomic groups.

The poverty-stricken student in a high school has been in a relatively worse position since World War II than he was before, since in the period of great prosperity that followed the war he has relatively fewer companions in economic distress. It is rare for a student these days to be unable to afford a decent dress for a party or money for lunch. The poverty-stricken student today, in his relative isolation from the social life of the school and community, is likely to be desperately unhappy.

On the other hand, it is fairly obvious why writers for adolescents have been little concerned with economic class relationships, at least with any "protest" element. In recent years, discussion of class relationships in general has been somewhat suspect. Certainly, writers who protest about the plight of the lower economic classes are likely to be accused of radicalism. Furthermore, the nature of the teen-age audience furnishes another explanation, for studies reveal that the adolescent since World War II has been economically and politically conservative.

Among junior novelists, the one who has made most artistic use of her characters' economic situation is again Mary Stolz, notably in her *Ready or Not* and *Pray Love, Remember*. The books deal, in sequence, with a New York City semitenement family in which the mother is dead. Though neither story conceivably could be called a "protest," Stolz, through skillful use of detail, makes the reader feel keenly the protagonists' feelings toward their environment—the moments of dull hopelessness in which the griminess seems to close in, the moments of elation, and the yearning for better things.

Always preoccupied with social themes but always the conscious storyteller, prolific Florence Means has produced a commendable story in *Knock at the Door, Emmy*. Emmy is the teenage daughter in an itinerant family living in a pickup truck that carries them from one work area to another. Eager for education, Emmy yearns to "settle down" somewhere, and she detects the same longing in her mother. The settling down is achieved in a story marked with a great sympathy, but not sentimentality, toward the characters—even the shiftless father—and a vibrant style. Despite her concern with the social theme, Means recognizes the need for incident, and there are exciting ones worked into the texture of the story, not dragged in. The rather coy and naïve love plot is the poorest feature of an essentially fine story.

A very similar theme is found in Doris Gates's well-known story for the preadolescent or early adolescent, *Blue Willow*. Janey Larkin travels from shack to shack with her stepmother and father, who is also an itinerant laborer. Janey longs for stability and for beauty in life, which the blue willow plate left her by her mother symbolizes. She realizes her hopes modestly in this thoroughly satisfying story. However, the book has never been greatly popular with young people, probably because it is not quite a children's story and not quite a story for adolescents. The net result is that its most ardent admirers are adults.

Relations among Nationality Groups

It is quite natural that World War II, in which some American soldiers died in places they had never before heard of, should have stimulated a mood of internationalism and an interest in peoples of other lands. This mood has been reflected since the war in books and magazines; more pages are devoted to foreign lands and peoples than ever before. In the high school English program there has been a definite trend toward more teaching of world literature.

The interest in life outside the boundaries of the United States has had little effect thus far, however, on the field of literature for adolescents. Fortunately, the travel tale in which Jane or Jack goes abroad and tells of the quaint customs in another country seems to be passé, but native American writers of fiction for adolescents are apparently unable to replace it with anything better, and the few books for adolescents coming from other countries prefer to deal with the romance of the past rather than with the realities of the present.

However, a distinguished contribution to fiction for adolescents is made by two books by Margot Benary-Isbert—*The Ark* and *Rowan Farm*—both treating, in sequence, the problems of life in devastated postwar Germany. In *The Ark,* the five members of the Lechow family, minus the doctor father, who is a prisoner of war in Russia, are assigned lodgings in two cheerless attic rooms of an aged widow's house. The story concentrates mostly on the two teen-age members of the family, Margret and Matthias, who obtain employment on Rowan Farm and lodging in an old railroad car, which they christen "Noah's Ark." Eventually the entire family comes to live in the Ark, and in the final chapter the father returns. *Rowan Farm* continues the story of the Lechows as they try to rebuild their family life in the rubble of West Germany. Margret, the main character in the sequel, is able, by the end of the book, to plan a trip to America. Mrs. Benary-Isbert's stories represent superior art in the junior novel. The real theme of both books is the importance of courage and the necessity for faith, under even the most adverse circumstances, that some parts of living can be good. Rowan Farm is in itself a symbol of the beauty to be found in life even in the midst of ruin and ugliness, and Margret's experience with the animals of the farm is a symbolic treatment of the mystic cycle of life and death. Underlying each book is a realistic picture of life in postwar Germany.

Postwar conditions furnish the setting, too, for versatile Emily Hahn's *Francie,* in which Francie Nelson, the belle of Jefferson High School, accompanies her father to England and spends a year in a girls' school under the grimness of British postwar austerity. Francie's traumatic experiences are blended into a suspenseful story in which Francie emerges as a well-dimensioned, if not likable, character. The sympathy for the English people is restrained and unsentimental.

Interesting in conception but somewhat disappointing in execution is Yoshiko Uchida's *The Full Circle,* a brief story of wartime Tokyo and the postwar period, from the point of view of a teen-age Japanese girl. The situation is high in interest, but the treatment is somewhat perfunctory and saccharine.

Junior novelists have written about the problems of various nationality groups within the United States and of immigrants, particularly about the "displaced persons" during World War II. Naturally, most of these books are didactic, their purpose being to create greater sympathy and understanding. This motive was given added impetus, no doubt, by a recent study that showed a sizable proportion of American teen-agers would keep foreigners out of this country.[8]

For younger readers, Valenti Angelo has produced two books that are charming but uniquely unsuccessful. They fit into that curious twilight category of books greatly admired by adults interested in books for young people but seldom read by the young people themselves. The two books, *The Marble Fountain* and *The Hill of Little Miracles,* are remarkably alike, though the former is set in Italy and the latter in San Francisco. Each features a teen-age Italian boy and his younger brother; in each case, one of the boys is artistically inclined; in each, there is a strong religious overtone. *The Marble Fountain* portrays family life in Italy just after World War II; *The Hill of Little Miracles* pictures family life in San Francisco. Both stories are episodic, relatively slow moving, and have sensitive characterizations. Their lack of excitement makes them "duds" with the early adolescent audience for which they were apparently intended. The illustrations, done by the author, give an unfortunately childish effect.

In the same category with Angelo's stories is Joseph Krumgold's 1954 Newbery Prize winner, *And Now Miguel.* Twelve-year-old Miguel's Spanish-American family are sheep farmers. Miguel longs to accompany the men on the annual drive to mountain pastures, and he admires his older brother, Gabrielle, who seems to do everything well. The strength of the book lies in its simple style, its warm portrayal of family relationships, and its

---

[8] H. H. Remmers and D. H. Radler, *The American Teenager* (Indianapolis: Bobbs-Merrill, 1957).

capturing of Spanish speech patterns—a feat to be commended in the finest adult fiction. Yet its lack of excitement and its burden of sheep-raising lore keeps the story from being popular with younger adolescent readers.

It is likely that the many books concerned with the problems of European immigrants, uprooted from their homes in World War II, will be ephemeral, but several novelists who write for adolescents have written better-than-average books about these problems. Tom Person demonstrated his ability in *The Land and the Water,* the very adequate story of the Zarina family, Latvian DP's, in the Delta country of the South. Teen-age Modris, who attends a small-town southern high school, is the main character in a story that is not particularly exciting but in which family relationships in an unusual and harrowing context are well developed. Modris's struggle to be accepted by his American peers and to contribute to his family's precarious financial situation is realistically resolved in a story appropriate for junior high school readers.

Highly original and intriguing in conception is Corinne Gerson's *Like a Sister,* in which Greta comes from Germany to live with her pen pal, Beth Peterson, whose father is a professor of sociology at a midwestern university. Remarkably, the story remains free of a patronizing tone as it skillfully develops, with amazing suspense completely free of melodrama, a plot more complicated than that usually found in the junior novel. First, it centers on Beth's difficulty in keeping up with Greta, rather than vice versa. Second, the romantic plot, involving Beth and her boy friend Hank, is true to the adolescent culture. Third, one strand of the plot, involving a German family in the town—potential melodrama—is resolved without resort to sentimentality or sensationalism. Greta emerges as one of the triumphs of characterization in the junior novel.

Also free of melodrama and improbability is Emma Jacobs' fine story of a teen-age Czech, *A Chance to Belong.* The struggle between the European family culture and American teen-age mores is clearly delineated here as Jan Karel risks conflict with his father to achieve status in the high school he attends. Music is his connecting link with his family as well as the means to recognition among his peers. In Anne Tufts's *The Super's Daughter,* a teen-age Czech girl is the main character, and the main value of this book is its picture of high school life in New York City. Most of the characters, including that of the protagonist, Meri Novak, are shadowy, and the story depends for interest upon a rather improbable mystery and a mild romance. More effective is the taut, simple story of Ewald Mand, *The World Is My Home.* In fact, the maturity of the content and style of this book, essentially the love story of an immigrant boy and an American girl, is a surprise, for the plot has a deceptively simple construction. A strong protest against the treatment of an Estonian DP group is prominent, to the detriment of both characterization and the resolution of the rather unreal love affair.

The problems of Spanish-Americans in the United States have been the focus for a number of junior novels. In this category, too, Florence Means has made a notable contribution, especially in *Alicia,* in which a Denver girl of Mexican heritage rids herself, while attending the University of Mexico, of her feelings of inferiority about her background. As usual, Mrs. Means does not let her message interfere with a good story. In this same area, Lucille Mulcahy captures the spirit and the idiom of the Spanish-American people in the Rio Grande Valley of New Mexico in her book, *Pita.* The plot of the story is slight, centering on teen-age Pita's problems at school and at home. Pita's father is the most interesting character in this book. Definitely in the protest vein is Phyllis Whitney's *A Long Time Coming.* After her mother's death, Christie Allard goes to live with her Aunt Amelia in the town in which her father, who had been divorced from her mother, owns a canning plant. The plant depends upon imported Mexican labor, and the story is mainly about the attempts of Christie and her friends to secure better living and working conditions for the Mexicans and to counter the prejudices of people like Aunt Amelia who consider the Mexican inferior. Although the various attitudes toward the Mexican laborers are skillfully identified, there is little characterization and some of the scenes are overdone. Christie's somewhat pallid romance with a young newspaperman is not too successful in injecting added interest in a story that is slow-paced and somewhat turgid in style.

Writers of fiction for adolescents have made interesting, and in a few cases, distinguished contributions to the literature of social protest. It seems likely that the problems of relationships among social and economic groups within the United States will claim increasing attention from writers both for adults and for adolescents. Writers of fiction for teen-agers can find a particularly fertile field in the artful portrayal of life in other lands, whose destiny has become so closely linked with our own.

POSSIBILITIES FOR STUDENT READING

(Books discussed in the preceding chapter are marked with an asterisk [*]. They are annotated only if the nature of their content was not made clear in the chapter. A indicates an adult book; E, an especially easy one.)

*Allee, Marjorie, *Great Tradition,* Houghton Mifflin.
   (Also *The House.*)

*Allen, Adam, *The New Broome Experiment,* Lippincott.   (E)

*Angelo, Valenti, *The Marble Fountain,* Viking.
   (Also *The Hill of Little Miracles.*)

Asch, Sholem, *East River,* Putnam.   (A)
   A Jewish family in New York City and a Jewish-Gentile marriage.

*Ball, Zachary, *Swamp Chief,* Holiday.   (E)
   (Also *Joe Panther.*)

*Beim, Lorraine, *Carol's Side of the Street,* Harcourt.   (E)

*Benary-Isbert, Margot, *The Ark,* Harcourt.
   (Also *Rowan Farm.*)

Blanton, Catherine, *Hold Fast to Your Dreams,* Messner.

Bro, Marguerite H., *Su-Mei's Golden Year,* Doubleday.
   A Chinese girl and her family lead in the modernization of their community.

Buckmaster, Henrietta, *Deep River,* Harcourt.   (A)
   A moving novel of slavery days. Georgia in the 1850's.

Carson, John F., *The Twenty-Third Street Crusaders,* Farrar, Straus.
   A gang of teen-age hoodlums is reconstructed.

Cook, Fannie, *Mrs. Palmer's Honey*, Doubleday.   (A)
A Negro girl's struggle to improve her lot.

*Dickens, Charles, *Oliver Twist*, various publishers.   (A)
A boy is forced into crime by Fagin's ring of criminals.

*Gates, Doris, *Blue Willow*, Viking.   (E)

*Gerson, Corinne, *Like a Sister*. Funk & Wagnalls.

Glasgow, Ellen, *In This Our Life*, Harcourt.   (A)
A Negro boy plays an important part in the story.

*Graham, Gwethalyn, *Earth and High Heaven*, Lippincott.   (A)

Guareschi, Giovanni, *The Little World of Don Camillo*, Farrar,
Straus.   (A)
Humorously told story of the struggle between a Catholic priest
and a Communist mayor in a small Italian town.

*Hahn, Emily, *Francie*, F. Watts.

*Hobson, Laura, *Gentlemen's Agreement*, various publishers.   (A)

*Hugo, Victor, *Les Misérables*, various publishers.   (A)
The monumental novel of Jean Valjean and his pursuer, Javert.

*Jackson, Jesse, *Call Me Charley*, Harper & Row.   (E)
(Also *Anchor Man.*)

*Jacobs, Emma, *A Chance to Belong*, Holt, Rinehart and Winston.

*Kaufmann, Myron, *Remember Me to God*, Lippincott   (A)

*Krumgold, Joseph, *And Now Miguel*, Crowell.   (E)

Lee, Harper, *To Kill a Mockingbird*, Lippincott.   (A)
A story of childhood in a Southern town and a Negro's unjusti-
fied conviction of rape.

Llewellyn, Richard, *How Green Was My Valley*, Macmillan.   (A)
The Morgan family in a Welsh coal-mining community and its
involvement in industrial strife.

*Mand, Ewald, *The World Is My Home*, Friendship Press.

*Means, Florence, *Shuttered Windows*, Houghton Mifflin.
(Also *Alicia* and *Knock at the Door, Emmy.*)

*Motley, Willard, *Knock on Any Door*, Appleton.   (A)

*Mulcahy, Lucille, *Pita*, Coward-McCann.

*Paton, Alan, *Cry, the Beloved Country*, Scribner.   (A)
A tragedy of race relations in South Africa.

*Person, Tom, *The Land and the Water*, Farrar, Straus.   (E)

Pillai, Thakazhi, *Chemmeen*, Harper & Row.   (A)
  Stark, tragic story of a girl in India who is forced to marry a
  man chosen by her greedy father rather than the man she loves.

*Rendina, Laura, *Lolly Touchberry*, Little, Brown.

*Shaw, Irwin, *The Troubled Air*, Random House.   (A)

*Sinclair, Upton, *The Jungle*, various publishers.   (A)

*Steinbeck, John, *Grapes of Wrath*, various publishers.   (A)
  The Joad family's trek from the Dust Bowl to disillusionment
  in California.

*Stolz, Mary, *Ready or Not*, Harper & Row.
  (Also *Pray Love, Remember.*)

*Tufts, Anne, *The Super's Daughter*, Holt, Rinehart and Winston.

*Tunis, John, *The Catcher from Triple A*, Harcourt.
  (Also *All-American.*)

*Uchida, Yoshiko, *The Full Circle*, Friendship Press.   (E)

*Whitney, Phyllis, *A Long Time Coming*, McKay.
  (Also *Willow Hill.*)

*Wilcox, Don, *Joe Sunpool*, Little, Brown.

*Wright, Richard, *Native Son*, Harper & Row.

HISTORICAL
BACKGROUNDS

6 ❧ # IN FICTION
FOR
ADOLESCENTS

A QUICK SURVEY of the shelves of any library or of publishers' lists is sufficient to illustrate the vogue of historical fiction, or at least of the historical romance. This vogue, a recurring one in the reading habits of Americans, is true of general adult literature as well as of literature for the adolescent audience. Firmly entrenched in the high school literature curriculum are such historical pieces as *Ivanhoe* and *A Tale of Two Cities;* such giants of the past as *Ben Hur* and *Quo Vadis* are still read. Since World War II, especially, the historical romance has captured the fancy of American readers, and at the time when a rather sensational naturalistic novel, *From Here to Eternity,* was circulating on a best-seller scale, Thomas Costain's *The Silver Chalice,* which is set in the early days of Christianity, had sold over 2,000,000 copies.[1] Among the best-known books of the post-World War II period are the historical novels of Costain, Lloyd Douglas, and Samuel Shellabarger.

The reasons for the recurring popularity of historical fiction can be traced to the functions of literature, the rewards sought in read-

[1] Cited in John T. Frederick, "Costain and Company: The Historical Novel Today," *English Journal*, XLIII (April 1954), 169–174 ff.

ing, which are discussed in earlier chapters. There is, certainly, an inherent fascination in looking backward as well as in looking forward. Just as the science-fiction piece is an escape into the future, so the historical novel is an escape into the past. The past, in general, induces a special kind of nostalgia on the part of most readers, and "the good old days" are still very much revered. Since the past has been lived through, it always seems more orderly, and seems to present less complexity than "the fast pace of nowadays." And subconsciously, too, the reader may feel a certain satisfying superiority as he or the author compares the past with the present.

The kind of people and the events that tend to be emphasized in the typical historical romance are exactly of the type that appeals to the adolescent mind. The characters are people of action —the man of great physical prowess, the woman of surpassing courage. To the average adolescent, the exciting events of the past are physical, stressing action and daring, melodrama and spectacle. Frequently the role of the martyr or of the person who is willing to fight for his cause against great odds is accentuated. These are roles much admired by the adolescent.

So far as teachers and parents are concerned, historical fiction may seem to possess advantages that some other types of literature do not. Even in entertainment many teachers and parents are much concerned with what is "educational," and the supposed opportunities to learn history may make historical fiction seem more "worthwhile" than contemporary romance.

Perhaps, too, part of the appeal of historical fiction may be found in the fact that it stresses certain broad themes or ideas that find sympathetic response among most readers. Underlying the fiction of the American past, for instance, is the "American dream," its extension and implementation, and the triumph of individual liberty over tyranny is the basic theme in many a historical novel. The worth and dignity of the individual is at the heart of American historical fiction.

Then, too, the typical historical romance affords a comfortable type of excitement, akin to that of viewing the Friday-night boxing match on television. Because the story is removed in time and because events already fully resolved are likely to receive more careful attention than are people, there is less likelihood of intense, and therefore possibly painful, identification than with some other genres. As John T. Frederick points out, " 'Spectacle' is the word that expresses the essence of traditional historical romance: spectacle as distinguished from drama."[2] The reader, then, is more likely to play the role of observer than of participant. Of course, as Frederick goes on to say, "In the best of historical romance the spectacle has meaning: in its totality it achieves grasp of an age, illustration of a general truth of human nature."[3]

Whatever the reasons, historical fiction possesses perennial appeal, both among adolescent and adult readers.

History and the Art of Fiction

If students are to approach historical fiction seriously, they must be made aware of a problem that lies at the heart of skillful reading, of discrimination in the genre—the relationship between history, historical facts, and fiction. Novelist John Hersey has commented cogently on this relationship:

Palpable facts are mortal. Like certain moths and flying ants, they lay their eggs and die overnight. The important flashes and bulletins are already forgotten by the time yesterday morning's newspaper is used to line the trash can to receive today's coffee grounds. The things we remember for longer periods are emotions and impressions and illusions and images and characters: the elements of fiction.[4]

Hersey is implying that historical fiction *is* fiction, not history or journalism; its responsibilities are to fiction. Further, he implies that good historical fiction is timeless rather than timely, and its essential concern is not for events but for people, for the truth of human character, which is unchanging—the constant in human experience.

[2] *Ibid.*, p. 173.
[3] *Ibid.*
[4] John Hersey, "The Novel of Contemporary History," *Atlantic Monthly*, CLXXXIV (November 1949), 80.

It is important to remember, too, that the function of historical fiction, as of any fiction, is not necessarily to set forth the literal truth, but rather only an impression of it. In good historical fiction, the major facts of a period must be adhered to, of course, but specific details and events may be secondary in the novel which, as James T. Farrell puts it, "re-creates the consciousness and the conscience of a period. It tells us what has happened to man, what could have happened to him, what man has imagined might happen to him."[5] Errors in minor details of the Napoleonic Wars are unimportant, for example, in *War and Peace*. The difference might accurately be defined as that between fiction and journalism, a problem apparent in many war novels. Jessamyn West has explained the failure of many war novels—and of popular taste—in terms of this difference:

. . . the reader's love of the "true story" is no help to the novelist. The wars produced more violence and cruelty, courage and devotion than the novelists of the world can equal. Firsthand accounts satisfy the reader's hankering for facts and convince him that reality is what happened at a named place on a specific day. So the novels he reads in quantity tend to be either nostalgic retreat from "the facts," or in them "the facts" are made even more irresistible by being attached to a narrative hook of a romantic-sexual nature which sinks deeply into frail flesh.[6]

The basic difference between the journalistic novel and that which rises above it lies probably in the complexity of characters and in the presence of an idea (or ideas) that gives unity to events. What a soldier did in a war is less important than why he did it, and in the great novel he becomes a symbol of humanity. The run-of-the-mill historical novel allows us to witness history; the truly good novel, to live it.

Another distinction is important in the relationship of historical facts and fiction: fiction, unlike history, may be highly selective, pretending to no rounded view. In a historical novel, some specific

[5] James T. Farrell, "Literature and Ideology," *English Journal*, XXXL (April 1942), 269.

[6] Jessamyn West, "Secret of the Masters," *Saturday Review* (September 21, 1957), p. 14.

phase of history may be viewed through the eyes of an individual character, and the reader therefore sees and understands only what the character sees and understands. In fiction, the final impression of an actual historical personage may be quite at variance with the scholarly consensus. For example, Gertrude Finney's *Muskets along the Chickahominy,* a competent historical novel for adolescents, views Bacon's Rebellion, and the character of Nathaniel Bacon, through the eyes of a young indentured servant who much admires Bacon.

It goes almost without saying, too, that in historical fiction there still is need for the imaginative creation of comic and heroic and tragic events. The story woven through whatever facts of history is more important than the facts themselves.

Historical Fiction in the School Program

Because of certain relationships it has to the school curriculum and to the reading development of adolescents, historical fiction can have considerable value in the high school program. "Core curriculum," in which there is often a merging of the content of social studies and English, has become relatively widespread, especially in the junior high school, and many senior high schools attempt, at least informally, to correlate the teaching of English with world history or with American and English history. Historical fiction is a particularly appropriate type of material for such programs.

In the field of social studies, especially in history, of course, historical fiction can be a valuable means, not only of enriching the program generally, but also of sharpening and deepening pupils' concepts of time, thus adding an important dimension to this study of the past. To many students, even after considerable exposure to American history, the American Revolution, for example, remains a rather remote and hazy mélange of tea in Boston Harbor, a midnight ride of Paul Revere, and patriots whose feet were frozen at Valley Forge. A novel like Esther Forbes's *Johnny Tremain* provides a moving close-up of that momentous time from the point of view of a realistic adolescent; understanding of the time and its issues as they entered the lives of people, which no history text can supply, is apparent in the imaginative work.

Through its stress on people and their reactions and emotions, thereby putting flesh on the skeleton of history, historical fiction, if it is good, can help develop an ability to see the past in perspective. Large movements and trends, momentous events, and great personages are, of necessity, the major stuff of history. It is for fiction to furnish the human element, the vision of the ordinary, historically insignificant individual. The main character in Emma Patterson's well-written junior novel, *The World Turned Upside Down,* for instance, is an eighteen-year-old farmhand in upper New York. Hearing vaguely of the outbreak of hostilites in the Revolution, he is unconcerned at the beginning, aligning himself with neither loyalists nor patriots; then the war comes to him and the issues are made real.

It is easy, however, to overstate the case for historical fiction, and mentioning certain limitations of the genre and cautions in using it is in order. One must remember that historical fiction *is* fiction. Though valuable as a supplement to the study of history, it can never be a substitute for history, though many teachers and laymen have been impressed by its apparent possibilities as a painless "backdoor" approach to history. Furthermore, many historical novels, even though set in the past, do not really have anything to do with the facts of history or with interpreting a period. In fact, at its worst, the "historical" novel may be merely a supposedly respectable framework for smut and sensationalism. Sex-laden *Forever Amber,* a best seller just after World War II, is one of the more striking examples of this.

Fare for the Adolescent Reader

Among the several almost "canonized" selections in the traditional high school literature program, as was stated at the outset of this chapter, are two historical novels—*Ivanhoe* by Sir Walter Scott and *A Tale of Two Cities* by Charles Dickens. For decades these two selections have been read and studied, *Ivanhoe* usually in the ninth grade and *A Tale of Two Cities* most commonly in the tenth, but occasionally in the twelfth. Since both novels are still widely studied, though apparently their prevalence is declining, *The English Journal,* official high school organ of the National Council of Teachers of English, has published recent reappraisals of them by competent critics. Major excerpts from these two essays are presented below:

Ivanhoe

When we return to *Ivanhoe,* we seem to enter a bigger and livelier world [than that of *The Lady of the Lake*], not because of the change of scene to medieval England, but because *Ivanhoe* seems to encompass more life and to be more skillfully constructed than *The Lady of the Lake.*

One very important reason for *Ivanhoe*'s superiority is its more varied and more exciting plot. In *The Lady of the Lake,* once we know the basic situation involving Ellen and her lovers and the threat of Roderick's rebellion, we realize that only a few things can happen. But in *Ivanhoe,* by having almost all of the main characters, except Rebecca, Lockesley, and Richard, together at Rotherwood from the first, Scott can have them interact more and make the plot more varied.

The second reason for *Ivanhoe*'s superiority is that it presents a broader historical panorama than *The Lady of the Lake.* There is a greater range of social classes and situations characteristic of the time. Scott manages to let us see a cross section of the period that he is describing, especially at Ashby when he not only shows us the splendor and excitement of the tournament itself in the costumes, the combat, and the ritual, but also some of the crowd's feelings in their reaction to Isaac and Prince John.

A still more important reason for *Ivanhoe*'s superiority is its lively characters. Just about every major figure in the book has some trait or traits that really differentiate him from anyone else. Furthermore, these particular characteristic traits seem to represent strong passions that control the characters' actions. Front de Boeuf has an animal courage and stubborn matter-of-fact belief in only the physical sensations of living that preclude any acceptance of spiritual values, and cause him to face death openly and brazenly. Prince John is a kind of simpering, fearful, and cunning child who, when his will is thwarted, has a tantrum. Both of these characters—as well as many others in the book—are plausible because their emotions are so deep and uncontrollable that they could act no other way.

Now we might think that with such passionate characters, such a wide range of historical events, and so skillful a plot, *Ivanhoe* would turn out to be a major work of fiction. However, I do not think that this is the case. First of all, Ivanhoe and Rowena, the conventional hero and heroine who supply the love interest (if we can call it that) and link together many of the plot incidents, are pretty boring. Rowena, as most readers seem to agree, is too coldly proud and wins everything, including her lover, too easily. Ivanhoe is really not much more interesting because he never says much except to comment on Rebecca's description of the storming of the castle. Even then he seems to be straining so hard in his questioning that he seems childishly zealous. Second, some of the characters, especially Bois Guilbert, seem to change personality too radically. Up until the time that Bois Guilbert begins pouring out his feelings to Rebecca at Torquilstone, he seems to have been a proud, cruel, independent, and brave man not given to reflection or doubt. However, he then turns out to be a very complex and unhappy person trapped by feelings of self-pity and self-abasement.

A third reason that *Ivanhoe* does not seem a major work of fiction is that it lacks a very consistent focus or thematic unity. It is true that Scott presents us with many representative aspects of medieval society but there does not seem to be any central problem(s) in terms of which these separate incidents and aspects are interrelated, as in *Waverley* or *Rob Roy,* where the historical incidents contribute to the psychological development of the hero. But in *Ivanhoe* the hero's experiences do not seem to enlarge his understanding or change any of his attitudes. Ivanhoe, for example, is reconciled with his father not as a direct result of anything that Ivanhoe himself has done or felt, but only because of Richard's intervention. Moreover, even if we grant that Scott does not intend Ivanhoe to be the psychological center of interest in the story, we have trouble finding such a center elsewhere.

A final criticism of *Ivanhoe* concerns its language. Undeniably there is some fresh, vigorous dialogue as in Wamba's jests, the repartee between the Black Knight and Friar Tuck, and Prince John's political discussions with Fitzurst. Most of the time, however, the language is flat and undistinguished. As the Black Knight, for example, travels through the forest after his victory at Ashby, Scott analyzes his condition:

> But the Black Knight had no mistress to meditate upon, or, being as indifferent in love as he seemed to be in war, was not sufficiently occupied by passionate reflections upon her beauty and cruelty to be able to parry the effects of fatigue and hunger, and suffer love to act as a substitute for the solid comforts of a bed and supper. He felt dissatisfied, therefore, when, looking around, he found himself deeply involved in woods, through which indeed there were many open glades and some paths, but such as seemed only formed by the numerous herds of cattle which grazed in the forest, or by the animals of chase and the hunters who made prey of them.

This language seems like mere formal exposition in which the author seems to be keeping his distance from his subject, though he analyzes clearly what is happening. Besides this impersonal, overly analytical description, there is a lot of high-sounding language in which characters express their feelings or thoughts. As Rebecca watches Ivanhoe while he is sleeping during his convalescence, she probes her feelings for him:

> Alas! is it a crime that I should look upon him, when it may be for the last time? When yet but a short space, and those fair features will be no longer animated by the bold and buoyant spirit which forsakes them not even in sleep: when the nostril shall be distended, the mouth agape, the eyes fixed and bloodshot; and when the proud and noble knight may be trodden on by the lowest caitiff of this accursed castle, yet stir not when the heel is lifted up against him!

This language, to say the least, is monotonously heavy, formal, and strained—and no character should have to be forced to speak in this manner. Yet there are many comparable passages in the book, and these, together with lapses in characters and the lack of any real unity except on the level of surface action, hurt the book a great deal. Our final impression of the book is that it is always interesting as spectacle but only sometimes interesting and revealing as a serious work of fiction.[7]

[7] Herbert Goldstone, "The Question of Scott," *English Journal*, XLVI (April 1957), 187–195.

A Tale of Two Cities

This particular novel was most widely accepted as a high school assignment about half a century ago. At that time, we must assume, it reflected contemporary literary enthusiasms. In the 1890's Freeman Wills' play, *The Only Way,* an adaptation of Dickens' novel, was an enormous success. I suspect that, for this reason, our pedagogical forebears found *A Tale* the most immediately relevant, the most "modern" of all Dickens' novels.

The fact that this novel is unlike most of Dickens' work may also have recommended it to teachers. There are more big scenes in it than in any of his other novels; there is less of the grotesque, fewer episodes and characters that the inexperienced reader might consider quaint or antiquated; and there is, almost uniquely in Dickens, a single plot that is unravelled with speed and concision, and which always dominates both the characters and their *milieux.* The novel's relatively simple construction makes it easy for the reader to get into and through the story; it invites an immediate and simple response.

Both the general approach and the structure of *A Tale of Two Cities* are shaped by Carlylean doctrines. Dickens chose the French Revolution as his subject because he, too, saw it as the event which ushered in the modern world.

Dickens . . . is encouraged by Carlyle's theory to regard the past primarily as a storehouse of lessons, a terrible moral drama. In constructing his novel—it seems clear—he conceived his problem as one of integrating the personal lives of his characters with the wider pattern of history. It is the principal scheme of the novel to show the individual fate mirroring and being mirrored by the fate of the social order. The lives of both Doctor Manette and Sydney Carton are, in a sense, parables of the Revolution, of social regeneration through suffering and sacrifice. The Doctor's return to life illustrates the stumbling course of the new order, released from its dark dungeon of oppression and misery, finding its place in a new and juster world. And Carton embodies both the novel's central narrative theme and its profoundest moral view: his past of sinful negligence parallels the past of eighteenth-century Europe; his noble death demonstrates the possibility of rebirth through love and expiation.

Dickens set himself the task of persuading his readers that they were not islands entire of themselves, but involved in the injustice that led to the Revolution, and in the violence that it set loose. "The world," Dickens is reported to have said, "is so much smaller than we think it; we are all so connected by fate without knowing it; people supposed to be far apart are so constantly elbowing each other; and tomorrow bears so close a resemblance to nothing half so much as to yesterday."

This notion of reciprocity between private and public, England and France, past and present, imposes a pattern of parallelism on Dickens' novel. It had to be a tale of *two* cities, not just a story of revolutionary Paris. Every device that ingenuity suggested was used to connect the seemingly placid world of England with the upheaval in France. Symbolically the point is emphasized by the footsteps which echo on the quiet corner of Soho where Lucie lives with her husband and father. These echoes, becoming increasingly ominous, finally mingle with the "headlong and dangerous footsteps . . . raging in Saint Antoine afar off." (Book II, Ch. 21.)

The difficulty in this attempt to yoke the worlds of London and Paris by violence together is that Dickens had to forgo his usual confident placing of English characters in English scenes. He was able to make use of a number of Englishmen, but he had to violate both fictional probability and historical possibility by transporting them all to Paris in the Year of Terror, 1792. Then, the absence of English backgrounds prevents, I think, the unhampered flowering of his comic spirit. The comedy that appears in *A Tale* is only a faint echo of the old Dickens.

In the absence of the comic spirit other means had to be used to vivify the novel, so it is no surprise to find that Dickens spoke of setting himself "the little task of making a *picturesque story,* rising in every chapter, with characters true to nature, but whom the story should express more than they should express themselves by dialogue." It is one of the great weaknesses of the novel that Dickens attempted to rely on plot rather than on character, but it is one of its strengths —as well as its most distinctive feature—that it became a novel of *pictures.* So marked is the painterly quality of *A Tale* that one's memory of it is dominated by a series of *tableaux vivants,* scenes without dialogue, but with a composition so clear that one tends to see them within the limits of a frame.

The general conception of *A Tale of Two Cities* is so grand that one is tempted to overlook the novel's technical faults. But faults there are, some of them unforgivable, many of them quite instructive. The elements of sentimentality and melodrama are no more persistent here than in some of the earlier novels, but as always, they are unpalatable to the modern reader. Lucie Manette's heart-rending reunion with the father she has never known is simply not prepared for:

> And if, when I shall tell you of my name, and of my father who is living, and of my mother who is dead, you learn that I have to kneel to my honored father, and implore his pardon for having never for his sake striven all day and lain awake and wept all night, because the love of my poor mother hid his torture from me, weep for it, weep for it. (Book I, Ch. 6.)

The illustrious analogue here is the reunion of Cordelia and Lear, but to define the differences between the two scenes is merely to become impatient with Dickens.

Some of Dickens' characteristic mannerisms grew all out of bounds in *A Tale*. Repetition was an endemic Victorian rhetorical device of which Dickens was always fond, but in no other novel is it so obtrusive. Observe the opening paragraph: "It was the best of times, it was the worst of times, it was the age of wisdom, it was the age of foolishness, it was the epoch of belief, it was the epoch of incredulity, etc. . . ." Perhaps some of the repetitions and parallels were intended to emphasize the interconnections of twin realms of the novel, but too often the device becomes merely a trick. It does not add to the reader's experience to find the titles of chapters in balanced pairs, "The Fellow of Delicacy" followed by "The Fellow of No Delicacy," and "Knitting" followed by "Still Knitting." These verbal devices evidence a curious lack of control, a tendency to depend for effect on mere smartness.

But if there are weaknesses in Dickens' technique, there is also strength in many of the smaller touches which give richness to the novel. Much of the effect of *A Tale* is a result of artful patterns of imagery. The pervading image of the road, for example, runs through the whole book. The first chapter, which opened with a general description of the period, ends with a reference to the figurative road along which all men will be carried in the years ahead of them. The second chapter, which begins the narrative, makes the figure of speech literal: "It was the Dover road that lay, on a Friday night late in November. . . ." When, in the course of the novel, we encounter many roads upon which the characters drive or ride, none, thanks to the explicitness of the opening chapter, is without metaphorical significance.

One of the powerful features of Dickens' art which should not go unmentioned is his strong sense of the lusts and guilts and passions which lie under the surface of human consciousness. It is notable that his treatment of the Revolution is free of sentimental notions as to the essential goodness of man. The Terror is conceived as both a cleansing and polluting force, but men are shown to be attracted to violence for its own sake.

The novel's chief weaknesses are the results of its excessive artificiality: its construction constantly calls attention to itself. But in reacting against these smaller details we must not forget that Dickens' main intention was to present a view of, to "add something" to our understanding of the French Revolution. And the more I consider this novel as an interpretation of that event, the more successful it seems to me. One may quarrel with this or that detail of documentation, but the historical view, in its broad outlines, is a sound one. Dickens suggested that "this terrible Revolution" was an inevitable response to injustice, but he showed also how revolutionary ardor produced its own forms of injustice.

A Tale of Two Cities is a profoundly thoughtful, if not a theoretical book. It is the sort of novel that should be enormously *usable* for young people and for their teachers. Its technical weaknesses are of a kind that can illustrate the nature and problems of fiction, but what is much more important, its conception can vivify for us the meanings of the past, can offer us a reading of history, humane and deep, by a great artistic intelligence.[8]

Other Historical Fiction

Any comprehensive analysis of historical fiction, either for the adult or the adolescent audience, would be impossible merely because of the quantity of titles in the past two decades. Few titles or authors stand out; a number of book lists that include sections on historical fiction are at the disposal of teachers, and a brief

[8] G. Robert Stange, "Dickens and the Fiery Past: *A Tale of Two Cities* Reconsidered," *English Journal*, XLVI (October 1957), 381–390.

annotated list for junior and senior high school students follows this chapter.

Many of the books for adolescents discussed here and elsewhere under the general label, "historical fiction," are not really historical fiction at all except in the sense that they take place in the past. Many such junior novels, and adult romances, too, make no real use of the historical period and its events, and no real historical personages are introduced. Such books, very numerous, belong merely to a species of adventure fiction that is perennially popular.

One authentic historical novel for adolescents stands alone in its conception and literary quality—*Johnny Tremain* by Esther Forbes. Out of her research on the pre-Revolutionary War years, the author, who won a Pulitzer Prize for her biography of Paul Revere, has wrought the authentic background for her story of a young Boston silversmith's apprentice who became involved in patriotic activities, including the Boston Tea Party, just prior to the outbreak of hostilities. Famous figures such as Paul Revere and Samuel Adams play important parts in the story.

However, *Johnny Tremain,* which is in rather wide use as common reading in grades eight to ten, is not a popularized history text. It is a genuine novel of exciting events and character. Teenage Johnny is one of the most interesting characters in junior fiction. At the outset of the story he is the completely vain and cocksure young bully. An injury to his hand ends his career as a silversmith's apprentice, completely changes his life, and involves him ultimately in the revolutionary movement. Johnny's personal tribulations are the major subject of the story, but the adolescent reader is able to live with Johnny through the stirring pre–Bunker Hill times in a manner that marks the best in historical fiction.

The frontier story, involving the settlers' battles against nature and the Indians, has been popular since the work of James Fenimore Cooper first appeared. Though Cooper's significance and achievement have been highly controversial among literary scholars, the issue has never affected the high school literature curriculum. High school teachers have given little attention to Cooper, and adolescents rarely read his books. The essence of Cooper's stories, however, has been reworked in countless novels for adults and adolescents. An appropriate representative of junior novelists in this category is Merritt Parmelee Allen, whose prolific output has been widely circulated. Typical of Allen's books, although somewhat better than many, is *The Wilderness Way*. In this story eighteen-year-old Laurent Delair accompanies La Salle on his ill-fated expedition that sought to reach the mouth of the Mississippi. The story is typically fast-moving—the major conflict between Laurent and his villainous cousin is introduced in the first few lines, and a hand-to-hand fight occurs in the first chapter. An above-average style and lavish use of dialogue mark a story based largely on the familiar capture-by-Indians-torture-and-escape plot. Most books of this type, those for adolescents and those for adults, treat the Indians either as noble savages or as savage brutes. Allen's stories are in the latter tradition, as this bit concerning an Iroquois Indian makes clear: ". . . his inflexible honesty and decency were in the best white tradition."

Among the better junior novels utilizing American historical background are two by Emma L. Patterson and Gertrude Finney. Patterson's *The World Turned Upside Down* features the upstate New York phase of the American Revolution. A teen-age farm boy is caught in the swirl of the war and becomes a rebel, although the father of the girl he loves remains a loyalist. The love affair is prominent in the well-executed and exciting plot. An excellently handled, and fairly complicated, plot also marks Finney's *Muskets along the Chickahominy,* which is set against the background of Bacon's Rebellion. The main character is a young man whose family had lost its estate in Virginia; he returns incognito as an indentured servant, becomes involved in the Rebellion, and falls in love with one of the daughters in the family to which he is indentured. Finney is also the author of another competent story, *The Plums Hang High,* in which an aristocratic young Englishwoman accompanies her husband to a midwestern frontier farm in the 1860's.

In the field of historical fiction with other than American backgrounds, four novels have had secure places for many years on recommended reading lists: *The Black Arrow* by Robert Louis Stevenson, *The Scarlet Pimpernel* by Emmuska Orczy, *Men of Iron* by Howard Pyle, and *The Cloister and the Hearth* by Charles Reade. Stevenson's story of chivalric adventure and intrigue has been perenially popular and has appeared in a paperback edition. In the suspenseful *The Scarlet Pimpernel,* set during the French Revolution, the dashing Englishman, known as the "Scarlet Pimpernel," leads a band that helps a number of French royalists escape the guillotine. Pyle's *Men of Iron* deals with the training of a young Englishman in the days of chivalry. *The Cloister and the Hearth,* more recommended than read, is a long novel of the medieval period, in which family life and church service are dramatized.

Marchette Chute, noted for her biographies, *Shakespeare of London* and *Geoffrey Chaucer of England,* has also produced two unique books of fiction in which she presents Chaucerian and Shakespearean backgrounds. *The Innocent Wayfaring,* set in the England of Chaucer's time, recounts the romance and adventures of a boy and girl, both of whom have run away from home, who meet on the road to London. The Shakespearean theater, with Shakespeare himself as a character, is the background for *The Wonderful Winter,* in which young Sir Robert Wakefield runs away to London and spends the winter acting in Shakespeare's company. Neither of the books has any great excitement, but both present authentic background with the verve characteristic of Chute. Both books are highly useful as supplementary reading for classes studying Chaucer or Shakespeare.

The books by Gladys Malvern that retell Biblical stories are also unique. *Behold Your Queen* is based on the life of Queen Esther of Persia, and *The Foreigner* is the story of Ruth and Naomi. Stories with religious background have been less popular with adolescents than with adults, but Malvern's books appeal to some girls.

A little-publicized but excellent and moving story climaxed by the Battle of Hastings is *The Fourteenth of October* by the Englishwoman who writes under the pen name Bryher. The career of a Saxon boy before, during, and after the Norman invasion furnishes the plot in this short but introspective, contemplative, and beautifully written book. Though there is not enough real action to satisfy many adolescent readers, the story would be very valuable for use with mature twelfth-graders.

POSSIBILITIES FOR STUDENT READING

(Titles discussed in the preceding chapter are marked with an asterisk [*]. They are annotated only if the nature of their content was not made clear in the chapter. A indicates adult books; E, especially easy ones.)

Aldrich, Bess S., *A Lantern in Her Hand,* Grosset & Dunlap.
  The story of a young bride who goes to live in pioneer Nebraska.

*Allen, Merritt P., *The Wilderness Way,* McKay.
  (Also *Johnny Reb.*)

Boyd, James, *Drums,* Scribner.   (A)
  A young man fights under the command of John Paul Jones.

Brink, Carol R., *Caddie Woodlawn,* Macmillan.   (E)
  A girl and her family on a Wisconsin farm in Civil War days.

*Bryher, *The Fourteenth of October,* Pantheon.   (A)

Carr, Harriet H., *Gravel Gold,* Farrar, Straus.   (E)
  A sixteen-year-old prospects for gold in Colorado in the 1850's with moderate success and much adventure.

Cather, Willa, *My Antonia,* Houghton Mifflin.   (A)
  Antonia and her Bohemian peasant family in Nebraska's pioneer days.

*Chute, Marchette, *The Innocent Wayfaring,* Dutton.
  (Also *The Wonderful Winter.*)

*Costain, Thomas, *The Silver Chalice,* Doubleday.   (A)
  A romance set in New Testament times.

Daringer, Helen F., *A Flower of Araby,* Harcourt.   (E)
  The adventures in Syria of an English Knight Templar's daughter at the time of the Crusades.

*Dickens, Charles, *A Tale of Two Cities,* various publishers.   (A)

Dunsing, Dee, *War Chant,* McKay.   (E)
  A teen-ager carries messages for the Army in the war with the Seminole Indians in Florida.

Edmonds, Walter, *Drums along the Mohawk,* Little, Brown.   (A)
  Warfare and life in the Mohawk Valley during the Revolutionary War. (Also *Wilderness Clearing.*)

Fast, Howard, *Freedom Road,* Duell, Sloan & Pearce—Meredith Press.   (A)

An ex-slave is elected to the U.S. Congress in Reconstruction days.

*Finney, Gertrude, *Muskets along the Chickahominy*, McKay.
(Also **The Plums Hang High*.)

*Forbes, Esther, *Johnny Tremain*, Houghton Mifflin.

Johnson, Annabel, and Edgar Johnson, *Wilderness Bride*, Harper & Row.   (A)
A Mormon girl is caught up in the violence of the Mormon displacement in Illinois and a love affair with a nonbeliever.

*Malvern, Gladys, *Behold Your Queen*, McKay.
(Also **The Foreigner*.)

*Orczy, Emmuska, Baroness, *The Scarlet Pimpernel*, various publishers.   (A)

*Patterson, Emma, *The World Turned Upside Down*, McKay.

*Pyle, Howard, *Men of Iron*, Harper & Row.

*Reade, Charles, *The Cloister and the Hearth*, various publishers. (A)

Richter, Conrad, *Light in the Forest*, Knopf.
A white boy, reared among the Indians and returned to his white parents, goes back to his Indian home and to divided loyalties.

*Scott, Walter, *Ivanhoe*, various publishers.   (A)
(Also *Quentin Durward* and *The Talisman*.)

*Sienkiewicz, Henryk, *Quo Vadis*, various publishers.   (A)
Persecution of Christians in Nero's Rome.

*Stevenson, Robert L., *The Black Arrow*, various publishers.   (A)

*Tolstoi, Leo, *War and Peace*, various publishers.   (A)
Only the best students should tackle this monumental novel in high school.

*Wallace, Lew, *Ben Hur*, various publishers.   (A)
A Jewish nobleman of the first century is taken prisoner by the Romans.

White, Stewart E., *The Long Rifle*, Doubleday.   (A)
A Pennsylvania farm boy runs away to become a mountain man; a saga about the fur trappers and the role of the Kentucky rifle.

FICTION
IN THE
LITERATURE
PROGRAM

THE DECLINE OF FICTION has become a fact of life in the literary world since World War II. In contemporary publishing, nonfiction titles far outnumber those of fiction, and magazines devote smaller proportions of space to fiction than they did even a few years ago. But although the post–World War II era may well be a golden age of nonfiction, fiction is far from moribund and its apparent decline need have little to do with the literature program in the secondary school.

In fact, it is quite possible that there has been no real "decline" in the popularity of fiction, only less reason on the part of the general public for seeking fictionalized experience in printed form. Television is now the chief medium for popular fiction, satisfying mass taste better than does the printed page. The popular-magazine story has lost its patrons to the television screen. For the high school teacher, television can be a boon as well as a depressant in teaching literature, for it furnishes a handy, interesting (to most students) avenue through which to approach the world of fictionalized experience, offering examples and comparisons through which understandings can be built and discrimination heightened, not only in televiewing but also in reading fiction. It comes as something of a revelation to the adolescent that fiction, that is, stories, are all around him in everyday life—in television, radio, motion picture, newspapers, conversation, and jukebox ballads —not just entombed in his anthology or in books in the library. In fact, a discussion beamed to this revelation is a good way to introduce a unit on fiction for younger students.

Because of this prevalence of fictionalized experience and because the pupil enters the junior high school with some natural interest in stories, fiction probably will be the keystone of the literature program in the secondary school, although students should certainly have broad experiences with the several literary genres. It is in the high school that many adolescents, naturally inclined to action and concerned with happenings, should realize, paraphrasing the philosopher Santayana, that one of the chief functions of literature is to turn events into ideas. It is only then that the student will be able to derive, in his own experience, the real rewards of literature discussed in the opening chapter of this book. Sterile teaching and poor choice of selections are the surest ways of guaranteeing that students will remain at the television level of fiction. And this is unfortunate, not because all television fiction is bad and all in books is good, but because the highest rewards of fiction come from that written by the serious artist and read by the serious reader. Through study of how to read fiction, in constant interplay with wide experiences in reading the novel and short story in their junior and senior high school years, many students will develop the ability to read serious fiction well.

Teaching the Skills of Reading Fiction

The short story and the novel, like the other forms of literature, pose special problems for the reader. Though there has been, in the past thirty years, a vast number of publications about the skills involved in reading and though reading-skill programs are now features of most high school anthologies, there is a great paucity of specific suggestions for teachers to follow in helping students to develop skill in reading fiction or the other literary forms. There are probably two major explanations for this. First, perhaps skill in reading fiction involves merely the application of much-discussed skills in vocabulary, "word-attack,"[1] and comprehension. Second, perhaps the process by which the mature reader truly reads fully a significant novel or story defies analysis, at least makes it impossible to enumerate the specific skills involved. Attempting the full description of such a process would be as impossible, perhaps, as delineating the process by which a music lover "got that way."

The relation of skills in reading literature to broader outcomes of appreciation is a knotty problem that cannot be examined in any detail here. It seems obvious that critical skill in reading fiction—knowledge of criteria for judging value, and ability to apply these criteria—does not guarantee that the reader will enjoy a book or a story, or be moved by it. A technically masterful novel or story may leave even some highly intelligent readers "cold." Undoubtedly other factors enter in—type of personality, point of view of the selection, the total context in which the selection is experienced, and a host more. Many writers have attempted to define "appreciation" in literature or to identify the factors in appreciation. For example, Robert C. Pooley writes: "Appreciation, then, I shall define as the emotional responses which arise from basic recognition, enhanced by apprehension of the means by which they are aroused."[2] I. A. Richards suggests some factors that may cause a faulty or immature literary experience: (1) failure to make out the plain sense of the selection; (2) misleading interpretations caused by a personal experience; (3) dependence upon or use of stock responses that may or may not indicate any real feeling about a selection; (This might be true, for instance, of a student who says that the story was "very convincing.") (4) sentimentality; (5) inhibitions or hardness of heart; (6) "doctrinal adhesions"—that is,

---

[1] "Word-attack" refers to the methods a student uses in trying to handle a word unknown to him which he meets in his reading. It may be of three kinds: phonetic analysis, structural analysis (as of prefixes, suffixes, roots), and guessing from context clues.

[2] Robert C. Pooley, "Measuring the Appreciation of Literature," *English Journal,* XXIV (October 1935), 628.

difficulty in overcoming the preconceived ideas and attitudes that
the reader brings to his reading.[3]

The whole matter of the interrelationship of a human personality and a piece of literature needs much study. Case studies may be
important in determining how certain individuals become very
mature readers of literature. Yet on the basis of what is now
known, the junior or senior high school teacher of literature needs
to identify the skills important in reading fiction and to provide
direction and practice in those skills. It is vital, first, that the student be made aware of the things that are important to think about
when one reads fiction. Then, naturally, the student must be given
much practice—criticized practice—in applying these processes of
thought to fiction appropriate to his level of experience, for the constant relation of one's experience to the printed page is essential in
any true comprehension. These processes of thought, which lead to
skill in reading fiction, seem to divide into two general categories:
those necessary to comprehend form and therefore to determine the
significance of a short story or novel, and those necessary to appre-
hend a variety of implied meanings inherent in fiction.

Reading to Comprehend Form

Because the novel or the short story is a particular way of recon-
structing experience, the special way in which the author has used
the form may be important for the meaning or significance of the
selection. Many students (and adults, for that matter) read only for
"the story," for the literal sequence of events. They tend to read all
stories in the same way, and if the given story does not jibe with their
way of thinking about what a story should be, they are likely to
complain that they "don't get it." Yet the same student who is impatient with form as a factor in understanding the selection may be
the boy who would never be content with knowing only the
amount of yardage gained on an around-end play in a football
game; he would want to know how the play was executed and
from what formation it was run, for this awareness would add to
his enjoyment. Or the impatient student may be a girl who is
sophisticated in music—at least in the form popular at the moment.

[3] I. A. Richards, *Practical Criticism* (New York: Harcourt, 1929).

She would never be satisfied merely to recognize the melody; she would be a keen critic of the artistry of the musicians and arranger in dealing with it. Analogies such as these, presented in class, may help students to see the importance of form in literature—at the least, they may break down some antagonisms.

High school students are frequently baffled by certain modern fiction of the highly symbolic or elliptical variety. For example, the author of this book has been most unsuccessful in teaching a favorite short story, Hemingway's "The Killers," to senior high school classes. Merely following the events of the story, the students come out blank and virtually snarling with frustration. On the surface the story seems stupid (a favorite word in the adolescent's vocabulary of literary criticism). Two sinister-appearing men turn up in a diner in a small town. They carry on a rather pointless conversation with the counterman in the diner. Finally they produce guns, holding the countermen and the cook prisoner, waiting apparently to kill one Ole Andreson, who usually eats at the diner. Ole doesn't come and the men give up and go away. Nick Adams, one of the waiters at the diner, goes to warn Ole, who seems resigned to his fate. The baffled young waiter goes back to the diner, where he exclaims to his partner, "It's too damned awful." The partner's reply is the last line of the story: "Well, you better not think about it."

Furiously, the students want to know why the men are out to kill Ole Andreson. And they want to know how the story *ends*— does Ole get killed or doesn't he? The impasse results from their failure to take into account the role played by the form of the story in expressing its meaning—a failure certainly excusable in the average adolescent, though not in the able. The mature reader realizes, probably from a previous reading of Hemingway that the author is pointing to the pervasiveness of evil in the world, and it does not matter at all, for instance, whether or not Ole Andreson actually gets killed nor why the men want to kill him. The psychological plot of the story involves Nick Adam's traumatic rendezvous with evil, and in terms of that plot the end is just right.

This the mature reader knows, but perhaps not until he reflects upon the story and, probably, rereads it. Much is learned about the way to read fiction *after* a selection has been read. In guiding the discussion of a story or novel that has been read, the teacher is giving important instruction in how to read the next selection. Often, perhaps, this role of class discussion is lost sight of in routine questioning or testing.

Studying Plot

What is the starting point in developing the over-all skill of organizing a selection of fiction in terms of its form and content? In the junior high school the students can learn of the various purposes that fiction may have: simply to entertain through a funny, exciting, or unusual story; to present some serious idea about life; to satirize or burlesque something; to create some kind of effect or impression; to portray or dramatize an emotion; to present an insight into a person's character. In the senior high school the student should learn something of the way in which the traditions of romanticism, realism, and naturalism have affected fiction, and he should have some experiences with historical, sociological, and psychological fiction. More specific ways of dealing with these matters are suggested in the following sections of this chapter.

Since students enter the junior high school naturally interested in "the story" in a piece of fiction, work with plot and its role in the art of fiction may be stressed in the early years, although in classroom work the various elements of fiction can never be considered in isolation from each other. Students will need practice with various methods of plot construction. As the writer has stated in another place:

Most will have little trouble with the plot which presents a straight chronological sequence of events, but they will need training in following the story which starts with a problem, regresses in time to tell how it arose, and moves forward in time to tell how it was solved; or the one which starts at the end, goes back to the beginning, and runs on to meet the starting point, the end of the person's life. In their early acquaintance with plots of this type, it may help students to draw jagged time lines to show the chronology of the story. In the novel, particularly the long nineteenth-century novels, students have the problem of following several plots involving various groups of characters through hundreds of pages. Simple charts showing the various plot strands and the characters involved may help, although the need for too many charts and diagrams may indicate that the novel is too difficult for the level of ability of the readers.[4]

The study of plot will involve students in some important matters of discrimination in reading fiction. For example, the point was made in Chapter 2 that the mature reader rejects improbability and too much coincidence in what he reads, recognizing the fact that in good fiction, as in the experience it reconstructs, there is a basis of cause and effect in happenings. A good study question for students reading fiction is: "Was there any preparation for this happening, any reason for it in what has gone before, or did this happen purely by chance or coincidence?" The literary matter of "foreshadowing" is the point here. After reading a "surprise-ending" story, such as those by O. Henry, students may enjoy looking back over the story to see whether the writer purposely led them astray in order to trick them at the end, or whether the surprise ending could grow logically out of the story.

Reading for Implied Meanings

A readiness to draw inferences, to read between the lines, is essential to successful reading beyond the literal story level. A typical response of adolescents to a teacher's or a classmate's interpretation is an astonished "Where'd you get that out of it?" To the inexperienced teacher highly trained in literature, it sometimes seems inconceivable that a student does not recognize an elementary matter of symbolism. Yet to many youngsters beginning junior high school English, the whole matter of symbolism is foreign, and it never occurs to them to look beneath the surface of happenings for implied ideas. They are often loud in their protest against the writer who doesn't "come right out and say what he means." The process of learning to think with literary material develops gradually through the junior and senior high school years—but it can develop.

---

[4] Dwight L. Burton, "Developing Competence in Reading," in Angela M. Broening (Ed.), *The English Language Arts in the Secondary School* (New York: Appleton, 1956), p. 185.

Using Clues to Setting

Often in fiction the setting is obvious. Yet occasionally, especially in maturely written short stories, the reader has to infer the time or place, and it may be most important that he do this. Simple stories of the Far North, the desert, the tropics, for example, in which there are obvious clues to setting, will provide training for junior high school pupils in making this type of inference. This training will make it easier for them to handle more subtle clues later, when it may be important for them to understand that a story about a pepper-eating contest is taking place in Mexico, or a certain Christmas story in Wales. Consideration of the geographical setting is important, too, in the local-color stories of American literature. The inference of time from clues is important occasionally, too. Certain excellent but "dated" stories of the World War II period, for example, would be bewildering to the student who had not determined the setting in time. Or a story such as Faulkner's "Race at Morning" would lose its impact if the reader did not determine from rather scanty clues that it took place many years ago.

Judging Character

Teachers are fond of asking students to "characterize" so and so from a selection read. This, too, will be a difficult task for the student who has not learned to work with a variety of clues. Discussion of ways to use such clues might be introduced by the question, "How do we arrive at our judgments of people in real life?" Students will usually answer this question with such responses as: "By the way they act." "By what they do." "By what other people say about them." "By the way they talk." "By the way they dress." "By the kinds of things they like to do." Then the teacher can point out that in fiction one arrives at estimates of character through the same kinds of clues, perhaps listing for the class "The nine basic methods of revealing a character," as identified by J. N. Hook:

1. Telling what kind of person he is.
2. Describing the person, his clothing, and his environment.
3. Showing his actions.

4. Letting him talk.
5. Relating his thoughts.
6. Showing how other people talk to him.
7. Showing what other people say about him.
8. Showing how other people react because of him.
9. Showing how he reacts to others.[5]

It is important for the teacher to point out the close relationship of characters and events in mature fiction. That is, a character is often revealed by his reactions in the crisis that provides a climax for a story. And in artistic fiction certain traits of certain characters lead to events. It is a mark of immature, formula fiction that this close relationship of characters and events is lacking, as, for example, when characters do highly improbable and unpredictable things merely for the sake of the plot.

Using Details to Determine or Illuminate Theme

Not all fiction is concerned with any definite theme—to cite an extreme example, the stories of Poe. However, it is important that students develop the ability to handle theme in mature fiction. Certainly no pat set of devices by which this ability could be developed can be outlined, so complicated are the factors involved in dealing with an author's theme. Yet, after students have an understanding of what theme in fiction is, they can be helped by being made aware of the way in which understanding the use of details can aid them to perceive it. Often there will be statements of the theme by the author or by characters. This is the case, for instance, in James Michener's novel of the Korean war, *The Bridges at Toko-Ri,* in which the theme—why American men had to fight and die in a strange, little-known country—is rather clearly stated near the end of the book. This statement of theme was overlooked by the girl who complained that she did not like the book because "it had such a sad ending." In view of the theme, there could be no other ending!

In order to deal with theme, and the general significance of a

[5] J. N. Hook, *The Teaching of High School English* (New York: Ronald, 1950), p. 160.

selection, high school students need to learn to judge details in terms of the author's attitude toward his material. These attitudes lie on a continuum between symbolism and naturalism. Of course, the problem of interpreting symbolism underlies the entire study of literature and is as important to the reading of fiction as to the reading of poetry or any other form of literature. To the symbolist, such as James Joyce or D. H. Lawrence, details are likely to be unimportant, or even meaningless, at the literal level, and this makes reading their work extremely difficult. Only a few high school students will be able to comprehend Joyce or Lawrence, for example, but a general acquaintance with symbolism and a habit of looking below the surface of details can begin in the junior high school. Seventh-graders may discuss the significance of the blue willow plate in Doris Gates's *Blue Willow,* for example, and eighth- or ninth-graders may consider the symbolic value of the black coffee in James Street's *Goodbye, My Lady*. Naturalistic writing, in which the author may be attempting to present a stark cross section, or "slice," of life, may be as baffling to adolescents as the highly symbolistic. It helps them to know the purpose of naturalistic writing. In the senior high school, students should learn something of the continuum of authors' attitudes toward their material. Preparation for reading the major writers of fiction includes placing them on this continuum.

An author's central meaning or theme in a piece of fiction, of course, may be dependent upon such devices as irony, satire, and allegory. In addition to explaining these devices, the teacher needs to provide practice in reading material in which they are used, material appropriate to the students' level of awareness. If this is done, the junior high school is not too early for introduction of these matters.

Approaches to the Novel

At all grades in the junior and senior high school, the novel has been important in the literature program, but because of the amount of time that must be invested in study of the novel, teachers have encountered some particular difficulties, both practical and philosophical. The practical problems center on the availability of material for class use. Library facilities vary widely from school to school. Some teachers have one copy per student of several novels and multiple copies of many at their disposal, whereas some teachers are virtually restricted to the selections in the anthology—and sometimes there is a shortage of anthologies! Editors and publishers have been loath to include full-length novels in anthologies because so much space is required and because no matter what the novel chosen for inclusion, many teachers are dissatisfied with the choice. Only in the books for the ninth and the tenth grades are full-length novels commonly included. However, a great boon has come to the teacher—the phenomenon of paperbound books. Use of paperbacks in the classroom and their inclusion in school and public libraries have become commonplace in the last few years.

Other problems in teaching the novel are philosophical ones. For a long time there has been among teachers a rather widespread suspicion of selections that are popular and that students find easy to read. Teachers have insisted upon choosing for common reading novels that really give them something to teach. However, the commendable zeal to provide challenging experiences has resulted frequently in the choice of novels that are appropriate only for the upper one third or one fourth of the class, and, in part, at least, are only frustrating to the rest. It is probable, for example, that *Silas Marner* and *A Tale of Two Cities* are more appropriate for the twelfth grade, if they are to be taught, than to the tenth, where they—*Silas Marner,* at least—are practically canonized items. However, many teachers have seemed to ignore the nature of a student's growth toward maturity in reading fiction, the gradual type of growth that makes it necessary for a girl to learn to read, say, *Seventeenth Summer* well before she can read *Wuthering Heights* well. A rather widespread burden of contempt for the "juvenile" and the contemporary has, to some extent, crippled teaching of the novel.

A major philosophical problem in teaching the novel, or any form of literature, for that matter, involves the teacher's view of his point of departure—whether he considers it to be the novel or the experience he wants the students to have. The classroom illustrations of approaches to the novel that follow in this chapter clearly show this bipolar view of the point of departure. Some teachers accept a certain novel, or group of novels, as their point of departure. Their problem becomes one, then, of getting the selection "across" to students, of making it meaningful and, if possible, interesting. Articles in *The English Journal* and other professional magazines over many years have shown the ingenuity and resourcefulness that teachers have mustered to meet this problem. Commitment to this point of departure in literature has resulted in production of "simplified classics," abridged or rewritten versions of famous selections. Though these books may have some uses in the general reading program, the disadvantages of using them in teaching literature seem to outweigh the advantages. It is questionable, for one thing, whether a really fine piece of literature can be simplified or even abridged without creating an entirely different piece of literature. There is a real danger that many students may get the idea that they are really experiencing *Les Misérables,* for instance, when they read a simplified edition. (There are even comic-book versions of this and other masterpieces!) Some students who might ultimately read a selection in the original may be discouraged from doing so through the early reading of the simplified version. It seems more legitimate to reason that if students are not prepared to read a certain selection in its original form, they should read another selection that, though of lesser merit or complexity, preserves its unity and integrity as a work of art.

Many other teachers, especially in recent years, have maintained that the point of departure is not any particular novel or group of novels but, rather, the kind of intellectual and emotional experience that a given group of students should have. For these teachers, then, the problem is that of determining what general kinds of experiences afforded by novels a certain class of students should have, and then of finding the selections most likely to provide those experiences.

No doubt this basic cleavage concerning point of departure in the literature program will continue to exist among teachers and others concerned with the reading and literary experiences of young people. Yet the research and experimentation of the past several decades seem to lend support to the viewpoint that the point of departure in teaching the novel should be determination by the teacher of the type of experience he desires his students to have, and then selection of the novels most likely to induce that experience. Considering the entire literary tradition, it is difficult to defend the position that any two or three novels are the *sina qua non* of the literary education during adolescence. It is quite obvious that, no matter what a teacher's opinion of a particular novel may be and no matter what position the book has held in literary history, it will be rewarding to a student only in terms of *his* reactions to it and of the value *he* perceives in his experience of reading it. It is unfortunately apparent that the great majority of high school graduates look back on their tenth-grade experience with *Silas Marner,* for example, as relatively unpleasant, even though there is little doubt that from an objective literary point of view the novel borders on greatness.

Novels for Reading in Common

Regardless of other differences of opinion, there seems to be one virtually unanimous point of agreement among teachers of literature: there should be *some* reading in common. Exactly what that common reading should be at each grade and how much of it there should be may be controversial, but the value of at least occasional experiences in a class's reading the same novel at the same time is universally acknowledged. At least one novel should be read in common in each grade, seven through twelve, although, as this book frequently has stated, there is no pat formula that can be used to prescribe which selections should be read in a particular class. No doubt, each novel chosen for reading in common should meet three general criteria:

1. Any novel chosen should furnish a profitable experience for a typical class, heterogeneous in its intellectual and esthetic potential. It should provide appropriate opportunities for the able without being either completely incomprehensible or unrewarding to those at the lower ranges of ability.

2. The work chosen should pose reading problems and demands that are, in large part, common to many other novels. That is, the unique or greatly experimental work might legitimately be ruled out for class study. Among the commonly taught novels, *Huckle-berry Finn* is such a book. To be sure, many students should read *Huckleberry Finn,* but the work is so much in a class by itself that it may lack real value for in-common study. Of particular value is the book that has a concrete, literal line of progression and at the same time a possible continual allegorical or symbolic progression, for example, *The Old Man and the Sea* and *The Secret Sharer.*

3. The novel must have some natural affinity with youth, with adolescence. There is, of course, no sure way by which this amor-phous quality of "affinity" can be judged, but it seems important that teachers consider it with as much insight as they can muster. For adolescents, however bright intellectually or mature socially and physically, are different, in general, from adults. There are certain themes, attitudes, mind-sets that are naturally more accept-able or comprehensible than others to young people. A work must be appraised carefully in terms of the resources of a given class for entering imaginatively into it and responding to it.

In order to give some practical help to teachers in choosing novels for common reading at the various grade levels, the author con-ducted a survey of all articles on the teaching of the novel that had appeared in *The English Journal* since 1946; surveyed recent sylla-buses and courses of study from many schools, cities, and states; con-sulted a number of reading lists published by the National Council of Teachers of English, the American Library Association, and other organizations; talked personally and corresponded with many teachers from various parts of the country. The following list of suggested novels for reading in common is a result of that study. Several somewhat obvious things should be pointed out about the list. First, there is nothing "objective" about the placement of the selections in the various grades; this placement was determined both in terms of common practice across the country and in terms of the writer's opinions about appropriateness. For example, *Great Expectations* appears in the tenth-grade list, although a cut version that appears in a widely used anthology is commonly taught in the ninth grade. On the other hand, *Old Yeller,* for instance, could be read before the ninth grade by many students. Second, it is obvious that some of the selections would be useful only for certain groups

—*Shane* for students of lesser ability and *The Dead* for highly able readers, for example. One of the real problems of selecting novels for reading in common by seventh- and eighth-graders is that boys and girls at those levels have such markedly different interests. Therefore, in the main, the selections for those grades have been suggested supposedly because of their appeal for both boys and girls.

In the list that follows, those books available in paperback edition when this volume went to press are marked with an asterisk. Readers may find that some of these marked titles are now out of print in paperback form and that others not so marked are now available in paperback.[6]

Seventh Grade

Buck, Pearl, *The Big Wave.* (A typhoon destroys a Japanese village.)

Henry, Marguerite, *King of the Wind.* (Story of a great Arabian horse.)

Knight, Eric, *Lassie Come-Home.* (The original story of the famous fictional collie.)

Krumgold, Joseph, *And Now Miguel.* (A boy and his sheep-farming family.)

Salten, Felix, *Bambi.* (The famous story of a stag in the forests of Austria.)

Sperry, Armstrong, *Call It Courage.* (A South Sea island boy proves his courage.)

Eighth Grade

London, Jack, *Call of the Wild.* (One of the great dog-and-man stories.)

Stevenson, Robert, *Treasure Island.*

Street, James, *Goodbye, My Lady.* (A boy and an unusual dog in the Mississippi swamp country.)

---

[6] Teachers should check in the most recent edition of *Paperbound Books in Print* (Bowker Company, New York, N.Y.).

Twain, Mark, *Tom Sawyer.*

Ullman, James Ramsey, *Banner in the Sky.* (A boy conquers a great mountain in Switzerland.)

Ninth Grade

Forbes, Esther, *Johnny Tremain.* (A young silversmith's part in the turbulent pre-Revolutionary War days in Boston.)

Gipson, Fred, *Old Yeller.* (Family life and an incorrigible yellow dog in pioneer days in Texas.)

Kipling, Rudyard, *Captains Courageous.* (A molly-coddle is rescued and "educated" by a ship's crew.)

Richter, Conrad, *Light in the Forest.* (A white boy is returned to his parents' civilization after years of captivity by the Indians.)

Schaefer, Jack, *Shane.* (A quality western.)

Tenth Grade

Annixter, Paul, *Swiftwater.* (A Maine woods boy, his ambitions, his family, and the girl in his life.)

Bagnold, Enid, *National Velvet.*

Godden, Rumer, *The River.* (An English girl in modern India.)

Hemingway, Ernest, *The Old Man and the Sea.*

Hilton, James, *Lost Horizon.*

Kantor, MacKinlay, *The Voice of Bugle Ann.* (A very different dog story.)

Steinbeck, John, *The Pearl.*

Eleventh Grade

Cather, Willa, *Death Comes for the Archbishop.*

Clark, Walter Van Tilburg, *The Ox-Bow Incident.* (A Nevada lynching in 1885.)

Crane, Stephen, *Red Badge of Courage.*

Faulkner, William, *The Bear.*

Hawthorne, Nathaniel, *The Scarlet Letter.*

Knowles, John, *A Separate Peace.* (An outstanding prep school story.)

Lewis, Sinclair, *Babbitt. (An attack on the narrowness of middle-class business culture.)

Melville, Herman, *Billy Budd.

Wharton, Edith, *Ethan Frome.

Wolfe, Thomas, *Look Homeward, Angel. (Childhood and youth of a North Carolina boy, in poetic prose.)

Twelfth Grade

Boulle, Pierre, *The Bridge over the River Kwai. (An ironic tale of World War II soldiers and their Japanese captors.)

Brontë, Emily, *Wuthering Heights.

Conrad, Joseph, *Heart of Darkness and *The Secret Sharer.

Dickens, Charles, *Great Expectations and *A Tale of Two Cities.

Gogol, Nicolai, *The Overcoat.

Golding, William, *Lord of the Flies. (A group of boys, marooned on an island, regresses to savagery.)

Hardy, Thomas, *The Mayor of Casterbridge and *The Return of the Native.

Joyce, James, *The Dead.

Koestler, Arthur, *Darkness at Noon. (The ordeal of a man forced to "confess" by the Communists.)

Paton, Alan, *Cry, the Beloved Country. (Race relations in South Africa.)

McCullers, Carson, *The Heart Is a Lonely Hunter. (Strangely assorted personalities come together in a Southern town.)

Wilder, Thornton, *The Bridge of San Luis Rey. (The patterns of the lives of five people killed when a Peruvian bridge collapses.)

Intensive Study of the Novel

The student's ability to read fiction will develop gradually through the junior and senior high school years. But his experiences in intensive class study of the novel are crucial because these experiences —and there is time for but few of them—will be the milestones toward perceptive reading of the mature novel.

Three kinds of abilities need attention in intensive study of the novel:

Those involving imaginative entry into the novel
Those involving perception of meaning in the novel
Those involving judgment of the author's skill in his medium

IMAGINATIVE ENTRY. First, in order to read a novel well, and in order to enjoy it, the reader must enter into it imaginatively, must empathize, as the psychologists put it. Some students are more imaginative than others, of course, more ready to suspend disbelief. But regardless of quickness of imagination or inherent flair for the nonliteral, all students are capable of imaginative entry into vicarious experience merely because they are human and because they have had experience.

Imaginative entry depends in large part on the use of correlative experience. Just as the novelist has to express emotion indirectly, so the reader has to cull up experiences in the *general* field of emotion represented. A man is killed in a novel and the reader, who must empathize with the killer, has never killed anyone. But perhaps he has killed an animal or has seen someone else kill one. The reader of *Huckleberry Finn* has not traveled down the Mississippi on a raft with a runaway slave and tussled with his conscience over knowledge of law versus feelings of personal loyalty, but probably he has been in some situation that involved a conflict between his relations with an individual and his relations with society or a group. The reader of *The Old Man and the Sea* probably has not spent a day and night upon the ocean fighting and finally subduing a giant marlin only to have it destroyed by sharks so that only a great skeleton is left, but perhaps he has realized the hollowness of a victory or has carried on a lonely struggle to achieve and no one has understood.

But the reader must *learn* to use experience. The secret of the success of the junior novels portraying adolescent culture is that they require only literal identification, no imaginative ordering of correlative experience. Perhaps this is as it should be in early adolescence. Mary or Joe reads a novel about a school like theirs, a family much like their own, people much like those they know, problems literally similar to those they are encountering. And they enter with zest into the world created by the novelist for it has true meaning and impact.

Abstract identification or entry, through the avenue of correlative experience, is quite another matter, but it is not beyond most high school students. Can imaginative entry into a novel be *taught?* Probably not, but it can be *promoted.* It can be promoted, first, by selection of those novels that offer a legitimate chance for the student to use his experiences as the touchstone for imaginative entry, and, second, by aid to the student in thinking about his experiences in connection with those portrayed in the novel.

There is one question teachers must live with: what basis does the student have for entering into the emotional experience of this novel through plumbing of correlative experience? Most seventeen-year-olds could not be expected to identify with Jake Barnes in his frustration over the impossibility of consummating his love for Brett in *The Sun Also Rises.* Nor can most adolescents understand why the attractive and wealthy Tom and Daisy Buchanan always seem so tired and bored in *The Great Gatsby.* But even the younger student can identify with Bucky Calloway, who in Annixter's *Swiftwater* meets the dreaded wolverine on his father's trap line, because most high school students already have had to face evil in obvious form and make decisions about it. And though *A Tale of Two Cities* presents a number of difficulties, its Sidney Carton is a natural for adolescent identification. His final grand sacrifice is of the stuff of adolescent dreams. Identification with Sidney Carton induces pseudo emotions, central in the esthetic experience. These pseudo emotions are none the less powerful but are more satisfying, as Aristotle said so long ago. The essential problem is to propel students from the launching pad of literal identification into the rewarding process of abstract identification, through making them aware that their experiences to date are the key to imaginative entry into a novel of whatever time, place, problem, or situation.

Thomas Hardy once wrote that the "writer's problem is how to strike the balance between the uncommon and the ordinary so as on the one hand to give interest, on the other to give reality." The student's problem is parallel: how to immerse himself in the experience of the work and yet retain his esthetic distance so as to organize the work for the perception of meaning. The word "easy" (a most slippery term when used in connection with literature) can best be applied to those novels in which very little organization for perception of meaning is required—the traditional romance, for example, in which the experience represented in the novel is exempt from the conditions that we know usually attach to experience. *The Prisoner of Zenda* is a good example.

PERCEPTION OF MEANING. The second emphasis, then, must be on helping the student build the equipment by which to perceive meaning in a novel, on acquainting him with the devices involved in the constant interplay of form and content. It is possible here merely to cite a few examples of things students must learn if they are to perceive meaning in a novel.

What is required in general might be called the method of hypothesis in reading a novel. That is, from the very first, the reader constantly has to hypothesize on the basis of what happens, what is said, what objects or scenes are introduced. The reading becomes a matter of continually positing and testing hypotheses. Some of these hypotheses will receive sufficient test in a few pages; others, not until the book is finished and the reader has reflected on it. For example, the hypothesis that Zeena's feigning of illness is used as a weapon to control Ethan Frome cannot be finally accepted or rejected until the end of the book. This is not to suggest that any two readers necessarily will come to the same conclusions or even raise the same hypotheses, but it is the process that is important. Student interpretations will be judged, then, mainly in terms of the process the student has used in arriving at his interpretation.

It is easy and natural for the immature reader to flow along with the plot of the story, going from episode to episode, without any real consideration of the value or use of the individual episode. Such a reading makes *The Red Badge of Courage,* for example, a rather flat tale of a farm boy at war. Episodes or scenes may be used for various purposes—to reveal character, to heighten effects, to provide meaning through allegory or satire, simply to satisfy the reader's curiosity about what happened to someone or what happened as aftermath to some event. The reader, then, must be willing to hypothesize about each scene. For example, the scene from *Swiftwater* mentioned earlier, the scene in which a boy fights with and kills a wolverine, is generally symbolic of the meeting with evil, the coming to terms with it, and is a key scene in developing the theme of a boy's growing up. In *Huckleberry Finn,* to take a far different example, individual scenes assume key importance. For instance, the scene in which Colonel Sherburn shoots Boggs and then faces down and disperses the mob that follows him to his house has broad meaning of itself in Mark Twain's view of the world. This meaning can be interpreted without reference to other things in the novel.

But, of course, individual scenes or episodes usually cannot be interpreted without reference to all the rest of the work, and the student must be willing to hypothesize not only about immediate meanings but also about the possibility of total allegorical or symbolic framework in a novel. Such seems necessary for a sophisticated reading of *The Old Man and the Sea* or Walter Van Tilburg Clark's *The Ox-Bow Incident,* to cite two novels rather commonly taught in high school, although students might profitably read these books at lesser levels of perception.

Interpretation of symbolism especially requires use of the method of hypothesis, though at mention of the word "symbolism" cautions may flicker across the backs of teachers' minds. For occasionally the bright and well-meaning student "gets hot" on symbolism and mires himself in a bog of symbols. And yet the reader of *The Great Gatsby,* say, who, early in the book, does not set up hypotheses concerning the use and meaning of the valley of ashes, the great dumping ground outside New York City, or of the billboard with the eyes of T. J. Eckleburg, cannot accomplish a full reading. The same thing is true of Conrad's *Heart of Darkness.* Here the ivory is a basic symbol. It accounts for the ruin of Kurtz and it symbolizes what may account for the ruin of mankind. Much is lost if the reader does not perceive this. It may be well in this instance to direct students' reading by telling them in advance that ivory is the basic symbol. Where they go from there will be up to them.

Hypothesis is important, too, in considering point of view. How much the narrator can be expected to know is a crucial question for the student to keep in mind if he is to read discriminately. But, more important, meaning in the novel may be definitely tied up with the nature of the narrator. Why did Mark Twain force himself to see the world through the eyes of Huck Finn, Stephen Crane through the eyes of Henry Flemming, Scott Fitzgerald through the eyes of Nick Carraway, Herman Melville through the eyes of Ishmael? Though final answers may differ, unless these questions are asked, the student is not on the track of important meaning.

A not insignificant function of the method of hypothesis may be that it is often a student's means of avoiding boredom and keeping his interest alive through dull parts of otherwise rewarding books. The author has always found it necessary to warn students about the openings of *The Secret Sharer* and *Heart of Darkness:* it takes patience to become engaged with a Conrad novel. It takes patience, too, to wade through the middle of *A Tale of Two Cities* in order to discover what it has to do with the end. In this context, the method of hypothesis may improve the student's morale if not his interpretation!

JUDGMENT OF CRAFTSMANSHIP. It was stated in the first chapter that the structure of literature in general, and thus of the novel, is to be found in its recurring themes and forms. It is legitimate, then, that intensive study of the novel give the student some skill in judging the author's technical skill. This matter was approached generally in an earlier section of this chapter. Yet a major problem needs to be stated again: Teachers may have given too great a prominence to this aspect of intensive study. The experience of many students in studying the novel is limited to a reading of the piece followed by discussion in which the work is criticized or dissected. Is it true to life? Were the characters lifelike? Was the plot probable? Was the author skillful in description? Of course, these are germane questions in the classroom, but they may sometimes signal a superficial approach to technique and an overemphasis on stock consideration of the traditional matters of setting, plot, characters, theme, and style.

A few illustrations may be appropriate. What about the much-used phrase—especially in student book reports—"true to life"? Of course, teachers know, and it is important to make students know, that it is verisimilitude, the appearance of truth or reality, that they are talking about, not reality itself. Literature is not life, and verisimilitude in the novel has to be judged not only by the reader's experience with life, but by life as presented in the work. Thus, is the coincidence that brings Stephen Kumalo and Jarvis together toward the end of *Cry, the Beloved Country* contrived, when we consider all that has gone before? In the same way, judgment of characters in connection with events must be based on internal consistency: Is Miss Pross's killing of Madame Defarge defensible in the context of the novel as Miss Pross has been portrayed?

Teachers have worked with legitimate zeal on characterization. It is all to the good—among other things it may affect students' attitudes toward television programs—that many students have been made aware of stereotypes of character. Yet it seems important to make a distinction between stereotypes and archetypes, which are so prominent, especially in modern literature. Representing a type of man, and evoking, in the words of the psychologist Jung, "a racial memory," the archetype may be greatly individual as is Joe, who, in *Great Expectations,* is a representative of the poetic approach to life, or as is Jay Gatsby, who is all of us who build our ambitions on illusions. The stereotyped character, on the other hand, lacks individuality and is based not on racial experience but on oversimplification and half-truths.

Finally, it seems apparent—and again it should be made apparent to students—that ability to judge an author's technique has nothing to do necessarily with a perceptive reading of a novel or with an impactful experience. A student may see clearly the neat parallelism in *A Tale of Two Cities* and still find the book tedious. He may detect the meticulous balance of scenes and characters in *Daisy Miller* and still be bored or puzzled. (Many high school students are bored or puzzled by Henry James.) He may even see that at every point in *The Secret Sharer* the literal progression of the plot is joined to the allegorical or symbolic level of the novel, and still not understand the work. Mere judgment of technique is butler to the masters—imaginative entry into a novel and perception of its meaning.

The Short Story in the Literature Program

Junior and senior high school English teachers universally find the short story the most successful form of literature with adolescents. Stories are eminently "teachable" partly because they are inherently appealing. Everyone from three to three-score years likes a story, whether in printed or visual form. Also, the magazine, the television screen, and the school anthology make the short story the most available form of literature. Furthermore, the form is especially suited for reading in common. Simply in terms of time investment, the story far above (or below) the level of individual students does not carry the same amount of penalty that the novel or drama or epic poem does; reading the short story gives the poorer reader a sense of accomplishment impossible for him to have from reading these longer forms. Many short stories can be read and discussed within one class period, and using a group of stories gives the teacher a chance to cover a great deal of ground in teaching the skills of reading fiction. Finally, study of short stories provides an excellent opportunity for motivating students' writing, as examples later in this section show.

Despite the ease with which it can be used in the classroom, however, the short story should not be overstressed at the expense of the novel, for it lacks the power of the novel. Although as has been pointed out the short story is to literature as the microscope is to science,[7] giving us otherwise impossible glimpses of experience, it cannot give the same opportunity for identification, for insight into human motivation that the novel affords. The short story's scope is "moral revelation"; the novel's, "moral evolution."[8]

Though the short story has been a major literary form since early in the nineteenth century, the last three decades have brought wide variety and experimentation in the genre, and high school students need definite training if they are to deal intelligently with many serious stories. It may be profitable to discuss with them, and illustrate by specific stories, the four "amalgamations" discussed by Mark Schorer: story method, character portrayal, attitude toward material, and style.[9]

The "older" story is narrative in method, like the older novel, proceeding, by and large, in chronological sequence with a tightly

---

[7] Ray B. West, "The Modern Short Story and the Highest Forms of Art," *English Journal,* XLVI (December 1957), 531–539.

[8] Mark Schorer, *The Story: A Critical Anthology* (Englewood Cliffs, N.J.: Prentice-Hall, 1950), p. 433.

[9] *Ibid.,* p. 431.

knit plot leading to a definite climax, denouement, and conclusion. In recent years the short story has often been dramatic rather than narrative in technique, presenting a single scene, often featuring a seemingly abrupt ending, as if the curtain fell while the characters were still in full action. The contrast between a Hawthorne tale and a *New Yorker* story shows the evolution in story method. In character portrayal the range is from the highly subjective to the highly objective. Short-story writers of the nineteenth century, particularly, furnished much direct background material about the characters, whereas in the modern story, as has been pointed out earlier, the author often forces the reader to infer the background from scanty clues to character. Dickens and Hemingway might illustrate the contrast of these extremes in character portrayal.

The author's attitude toward his material, ranging from naturalistic to symbolistic, has been discussed earlier in this chapter. The fourth "amalgamation" which Schorer identifies is that in style, from "low" to "high." Hemingway, again, illustrates clearly the "low" style. That is, his stories are written in the language his characters speak. Part of Hemingway's effectiveness lies in his ability to reproduce the speech patterns and idioms of the kinds of people he writes about. O. Henry, perhaps, is a good example of the "high" style. Though he may write about a New York City tramp, as he does in "The Cop and the Anthem," the speech patterns and vocabulary are still O. Henry's.

Classroom Illustrations

Because units of short stories and aids to teaching individual stories are widely available to teachers in the many anthologies on the market, a detailed discussion of classroom approaches to the short story seems unnecessary here. However, some techniques that have proved effective in actual teaching situations are suggested below.

STUDY OF MAGAZINE FICTION. Although the amount of space given to fiction in magazines has been decreasing in favor of the nonfiction article, still, because of the wide distribution of magazines in the United States, the short story is virtually at everyone's fingertips:

More short stories are bought and read today than any other form of literature. In fact, when historians write about the twentieth century they may well decide that the short story is the typical and representative literary form of this age, just as the drama has been the great literary form in some periods and the poem in others.[10]

Study of magazines, valuable in itself in high school classes, can be tied in profitably with the study of short stories as students build criteria for themselves by which to distinguish poor, mediocre, and superior fiction. A senior high school class might be divided into three groups, each group to study the fiction in a certain class of magazines. Group I might consider such periodicals as the *New Yorker,* the *Atlantic Monthly,* and *Harper's,* and possibly even some of the literary magazines. Group II could study such middle-grade "slicks" as the *Saturday Evening Post* and *Redbook,* while Group III would consider low-grade "slicks" and even the pulps. Each group would work out a descriptive "profile" of the fiction appearing in its group of magazines, with generalizations concerning plot, characters, theme, and style. Each group could then make a report to the class, and the profiles would be compared. General differences in the fiction in the various groups of magazines will become apparent, although students should be given to understand, naturally, that occasionally a truly outstanding story appears in the *Post,* for example, while a bad story may turn up even in one of the literary magazines.

This device helps students at least to see the differences between commercial-formula and serious fiction. The reports by the groups of students probably will bring out points of difference such as those listed below, which were established by the writer's own analysis of large numbers of short stories from magazines generally considered to be "high quality" or "low quality."

1. The "low quality" stories not only have very definite plot structure but rely on several stereotyped plot patterns. Plots deal more frequently with romantic love and crime than with any other subjects.

[10] Wilbur Schramm, *Great Short Stories* (New York: Harcourt, 1950), p. 2.

Stories from "quality" magazines tend to have looser plots and much greater variety of subject matter.

2. Stories from "low quality" sources tend to resolve problems very conclusively and definitely. Endings are satisfyingly final. (Of course, marriage is the usual ending for the love story.)

The stories from more literary sources frequently present no definite solutions to problems. (To the immature reader, endings often seem abrupt and mystifying.)

3. Coincidence and improbability often characterize the stories from "low quality" sources, though they are usually cast in a realistic framework.

4. Physical action is paramount in the "low quality" stories. The stories from "quality" sources often rely on psychological action.

5. The "low quality" stories rely on character stereotypes.

PLOT SUMMARY DEVICE. The author has found that the material reproduced below is useful in promoting discussion and in illustrating important points of difference between the mature and the immature short story. The material may be used, too, as an evaluating device at the end of a unit on short stories. Each item below summarizes a story up to a certain point; then three possible completing summaries are given. The student rates these three in order. The ranking of the completing summaries in each item was agreed upon unanimously by twenty college and high school teachers of English. This ranking is given in parentheses after each summary ("best" is 1; "poorest," 3).

PLOT SUMMARY EXERCISE[11]

Directions to students: After each Roman numeral below is a summary of a short story. The summary of the story stops at a certain point. Then three summaries—lettered A, B, C—are given of how the story could be developed from that point. Decide which of

11 Teachers have permission from the publisher to reproduce the following exercise for use in individual schools.

these three versions would be the best development of the story—
that is, which most probably would give the best-quality story. Then
decide which would be second best and which poorest. Rank the
summaries by putting a number before each letter—1 for best, and
so on. Be ready to defend your choices.

I. At Midwestern University, fraternity and sorority initiation
   week for freshman pledges was coming to an end. Jerry
   Barnes was thankful that this was his last evening of initiation. He had been doing zany stunts all week. Now he had
   been assigned his last stunt. He was to go to the streetcar
   stop, stop the streetcar as if he wanted to get on, and then
   put his foot on the step, tie his shoe, and thank the streetcar
   operator for the use of the car. So Jerry, following instruc-
   tions, stopped the first streetcar. He calmly put his shoe on
   the step and began to tie it, but the irate operator, accus-
   tomed to college pranks, saw what Jerry was doing and
   kicked his foot.

   A. Jerry sprawled backward into the street. As he scrambled
      to his feet, he realized that a pretty girl who had just gotten
      off the car was laughing. She asked if he was being initi-
      ated. He explained as they started down the street, and
      He told her the worst one was having to go in and
      do. He told her the worst one was having to go in and
      ask silly questions of old "Frozen Face" McDougal, his-
      tory professor. He told her what a pill "Frozen Face"
      was. She accepted his invitation to have a coke, and after
      they sat down in the drugstore, he asked her what her
      name was. "Helen McDougal," she answered, smiling.
      " 'Old Frozen Face' is my dad!" Jerry, completely em-
      barrassed, apologized heartily. The girl laughed gaily and
      invited Jerry to her house "to see how Dad really is."
      Jerry found that Professor McDougal was very human,
      and he left that evening having made a date for Saturday
      with Helen. (2)

   B. Jerry sprawled backward into the street. Hearing some-
      one laugh, he looked up to see a pretty girl on the curb.
      "Are you being initiated?" she asked. Jerry told her about
      the initiation and they walked down the street together.
      He told her of all the stunts he had had to do, and she
      accepted his invitation to have a coke. After the coke, she
      invited him to her sorority house. When they reached the

house, she said, "I'm afraid you'll have to go now. We're having a meeting. I'm sorry, but you'll understand. I'm being initiated, too, and I had to pick up a boy and get him to walk home with me!" (1)

C. Jerry lost his balance, slipped, and fell, his legs going under the car, which had already started. He lost consciousness as the wheels passed over him. As Jerry recovered in the hospital, something happened to his thinking. When he finally left the hospital with an artificial leg, he knew what his purpose was. He returned to school and started a one-man campaign against the initiation week. He was determined to save others from being victims of silly and dangerous stunts. At first, he made himself very unpopular. A fraternity group threatened him. But gradually he turned sentiment to his side. Finally, through his efforts, the university outlawed the initiation week, and at a convocation, Jerry was commended personally by the president of the university. (3)

II. Grizzled Harp Williams, veteran cab driver, returned to work on the afternoon shift feeling that life no longer had any purpose. The afternoon before, he had attended the funeral of Jane, his niece, who for years had been Harp's main interest in life. Jane had been killed in an automobile accident. She had been left in Harp's care when she became an orphan as a little girl. Harp, before the coming of Jane, had been left alone when his wife ran away with another man. Now Harp felt a great need to talk to someone about his sorrow. He tried to talk to his first passenger, a young woman. But the young woman was very upset about something and Harp dropped his efforts to talk to her. The next passenger was a well-dressed man, and again Harp tried to begin to talk. But the man explained brusquely that he had troubles of his own. Then three young men, very gay and noisy, entered the cab and Harp had no opportunity to talk to them. As the evening went on, many other people engaged the cab, but no one was inclined to listen to Harp.

A. Finally an elderly woman engaged the cab. And at last Harp found a listener. He poured out his sorrow. Eventually, greatly agitated, the woman told Harp to stop the cab. In tears, she revealed that she was his wife who ran away years before. She said the other man had deserted her, and she had been lonely for years, but too proud to go back to Harp. She begged Harp to take her back now and let her ease his sorrow. Overjoyed, Harp accepted, and the two decided to begin again. (3)

B. When his shift ended, Harp checked in his cab and lingered around the central garage, hoping to talk to someone among the other drivers. But they were all anxious to get home. Finally, Harp returned to his very empty apartment and went to bed. (1)

C. Harp finally fell silent, realizing that no one else was interested in his sorrow. He mechanically finished his shift. When it ended, Harp drove his cab to a lonely part of the harbor and drove off a pier into the deep, icy water. (2)

III. Old Mr. Farnsworth, millionaire, wasn't given too long to live. He had no particular illness, the doctors said, but his mind was slipping badly. The old man had no important reason for living longer. He had a million dollars with nothing in particular to spend it for. His wife had divorced him many years before. His niece and her husband, with whom Mr. Farnsworth lived, were engrossed with their own concerns. They were instructed not to let the old man out of the house alone. But one stormy night, Mr. Farnsworth was taken with the desire to go out. About midnight he managed to slip out of the house. An hour later he was hopelessly lost and half frozen in the swirling snow. A youngish woman, probably a waitress on her way home, encountered the old man groping along the deserted street. He was unable to tell her where he lived, so the woman took him to her little apartment. She installed him near a warm radiator and made coffee.

A. Meanwhile, Mr. Farnsworth's absence had been detected and the distraught niece and her husband had the police start a thorough search. Early the next morning the old man was found walking happily along a street some distance away. He told the amazed officers a strange story about a young woman who had taken him in and given him coffee. He had stolen away after she had gone to sleep in a chair. He couldn't remember where she lived now, but he insisted that his niece advertise for the woman and offer a $10,000 reward. A few months later when the old man died, the reward was still unclaimed as his disgusted niece had told her friends it would be. (1)

B. In a few minutes the old man went to sleep. Unable to find any identification in the clothes he wore, the puzzled young woman made him comfortable on the couch and dropped to sleep herself in a big chair. In the morning the old man's mind was clear. He was humbly grateful and gave the young woman his niece's telephone number. While they waited for the niece's husband to come, the young woman made breakfast and they talked. She told him about her job at the restaurant. When the old man was safely home again, he sent for his lawyer with more animation than he had shown in months. Within two days, Mr. Farnsworth had bought an attractive restaurant and installed the young woman as manager. With great enthusiasm, he went to the restaurant often and watched from a private little booth. The doctors changed their predictions. (2)

C. After talking happily for a few minutes, Mr. Farnsworth dropped to sleep. The puzzled young woman went through his pockets for identification. She found his wallet and a little diary the old man was fond of writing in. As she looked through the diary, she grew pale and trembled, and she began to shake with sobs. Now she knew who her father was, whom her mother had always refused to discuss! Here he was, in her apartment, and he was a millionaire! She put back the diary and wallet and made the old man comfortable on the couch. As she regarded him, she thought bitterly of her own life, her job in the disreputable cafe. She did not sleep. In the morning the old man's mind was clear. He was very grateful and began to thank the young woman. In tears, she told him who she was. The old man became very angry at what he thought was a trick by an unscrupulous woman. He stamped out, throwing a little money on a table as he went. He told the woman it would have been more if it had not been for her shabby trick. (3)

IV. Down on the street, newsboys were hawking "Extra! Extra!" In his apartment four stories up, John Ward heard them and knew that soon his wife would ask him to go down and get a paper. Newspaper extras had a fascination for Mrs. Ward.

Her curiosity refused to let an extra go by unread. So it was
always John's duty to go down the four flights for the paper.
To John this was something of a symbol for the bored routine
his three years of married life had been. To offset his boredom
and to avoid the acid of his wife's tongue as much as possible,
John spent more and more time in the big chair reading
stories of exotic, far-away places and exciting adventures.
Soon John's wife heard the newsboys, and John was sent on
his usual errand. He got his coat from the bedroom, waking
his four-month-old son, Elden. John heard him begin to cry
as he went down the stairs.

A. As John walked down the dingy hallways of the apartment
building, an idea took hold of him with such force that
he ran down the last flight of stairs and fell into a rapid
stride in the foggy street. He was through with boredom,
with his wife's nagging, with the dismal apartment! He
was not going back! The Navy or a merchant ship! Pictures of Singapore, Constantinople, Buenos Aires rose before his eyes. He would send money to his wife, exciting
gifts to Elden. After he had covered several blocks, John
began to feel the cold dampness of the night. Lights were
going out in the apartment buildings. John's pace slack-
ened. Finally he turned around. When he arrived at his
apartment with the paper, Elden was still wailing. His
wife indignantly demanded to know why he had taken
so long. (1)

B. By the time John reached the street, the newsboy was a
couple of blocks away. John caught up to him. The extra
dealt with a murder on the East Side. As John turned
back through the chill fog, he heard a foghorn out in the
harbor. The sound stirred something within him. Visions
rose before his eyes of Singapore, Constantinople, Buenos
Aires. Suddenly he turned and walked rapidly in the opposite direction. Three months later an envelope post-
marked "Singapore" was delivered to Mrs. Ward. The
envelope contained only money. But the return address
read, "Apprentice Seaman John Ward." (2)

C. As John walked down the damp street after the newsboy,
a foghorn sounded out in the harbor. Something stirred
within him, and then the idea came to him with a sudden
flash. John never returned to his apartment. He enlisted

in the Navy, and his dreams came true of visits to Singapore, Hongkong, Constantinople. Eighteen years went by and John was a Chief Petty Officer on the battleship *Indiana*. Then came the war. One day a group of new seamen came aboard. There was one named Elden Ward. John discovered with a shock that it was his son. John kept the secret as the battleship entered combat waters. One day the ship was attacked by Japanese planes. Part of the deck was set on fire, and Elden, knocked unconscious, was trapped by the flames. John saved him, but was fatally injured by enemy bullets. Just before John died, he called Elden to his side, told him who he was, and asked forgiveness. Elden forgave him and determined to be as great a sailor as his father. (3)

V. Victims of bad train connections, James F. Webster and his two business associates, Hal Russell and Winston Crane, found themselves faced with a five-hour stopover in the little town of Hutchins, sixty miles away from their home city. This loss of time was a great irritation to James F. Webster who had never lost any time in his life. It was his ability to make every minute count that had made him president of the company at thirty-six. He hadn't even taken time to marry any of the attractive young women who had come into his life. The three men decided to take a hotel room and clean up. There was only one room left vacant at the town's one hotel, not a very good room, but they took it, resignedly. Mr. Webster took a bottle of expensive liquor from his suitcase and suggested a drink. There was no room service, so Mr. Crane volunteered to go for some soda. The other two sprawled in chairs. Mr. Russell reached down and picked up a crumpled piece of paper lying on the floor. He smoothed it out and examined it lazily. Then with a smile he handed it to Mr. Webster. On the paper was scrawled "Cash on hand . . . 17.60." Then there was a column:

Jimmy's doctor bill	163.50
Back rent	52.00
Owe Thompson	15.00
Grocery	17.00
Need	246.00

Then there followed some aimless doodling. Then the notation, "Try to borrow from Mr. Hadkins."

A. Mr. Webster looked at the paper with boredom and tossed it on the table as Mr. Crane arrived with the soda. As they sipped their drinks, Mr. Webster grunted, "What a place to spend five hours!" He picked up the paper again and toyed with it idly. He noticed that the calculations had been made on the back of an envelope. On the other side was the address:

> J. A. Manley
> Hopkins Falls
> Illinois

Mr. Webster, grinning, called the desk and asked to have a call put through to J. A. Manley in Hopkins Falls. When the call came through, Mr. Webster asked an amazed Mr. Manley if he had gotten the loan from Mr. Hadkins. When the answer was that he had not, Mr. Webster said, "Well, you will," and hung up. Handing Mr. Crane the paper, he took a coin from his pocket. "A little game of chance," he grinned. "Loser sends Mr. Manley the money he needs." Groaning, the others agreed. Mr. Webster was the loser. "First time I've lost on a coin in a long time," he complained as he reached for his checkbook. (2)

B. Mr. Webster read the note with boredom. He noticed that it was written on the back of an envelope. On the other side was the address:

> J. A. Manley
> Hopkins Falls
> Illinois

He knew the town. It was a suburb of his home city. Suddenly he picked up the phone receiver and sent a telegram to J. A. Manley, Hopkins Falls, Illinois: "COME OFFICE J. F. WEBSTER ILLINOIS PRODUCTS CORP. TOMORROW STOP HAVE OFFER FOR YOU" The next day, a pretty but puzzled young woman was presented to Mr. Webster, who asked if she had gotten the loan from Mr. Hadkins. More amazed than ever, the woman said that she hadn't. Mr. Webster explained everything and offered her a position which the delighted young woman accepted. A few months later, the newspapers carried the news of Mr. James F. Webster's engagement to Miss Jane Manley. (3)

C. Mr. Webster read the paper. "Well, do you think the guy got the money from Mr. Hadkins?" he asked Mr. Russell with a smile.

"Naw," yawned Mr. Russell, "Mr. Hadkins probably told him he was sorry, but times weren't good and he had expenses of his own."

"You're too pessimistic," Mr. Webster answered, "Hadkins probably gave him the money interest-free."

"Nuts," rejoined Mr. Russell. "The old skinflint probably has a mortgage on the house." Just then Mr. Crane came back. "We'll leave it up to Win to decide," Mr. Russell grinned. He handed the paper to Mr. Crane, who looked at it blankly and said, "I don't get it." The others laughed and Mr. Crane looked at the paper again. Then he said, "Oh, I see. It's added up wrong!"

Mr. Russell snatched the paper. "By Gad, it *is* added wrong!"

As the other two men roared with laughter, Mr. Crane said, "I still don't get it." (1)

VI. Keith Mason had become very unhappy and depressed. After his return from combat duty in the Army, Keith had gone back to his old job at the factory. But he could see that it was a blind-alley job and would get him nowhere. Keith, who had been wounded in action, had become very bitter, feeling that combat veterans weren't being treated as they should.

A. To add to his bitterness, Joyce Markel, Keith's girl friend for two years, began dating a young insurance salesman with a flashy convertible. One day Keith happened to meet an old Army friend who told Keith that he was on his way to Arabia to work for an oil company. He told Keith that the company was hiring former combat soldiers at tremendous wages to do dangerous work in Arabia. He took Keith to the local representative, and Keith, too, was hired. They went to Arabia, where they were assigned to run a locomotive hauling oil across desert country infested with hostile tribes who wished to drive out the companies. Several times their train was attacked, and once Keith was shot through the shoulder. After three years, Keith had $50,000 in wages and bonuses, and he returned home. There, he bought a lumber company and became a successful businessman. He began going with Joyce again and they planned to be married. (3)

B. One day Keith had a long talk with an old fellow work-man at the factory. The old workman advised Keith to quit his job, get a G.I. loan, and start his own business. Keith did get a government loan and started a small trucking business. A large rival trucking business tried to run him out of business, even hijacking one of his trucks. Keith was almost ready to give up, but with the help of some friends he exposed the people trying to run him out, and he finally made the business a success. (2)

C. Keith's mother, who was worried about his state of mind, had a talk with Keith and persuaded him to go to night school under the G.I. Bill of Rights. Keith did this reluctantly to please his mother. He learned pipe fitting and plumbing, and was apprenticed to a local pipe fitter. The pipe fitter had a sound philosophy of life, and Keith found that he enjoyed associating with his employer, and that he was enjoying his work. Keith became very skillful at the work, and his employer told him that he would be promoted to journeyman in a year with a possible advancement to master pipe fitter in seven years. Keith found that he had stopped worrying about the treatment of combat veterans. (1)

VII. I had been seeing Sorenson at lunch for several weeks before our conversation got beyond the point of exchanging pleasantries. He and I usually sat next to each other at lunch. I eat at the Capitol Cafe, which is the kind of place that has a steady lunch clientele of clerks and bookkeepers like myself who have to live economically. We eat at large tables and everyone gets used to sitting at the same place each day. I had been interested in Sorenson from the beginning. He invariably ordered the cheapest thing on the menu. He never had a desert or a cigar. He always seemed quite preoccupied. Our conversation became more familiar at each lunch time. I found out what firm he worked for. One evening he invited me to his home for dinner, where I met his wife, a plain, quiet little woman. One hot day he told me his secret. For years he had been saving, skimping on every penny, to buy a little piece of land on which there was a supply of marble about which only he knew. Enough marble, he said with his cheeks flushed, to make him a small fortune. With shining eyes, he confided that in a few weeks he would have the necessary money. An insurance policy was to come due and it would enable him to buy the property. After that, we often talked about it. And as the day grew near when he would buy the property, I began to envy him and share his excitement. Through the years, I had often dreamed of a stroke of luck that would take me out of my humdrum existence.

A. One day, near the appointed time, he came to lunch, his face strained and grey. He told me that the property had gone up in price, and that he would lack $3000 of being able to pay the price. A loan was impossible; he had no security. He dared take no one into his confidence, he said. Suddenly a thought stabbed through my mind. I had a little over $3000 in savings. Hesitantly, I suggested that he accept me as a partner. He stared at me and then, as tears came to his eyes, he said, "Of course! I should have thought of you! But I had no idea. . . ." So I turned over the money to him and we signed the agreement. The next day I wanted to discuss some details with him, but he didn't appear at lunch, so I decided to go to his home that evening. He looked startled when he saw me. I noticed that he and his wife were packing. Suddenly I became suspicious. But he drew a pistol and forced me into a room which he locked. When I finally got free and reported to the police, I found that I was only one of a number of victims. The police had been looking for him for months. (2)

B. One day he didn't appear at lunch, nor the next. Curious, I called at the offices of his firm and inquired about him of a young man at a desk. "Oh, Old Marble is sick," the young man said.

" 'Old Marble'!"

"Yeah," the young man grinned. "Hasn't he ever told you about that marble that he's going to get rich on?"

"Well, yes, he has. . . ."

"I thought so," the young man laughed. "He's been telling that for twenty years. That insurance policy is always about to come due. He's told that so much he believes it himself. I think that's what keeps him going." (1)

C. A few days before Sorenson was to have his money, my firm sent me out of town on a business errand. I thought of him, envying him after I arrived home and he no longer appeared for lunch at the Capitol. I heard from him a month and a half later. He called one night, jubilant. He had allowed quarry operations to begin on his land; there was already a handsome profit. I couldn't help being chilly in my response. His success made me despair even more of my own lot. A year passed. One morning as I was reading the *Inquirer* hurriedly, some lines of print leaped out at me. ". . . week-end death toll was brought to twenty-four when F. J. Sorenson, president of Sorenson Marble Company, and his wife were killed when their car was struck by a train at. . . ." Two days later, a lawyer called at my office. Sorenson had no relatives. In his will I was the only beneficiary after his wife. I now owned the controlling interest in the Sorenson Marble Company! In later days I thought often of those lunches at the Capitol. I named my summer mountain retreat "Sorenson Lodge." (3)

VIII. Jerry Murphy, a leading senior at a large city high school, is known to be very prejudiced against Jews. When he blocks the entrance of Morris Roth, a Jewish boy who is editor of the school newspaper, into Pen and Shield, boys' honor society, a feud develops between Jerry and Morris. Morris writes several bitter editorials against anti-Jewish prejudice.

A. One day Jerry becomes involved in a serious violation of school rules, and his case is referred to the student-faculty discipline committee of which Morris is a member. Morris discovers that Jerry was framed by a group of Jewish boys. Morris is torn between his hatred for Jerry and his obligation to be fair in his committee work. Finally, he reveals the plot against Jerry to the committee, and Jerry is cleared. Thus, the feud is ended between Jerry and Morris. (2)

B. One day, as Jerry is walking home from school, he is attacked by three Jewish boys who plan to beat him up. Morris happens to come by at the time. Seeing the three boys ganging up on Jerry, Morris enters the fight on Jerry's side. The two beat off the three Jewish boys, and Jerry is very grateful to Morris. At the next meeting of

Pen and Shield, Jerry proposes Morris for membership, and Morris is accepted. From that time on, Jerry is no longer prejudiced against Jews. (3)

C. Both Morris and Jerry are appointed to the student-faculty discipline committee that decides what action to take on serious violations of discipline in the school. A particularly difficult case, involving both Jewish and non-Jewish boys, is brought before the committee. Through their work in handling the case, Jerry and Morris develop respect for each other and understand better each other's outlook. (1)

IX. Sylvia Benson, a senior at Grand Rapids High School, had become very enthusiastic about writing. When her English teacher tells her that she has natural talent for creative writing, Sylvia decides to devote her life to it.

A. Sylvia tells her parents of her decision to dedicate her life to writing. Her father tells her that he thinks this is a fine idea, but that she must have an education to become a writer. He points out to her that she shouldn't neglect her other subjects, as she has been doing, if she wants to prepare to become a writer. At the end of the story, when Sylvia is in the middle of some writing, her mother comes in and reminds Sylvia about doing the dishes. Sylvia is exasperated and says, "Do dishes when I'm in the midst of inspiration!" Her mother smiles as Sylvia goes to do the dishes. (1)

B. Ecstatically, Sylvia devotes all her time to her writing. She confidently enters the state writing contest held annually for young writers. She tells her boy friend, handsome Bob Paine, that she no longer can see him since she has to spend her time on her writing. However, Sylvia fails to win the state contest; she doesn't get even Honorable Mention. Bob, when he sees the results in the newspaper, goes to Sylvia's house where he finds her in tears. She asks him to forgive her, and he generously tells her that she only had to learn her lesson. (2)

C. Sylvia spends most of her time on writing, neglecting her other school subjects. Her parents object to this and think that her enthusiasm for writing is silly. When Sylvia's school marks go down, there is a scene in which her parents forbid her to spend any more time on writing.

But Sylvia continues to write secretly, preparing a story to enter in the annual state writing contest. Sylvia wins the contest. Her parents learn this after she has gone to school one morning, when they see her picture on the front page of the newspaper. The accompanying story quotes the judges as saying that Sylvia is the outstanding young writer in many years. When Sylvia comes home that evening, her parents apologize and tell her that they realize now that they were wrong. Sylvia is completely happy when she is awarded a writing scholarship at a prominent college. (3)

X. Branda Milanovich is the only child of Rumanian immigrants. The Milanovich family once had been important in Rumania, but now Branda's father works as a machinist and they live in a small apartment. But the parents retain their aristocratic pride, and sacrifice in order to send Branda to wealthy, sophisticated Norton Collegiate School for Girls. Branda is unhappy at Norton because she is not accepted by her classmates, although she tries to be friendly.

A. Branda notices several other girls at Norton, who, like herself, just don't seem to fit in. Suddenly getting an idea, Branda invites these girls to her home. They have a good time, and the other girls are delighted with the European food Branda's mother serves and with her stories of life in Rumania. From that time on, Branda becomes the leader of her own little group. (2)

B. Left out by her sophisticated, well-dressed classmates, Branda goes her lonely way. One day the Norton girls become very excited about an assembly at which a Russian countess is to speak. The girls are amazed—and so is Branda, who hadn't known about the plan—to discover that the Russian countess is Branda's mother. From that time on, Branda is accepted by the group. (3)

C. Finally, Branda decides upon a bold stroke. She invites six of the most prominent Norton girls to her home for tea. The surprised girls tell Branda that they will come if they can. However, they get together and decide not to go. Most of the story concerns Branda's thoughts as she waits for the girls to come. Finally, she gives up and puts the tea things away. She realizes now that there are class lines in America similar to those her father spoke about in Rumania. (1)

SKELETON UNIT. A brief outline is given below of an introductory unit on the short story, taught in the ninth grade.

I. The class discussed:
   A. Sources of stories: oral tales, books, magazines, comics, TV, radio, movies, songs, and so on.
   B. Characteristics of stories they liked.
   C. How incidents that occur in everyday life might be made into plots of stories.

II. The following guide sheet was given to the class.

The Short Story

Why read stories—just for "kicks," to pass time, because the English teachers say so? Partly for all these reasons, as well as for some others, but the fact is that almost everybody likes a story—whether it be told by a friend in a "bull session," on television, in a movie, or in print by a professional author. Different kinds of stories do different things for different people, but in general, the short story is one way of looking at life, at human experience. In literature, the short story does about what the microscope does in science; it allows us a chance to see or understand things about life that we might not otherwise see or understand, just as the microscope allows us to see things we could not see with the naked eye. The good short story entertains us at the same time that it teaches us more about life. One of the main purposes of this unit is to help you learn to read short stories better, so that you can get more out of them.

Every short story must have a plot, characters, a setting, and some of them have a "theme"—a certain definite idea about life that the story is trying to put across. However, stories tend to stress one of these several things. We will read some stories that stress plot, some that stress character, and some that stress theme. The questions below are to guide you in reading stories during the unit.

A. The Plot Story

1. Is there suspense in the story? Does it keep you on edge? If so, how does the author do this?
2. Can you find a definite "turning point" in the story?

3. How does the main character solve his problem? Overcome obstacles?
4. Does the plot have a logical series of happenings? Or do many things happen just by chance or coincidence?
5. Does the ending satisfy you? Or do you feel cheated by it?
6. Which is more important in the story—physical action (what the characters do) or mental action (what the characters think or feel)?

B. The Character Story

1. Are the characters like real people in the way they act and talk? Are there any "stereotypes"—such as the "typical" teen-ager who isn't really like most teen-agers at all?
2. Are any of the characters like real people you know or have known?
3. Are the actions of the characters in line with the kind of people they seem to be?
4. How does the author let you know what kind of person a character is, what his traits are, and so on? Does the author *tell* you directly? Or does he show you what a character is like by what the character does, what he says, what others say about him?
5. Do any of the characters change in the way they think or feel during the story? If so, do you think there is a good reason for the change?

C. The Theme Story

1. What is the "moral" or idea of the story? Have you read any other stories with this same idea or moral?
2. Does the story make you think?
3. Does the ending puzzle you? If so, try to figure out why the author ended the story as he did.
4. Does the author make his idea pretty obvious? Or do you have to "read between the lines"?

III. After discussing different kinds of "plot" stories they had read, including the horror story, the class listened to a tape recording of Poe's "The Tell-Tale Heart."* The story was

---

* The excellent recording of Gilbert Highet's reading of "The Pit and the Pendulum" might have been used. This record is available from the National Council of Teachers of English, Champaign, Ill.

discussed. Characteristics of the good "plot story" were discussed.

IV. The class members read Stockton's "The Lady or the Tiger" and defended their choices of the "right" ending. The teacher guided discussion to the relationship of character and plot.

V. The class was divided into three groups to carry out a project on "character" stories. The students were divided by ability, and each group was assigned an appropriate story from the anthology. Each group had to decide on the main traits of the principal character(s) and present them to the rest of the class through a skit or dramatization, group discussion, or "interview" with the main character.

VI. After a discussion of "theme" in the short story, the teacher read De Maupassant's "The Necklace" to the class. Discussion centered on the ending of the story.

VII. The class read MacKinlay Kantor's "That Greek Dog" as an example of the "theme" story that deals with a social problem.

VIII. Each student chose from the anthology one story not read during the unit and wrote a short paper evaluating it. In writing the papers, the students made use of the questions on the guide sheet.

WRITING ACTIVITIES. Study of short stories can provide a good context for creative writing. Not only does the reading suggest and motivate writing assignments, but the attempts at writing may help students to learn to read fiction better, as Cleanth Brooks suggests: "I am interested in creative writing, then, not because it may teach a few students to become able writers, but rather it may teach many to read."[12]

In addition to the original short stories, parodies, descriptions, and character sketches that students may write, there are some other activities that tie in with the skills of reading the short story. For example, pupils in the junior high school might end a unit on the short story with a "group" story. Using this device, the teacher puts on the blackboard the details the class suggests about the characters, setting, and theme or problem for a story. Then the in-

[12] Cleanth Brooks, "Place of Creative Writing in the Study of Literature," *Association of American Colleges Bulletin*, XXXIV (May 1948), 231.

dividual pupils each write a story, tying the material together and providing an ending. Another device, usually successful at any level, is to have students write the ending for a story, the begining of which the teacher has read to the class. After the students' endings have been written and discussed in class, the teacher can read the author's ending. Often, too, certain short stories can trigger very specialized kinds of writing assignments. After reading "The Secret Life of Walter Mitty," one group of students, for instance, wrote papers in which they put themselves into a situation that met their fondest daydreams.

TEACHING SUGGESTIONS FOR SELECTED MODERN NOVELS

Shane by Jack Schaefer
(Eighth or ninth grade.)

    I. The novel
        A. Outline the novel by arranging the following plot incidents in the order in which they occurred.
           1. Ledyard tries to overcharge for the cultivator.
           2. Shane fights Chris and breaks his arm.
           3. Fletcher and Wilson come to the ranch and threaten Joe.
           4. Shane and Joe fight Morgan and Curly.
           5. Shane knocks out Joe, straps on his gun, and goes to town.
           6. Fletcher returns with the gunslinger Stark Wilson.
           7. Shane meets Chris and walks off with cherry soda pop.
           8. Shane arrives at the Starrett ranch.
           9. Shane's gunfights with Stark Wilson and Fletcher.
          10. Bob discovers Shane's gun kept in his blanket.
          11. Chris comes back to the Starretts to take Shane's place.
          12. Shane and Joe cooperate in removing the stump.
          13. Shane shows Bob how to use a gun.
        B. Choose one of these as the turning point of the book. Be able to justify your statement. Is the turning point the same as the climax of this novel?

    C. Describe the following characters in two or three sentences each. What is the relationship of the characters to each other?
      1. Marian Starrett
      2. Joe Starrett
      3. Red Marlin
      4. Chris
      5. Stark Wilson
      6. Henry Fletcher
    D. What do you think Shane's past life had been? What was Shane running away from? Cite evidence in the book for your answer.
    E. After reviewing the concept of a "symbol," consider Shane as a symbol. What does he represent? Do any of the other characters represent an idea or a human quality?
    F. List several ways in which Shane changed the lives of the Starretts and the homesteaders in general.
    G. What do you think happened to Shane after the end of the book?

II. Collateral work
    A. Describe in an essay how the novel might have been written from a point of view other than that of a young boy.
    B. Compare the hero Shane with one of the following characters. You should tell how Shane is similar to and different from one of these heroes:
      1. Palladin
      2. Matt Dillon
      3. Robin Hood
      4. Davy Crockett

The Pearl by John Steinbeck
(Tenth or eleventh grade.)

    I. The novel
    A. Is this fable or parable? Explain.
    B. Of what is the pearl symbolic? Does it represent the "pearl of the world"?
    C. Is there ancient myth here?
    D. What is the tone of the novel and what does this tone contribute? How does Steinbeck achieve this tone?

  E. Of what significance is the setting of the novel? Of what significance are the ethnic characteristics of Kino and of his oppressors?

  F. Is there a theme in this novel? Is there a statement of theme?

  G. What are symbols of good and evil in the work? What do the various characters represent?

  H. Is there any irony in the comparison between Kino and the doctor?

  I. What is the relationship of Kino and Juana to their group?

  J. How does this novel compare with other novels by Steinbeck? Is the outlook essentially romantic? Is the style basically naturalistic?

II. Collateral work

The following novels all deal with themes of good and evil. Choose one of the novels for collateral reading and in an essay compare and contrast it with *The Pearl*. Or the novels may be utilized for small-group reading, with the comparison presented in an oral report.

  A. Walter Van Tilburg Clark, *The Track of the Cat*.

  B. Charles Dickens, *Oliver Twist*.

  C. George Eliot, *Silas Marner*.

  D. Edna Ferber, *Giant*.

  E. John Hersey, *A Single Pebble*.

  F. William Dean Howells, *A Hazard of New Fortunes*.

  G. Sinclair Lewis, *Arrowsmith*.

  H. Herman Melville, *Moby Dick*.

  I. Ayn Rand, *The Fountainhead*.

  J. Upton Sinclair, *The Jungle*.

A Separate Peace by John Knowles
(Tenth or eleventh grade.)

I. The novel

  A. Who is the main character or protagonist? Is this a study of Finny or of Gene?

  B. Do we really get to know Gene? Is he left shadowy purposely? What is his motivation in pushing Finny off the tree? What mistake does he make about his relationship with Finny? Does he ever understand Finny?

    C. Consider the "roundness" of other characters such as Leper and Brinker. What do they represent?

    D. What is the significance of Leper's going to war? Discuss the meaning of the later meeting of Leper and Gene.

    E. What is the theme of the book? What is the significance of the title? What "separate peace" is negotiated? What symbolic moment is tied to the theme? Cite passages that further the theme.

II. Collateral work

    A. Write an essay discussing the novel in relation to a theme of conflict between innocence and reality.

    B. Any of the following is suitable for small-group reading and oral presentation in its relation to *A Separate Peace:*

        1. Joseph Conrad, *The Secret Sharer.*

        2. Herman Melville, *Billy Budd.*

        3. J. D. Salinger, *The Catcher in the Rye.*

    C. Other related novels for group reading or for individual reading, with oral or written reports, include:

        1. Dorothy Baker, *Young Man with a Horn.*

        2. Henry Fielding, *Tom Jones.*

        3. Rumer Godden, *Greengage Summer.*

        4. James Joyce, *Portrait of the Artist as a Young Man.*

        5. Conrad Richter, *A Light in the Forest.*

        6. Betty Smith, *A Tree Grows in Brooklyn.*

        7. John Steinbeck, *East of Eden.*

The Old Man and the Sea by Ernest Hemingway
(Tenth or eleventh grade.)

I. The novel

    A. Is this a tragic novel? In what sense is the novel tragic? Consider Aristotle's definition, for example.

    B. Is this work a novel of affirmation? in what sense?

    C. Is Santiago a hero? a tragic hero? an epic hero? In what ways is he an extraordinary man? Does he differ from other Hemingway heroes, or in what ways is he like them?

    D. Is there allegory here? Is there a theme?

    E. What is the significance of Santiago's experience to others?

F. What is the relationship between the boy and the old man?

G. What does the novel say about the relationship between man and nature?

H. Is there religious symbolism pervading the novel?

I. Discuss the possible meanings of the sharks, the skeleton of the great fish, the lions in Santiago's dream.

J. Find specific examples of the following aspects of Hemingway's unique style in the novel:

   1. Use of simple and compound sentences
   2. Naturalistic concern for authenticity of detail
   3. Sparse, objective, masculine tone and over-all style

II. Collateral work

Write an essay in which you consider the novel in relation to the following: The honorable, honest man is scarred and battered by the forces of existence. He realizes the futility but struggles only to lose. In the struggle, however, is the only meaning of life, and in the struggle, man reveals his stature and dignity. Is Hemingway's final theme dealing with the dignity of man in the face of the adversity of life?

The Ox-Bow Incident by Walter Van Tilburg Clark
(Eleventh grade.)

I. The novel

A. Relate the time and place of the novel to the conflict with the character or characters. Would the theme of the book be meaningless if the time or the place were changed?

B. What is the nature of the characters that brings them into conflict? Is there a main character or a protagonist? Are the characters representative of a minority group? What characters specifically represent groups and which characters are more representative of all man?

C. Is the conflict with other men as individuals—as groups— or with intangible attitudes and institutions within the society?

D. What is the outcome of the conflict? To what extent does the character control the outcome? To what extent does "fate" or destiny control the outcome?

E. How does the author feel about man as indicated by this work?

F. How does the author present the ideas? Does he give the situation without comment? Does he interpret the actions and situations of the character?

G. Is the conflict in the novel a contemporary problem? Is the conflict also one that has always been present?

II. Collateral work

Accept the hypothesis that this novel is an allegory of humanity approaching the democratic life. In an essay choose three of the following characters and defend or reject them as representing the characteristics listed below.

Art: Everyman.
Gil: The good-natured, simple but emotional type.
Farnley: Meanness and viciousness.
Canby: Vested neutrality.
Davies: The ineffectual, liberal, intellectual reformer.
Osgood: The ineffectual representative of religion.
Smith: The status-seeker.
Gabe: The completely stupid follower.
Mapes: Organized religion that has become corrupt.
Tetley: The fascist.

The Bridge of San Luis Rey by Thornton Wilder
(Eleventh or twelfth grade.)

I. The novel

A. The setting is significant in that it is remote in time and place, thus indicating perhaps a romantic outlook. The idea of universality is implied so that the reader looks for meaning in terms of pervasive ideas rather than specific commentary on a certain period in history.

B. The inner life and the outer life of the characters are narrated with objectivity. The author makes no didactic commentary.

C. The concept of truth presented is that of an absolute or divine truth.

D. The universe is viewed as having a plan or an ordering by a divine being. Each character, having reached a kind of climax in his life, had to die. Love is regarded not as an entity in itself but as a link—love links the living and the dead through memory. The love as a link is enough; it acts as a kind of end by being a means.

E. Man is viewed as having relatively little free will and control of his destiny. The view is not pessimistic, however, but positive, since love is central in the order of the universe.

F. Art and the imagination and the "poetic view of experience" enter into the characters of Uncle Pio, who has a need to create; Perichole, the actress; and to some extent into the literary letter writing of Dona Maria. Implied in the work are ideas on the function of the arts and the beauty of the imagination.

G. Generally the novel discusses manifest forms of love—love that is not completed—but the existence of the love is enough. Thus, the idea of unfulfilled love as good in itself would place Wilder generally in the romantic mode.

II. Collateral work
A. Speculate on what would have been the fate of a character had the bridge not fallen. You must remain faithful to the character as portrayed in the novel.

B. Discuss the symbolism of the bridge in these terms:
1. Its calamity brought forth a revelation of love among men. These five accident victims are raised to a "universal" level through their means of proving this love in Juniper's investigation.
2. The bridge not only brings together suffering humanity but closes the gap between this world and the next.

The Bridge over the River Kwai by Pierre Boulle
(Twelfth grade.)

I. The novel
A. Consider the novel in the tragic-ironic mode. Is Colonel Nicholson a tragic hero? Consider these four typical situations of the tragic hero in relation to Colonel Nicholson.
1. The hero's role is basically but not solely a guilty one.
2. While above the average man, the hero is not completely good and just.
3. The hero is destroyed through fate or external evil, but he is not overcome with this evil.

      4. From one point of view the hero's action is guilty. From another point of view his action is innocent.

B. Consider the symbolism of the bridge. For each of the separate characters, the bridge takes on a personal meaning. The construction of the bridge may be in a larger sense considered as a means of artistic expression or as creativity. Relate each of the following statements about art to the individual perceptions of the bridge in the novel.

    1. Art is a means of escape to the world of ideals.
    2. Art is an expression of the reality of the spirit.
    3. Art is a social sharing of man's best experiences.
    4. Art is the language of emotional attitude.
    5. Art is the imaginative expression of a wish.
    6. Art is a secondhand copy of reality.
    7. Art is the play of the man.

C. Consider the novel in a unit dealing with war in literature.

    1. Discuss the setting historically and geographically and its significance.
    2. Discuss the effect of war on an individual character and/or a particular group.
    3. Discuss the conflict or conflicts in the novel. Is there resolution?
    4. Does man have a choice as to his fate in this novel? Can the characters change their destinies?
    5. What seems to be the author's point of view toward the issue of war?
    6. How is the story told? Who tells it? Is it told in chronological order, by flashback technique, or the like?
    7. Discuss the author's use of symbolism and of figurative language.
    8. Can you see any relation of the structure or form of the novel to its effectiveness in communicating the theme?

II. Collateral work

Consider the novel's presentation of man in relationship to the universe. In an essay discuss one of the following concepts in connection with the novel.

A. Men are continually in competition for honor and dignity.—THOMAS HOBBES

B. Man is wholly and throughout but patch and motley.—MICHAEL DE MONTAIGNE

C. Man in nature is the mean between nothing and everything.—BLAISE PASCAL

D. All events are interdependent and necessary.—BENEDICT SPINOZA

E. Perceptions are according to the measure of the individual—not according to the measure of the universe.—FRANCIS BACON

F. Struggle is an indispensable accompaniment of progress.—IMMANUEL KANT

G. Man functions as an harmoniously operating "divine machine" in a "best of all possible worlds."—WILHELM LEIBNITZ

H. Things are good or evil only in reference to pleasure or pain.—JOHN LOCKE

I. A cause contains as much reality as its effect.—RENÉ DESCARTES

J. Good is obtained by harmonizing ideals and natural objects.—PLATO

Cry, the Beloved Country by Alan Paton
(Twelfth grade.)

I. The novel

In this particular novel there seem to be nine characters —two main characters and seven very important minor characters, who should be considered separately and individually. The following questions could be asked in general about each:

A. What kind of person is he or she?

B. Describe this person, in particular the clothing and the environment.

C. Briefly give his importance in the novel.

D. Show the interrelationship among these characters.

    1. Stephen Kumalo

    Is he kind or unkind, patient or short-tempered, generous or selfish? Back up your opinion with examples. Did you feel sympathetic toward him? Would you say he is the main character—why?

2. James Jarvis

What do you learn about James Jarvis in Chapters 18 and 19? Does he know his son? What sort of man is he portrayed as? What do you think he felt upon learning of his son's death? Is there a great change in his attitude? Could this man be typical of the white man in Africa?

3. Arthur Jarvis

Did we meet or read of this character? Could he be considered a living character or one we meet through the eyes of other characters? Why was he important? What was his contribution?

4. Msimangu

Would you say this character was interesting? What do you think he means when he says, "I am a weak and sinful man, but God put His hands on me, that is all"? Why was he kind to Kumalo? What does this show about his character?

5. Absalom

How do we know this character? What do we learn about him from the interview at the prison? during the trial? before he dies? What does this character contribute to the novel?

6. Gertrude

What is your opinion of this character? Did she really repent or not? When she left, did you believe that she was going to become a nun? Why or why not?

7. The young white man at the prison

Why is this man important? Is he honestly helpful or does he want to keep from failing or having the sense of failure in this case? What is his attitude in general?

8. John Kumalo

What sort of person is he? Why was he cruel to his brother? What was his general attitude? What happened in the last meeting between the two brothers? What was your opinion of this event?

9. Stephen's wife

Though this character is mentioned in only two places, why should she be considered a very important minor character? What is Paton saying about her when he writes, "Then she sat down at his table, and put her head on it, and was silent, with the patient suffering of black women, with the suffering of oxen, with the suffering of any that are mute"? What more do we learn about her in Book III?

II. Collateral work
A. Discuss the thread of fear that runs throughout the novel.
B. In an essay discuss the paradoxical statements that are made in the novel:
   1. In Chapter 6, Msimangu's statement: "I am not a man for segregation, but it is a pity that we are not apart."
   2. In Chapter 22, the paradox concerning the law, justice, and being just.
   3. When Jarvis, in Chapter 32, learns that there is to be no mercy, he says: "I do not understand these matters, but otherwise I understand completely."

Lord of the Flies by **William Golding**
(Twelfth grade.)

I. Preparation
A. Discuss the possibility and plausibility that the events told in the story could actually occur in this nuclear age.
B. Instruct the students to read the novel so they can visualize the problem and the actions and decisions made to overcome it, evaluate these actions, and offer alternatives based on their own viewpoint and experience.
C. Define the British expressions that might present problems in reading and understanding the novel.

II. The novel
Class discussion of the book, either chapter by chapter or on the basis of three identifiable areas of the book: the world of the game; the world of fear; and the world of reality or destruction and evil. The following are representative questions from the chapters:

A. Chapter 1
   1. How is the glamour of the situation and the island conveyed to the reader?
   2. What suggestions are there that this glamour may be an illusion?

     3. How successful is the beginning government likely to be, and why?

B. Chapter 2
     1. How secure are the rules of government and on what are they based?
     2. Why do the characters feel that the other side of the island is unfriendly?
     3. Where does the blame for the child's death lie?

C. Chapter 3
     1. How would you describe the nature of the conflict between Jack and Ralph?
     2. What is the nature of Simon's experience and feeling?

D. Chapter 4
     Can degrees of seriousness and danger be distinguished?

E. Chapter 5
     1. What are the expressed attitudes toward the "beast" and what attitudes to life as a whole do they imply?
     2. What does "man's essential illness" mean to Simon?

F. Chapter 6
     1. What is happening to the importance of the rescue?
     2. What does the sign from the adult world mean?

G. Chapter 7
     1. What is the difference in Ralph's view of themselves and of the sea? Why does it produce such strain?
     2. Why is the ritual dance in this chapter different from other ritual dances?
     3. What is the effect of schoolboy language at this point?

H. Chapter 8
     In what ways can we now see that this novel is more than a boy's adventure story?

I. Chapter 9
     What on the mountain is a sign of man's inhumanity to man?

J. Chapter 10
     Why do none of the children fully recognize what they have done and its significance?

K. Chapter 11
     1. What is the full symbolic meaning of the conch?
     2. What power and desire have finally been liberated in the children?

   L. Chapter 12
      Is the conclusion just a trick to make a happy end-
      ing, or does it serve deeper purposes?

III. Collateral work
   Relate one of the following statements to the novel. Accept
   or reject the statement, using specific illustrations from the
   novel as evidence for your conclusion.
   A. A democratic society must be mutually organized for the
      survival of all the members.
   B. Each member must contribute to the general welfare of all.
   C. Leadership in a democratic organization entails a respon-
      sibility to all members.
   D. The more capable members must assume the guidance and
      control of the less experienced or less capable members.
   E. Cooperation in a democratic society must be maintained
      or chaos will result.

USEFUL COLLECTIONS OF SHORT STORIES

Best Short Stories, edited by Eric Berger (New York: Teen Age
   Book Club,[13] 1960, paperback).
   A book of short stories with twist endings.

Beyond Time and Space, edited by August Derleth (New York:
   Farrar, Straus, 1950).
   Old and new science fiction pieces.

Big Woods (New York: Random House, 1955).
   The hunting stories of William Faulkner. Contains "The Bear,"
   "The Old People," "A Bear Hunt," "Race at Morning." Excellent
   for use in the eleventh and twelfth grades.

A Book of Stories, edited by Royal A. Gettmann and Bruce Harkness
   (New York: Holt, Rinehart and Winston, 1955).
   Designed for college students, this collection will be useful with
   selected high school classes. Excellent teacher's manual.

Chucklebait, edited by Margaret Scoggin (New York: Knopf,
   1945).
   Humorous stories of adolescent life. (Also *More Chucklebait.*)

Hit Parade of Short Stories, edited by Mary Dirlam (New York:
   Teen Age Book Club,[13] 1953, paperback).

[13] The Teen Age Book Club, 50 West 44th Street, New York 36, N.Y.

A fine collection of stories that appeared originally in *Scholastic Magazine*.

The Hunting Horn, edited by Paul Annixter (New York: Hill & Wang, 1957).
A fine collection of dog stories.

Out West, edited by Jack Schaefer (Boston: Houghton Mifflin, 1955).
An unusual and varied collection of quality western stories, edited by the author of *Shane*.

Short Stories, edited by Edwin H. Sauer and Howard Mumford Jones (New York: Holt, Rinehart and Winston, 1962).
A varied collection of British and American Stories, past and present.

Short Stories for Our Times, edited by Simon Certner and George Henry (Boston: Houghton Mifflin, 1950).
Stories that stress the social and personal concerns of young people.

Stories, edited by Frank G. Jennings and Charles J. Calitri (New York: Harcourt, 1957).
A splendid collection, highly varied in form, theme, and difficulty, with a good teacher's edition.

Stories from Seventeen, edited by Byrna Ivens (Philadelphia: Lippincott, 1955).
Sensitive stories of adolescence, reprinted from *Seventeen*.

Stories for Youth, edited by A. H. Lass and Arnold Horowitz (New York: McGraw-Hill, 1950).
The stress is on human values—one of the best anthologies for teen-agers.

The Story: A Critical Anthology, edited by Mark Schorer (Englewood Cliffs, N.J.: Prentice-Hall, 1950).
A resource for the teacher. Furnishes insight into the art of the short story and contains some directly teachable material.

The Story Survey, edited by Harold Blodgett (Philadelphia: Lippincott, 1953).
A collection of mature American, European, and English stories. Useful with advanced high school students.

Teen-Age Tales, Books 1–5, edited by Ruth Strang and others (Boston: Heath, 1954–1956).

Time to Be Young, edited by Whit Burnett (Philadelphia: Lippincott, 1948).
A collection of celebrated stories of the growing-up process.

Tomorrow the Stars, edited by Robert Heinlein (New York: Doubleday, 1952).
Fourteen good science fiction stories.

Twenty Grand, edited by Ernestine Taggard (New York: Bantam Books, 1962, paperback).
A group of stories with great range in subtlety and variety. Several involve teen-agers.

Youth, Youth, Youth, edited by A. B. Tibbets (New York: F. Watts, 1955).
A brilliant collection of stories dealing with the problems of adolescence.

BIOGRAPHY
AND ESSAY IN

8 ❧

THE
LITERATURE
PROGRAM

BIOGRAPHY, UNLIKE FICTION, is not an inherently popular form of literature. The general public *is* interested in people, but the popular taste in recent years has run to the personal narrative of adventure, which often has true literary merit, and to autobiographical confessions of the "I was a Communist" or "I was an alcoholic" variety, which have nothing of literary artistry about them. An occasional biography of high quality—such as Arthur Mizener's *The Far Side of Paradise* or Robert Sherwood's *Roosevelt and Hopkins*—catches the public fancy, but in general the reading of serious biography is limited to the intelligentsia and the specialists.

Compared with the novel, short story, poem, or play, biography is a minor form of literature, although school anthologies determinedly include selections from biographies, past and current, and teachers dutifully present the form in their classes. There is justice in this, for biography, which is actually more popular among adolescents than among adults, presents some important possibilities and advantages as well as some problems when it is used in the high school literature program. The first section of this chapter examines these problems and possibilities, and briefly surveys the field of junior biography.

Biography in the Literature Program: *Problems and Opportunities*

Foremost, perhaps, among the problems posed by teaching biography as a literary genre is the fact that between excellent mature biography and most junior biography is a wide hiatus, much wider even than that between the better junior novels and mature novels of superior caliber. The best of adult biography, at least since World War II, is in the tradition of the scholar and the historian. The result is that it is often difficult reading—requiring analysis and reflection. This is surely no argument for the exclusion of mature biography from the high school, but for the average and below-average readers, it often may not be feasible.

Not only are the best of biographies often weighty in style and formidable in organization; they tend naturally to deal with mature phases of life and the conflicts and emotions that accompany these phases. Almost always, the person of eminence, about whom a biography is likely to be written, has attained his eminence and made his greatest contributions in later life. For example, even in Mabel Robinson's *Runner of the Mountain Tops,* a biography of Louis Agassiz for the teen-age audience, the mature phases of the great naturalist's career have to be given main stress, not his boyhood and youth. Thus, biography often offers little inherent appeal to adolescents or chance for identification by them.

Then, too, the mature biography of the statesman or scientist or specialist in any area may demand a background of knowledge beyond that of the average adolescent. For that reason, biographies are especially difficult to use for reading in common. Also, for the adolescent reader, the adult biography, often organized in expository rather than narrative fashion, may be an unnatural kind of reading, far from the tradition of the well-constructed plot or the happy ending. Biography may well be a more valuable adjunct to the social studies or some other class than it is to the English class. Of course, the nature of adult biography points out clearly one responsibility of the senior high school English teacher: to teach students to read it as a distinct form of literature for purposes that may serve more than simple enjoyment.

Yet biography used in the high school program also offers some advantages that go beyond the general purpose of widening reading horizons. For some adolescents, biography or autobiography has greater impact than fiction because the people and events are, presumably, real. The literal-minded student who has not yet developed a clear perception of why good fiction gets at the truth of human experience may be more impressed by the biography than by the novel. This is particularly true of adolescents who have a certain handicap, especially a physical one. To such students, the inspiration of a story like that of Helen Keller or of Glenn Cunningham, as told in David Boynick's *Champions by Setback,* or that of the girl who loses a limb in Louise Baker's *Out on a Limb* may be nothing short of phenomenal. The reality of the biography may make identification easier for some readers.

Then, too, biography, particularly that written for the juvenile audience, often features the kind of heroism, idealism, and martyrdom that the essentially romantic mind of the adolescent especially admires. The person who fights for what he believes against great odds is a hero to the adolescent—probably to the adult, too, for that matter—and this theme is present in many of the junior biographies. This is, no doubt, the key to the popularity of Tom Galt's *Peter Zenger, Fighter for Freedom,* which deals with the career of an early champion of freedom of the press in America.

Certainly, biography offers an opportunity to meet students' differing individual interests in various fields. For example, Madeleine Goss has written some excellent biographies of great musicians. There are many biographies of sports heroes. No matter what his interest, the adolescent can find it represented in biography. For this reason, biography is valuable in enriching study of science, social studies, and other subjects, and may be very useful in the core curriculum.

Reading and study of biography can also provide some natural motivation for writing about personal experience. Both literature and writing contribute to the student's awareness of the significance of his own everyday experience, and the two come together naturally in connection with biography or autobiography. After reading autobiography, perhaps, students may be better prepared to write thoughtfully about aspects of their own personal experience, and writing an autobiography might be the culminating activity in a class unit on biography and autobiography.

Approaches in Teaching Biography

"Transition" fiction for the junior high school was discussed in an earlier chapter. The problem of the transition from fiction to biography is important, too, and can best be approached in the junior high school through biographies that are fictionalized or that use the techniques of fiction. Biography for the early junior high school should have the same qualities as fiction for that level: action and excitement, human daring and courage, humor and human interest. Fictionalized biographies such as those of Sitting Bull, Kit Carson, and Buffalo Bill by Doris Shannon Garst are especially appropriate. Not only the content but the style must be considered in choosing "transition" biographies. Some relatively mature biographies utilize the techniques of fiction. For example, compare the passages below, which open biographies of Garibaldi and Leonardo da Vinci, respectively:

A chill autumn rain was falling; the bitter wind swept it in gusts against his face as he turned into the quiet shabby street. He had left the noisy, lighted wineshops of the harbor quarter behind him. . . .
    The young sailor paused for a moment beneath a flickering gas light, examining the superscription of a letter.[1]

When you go to Florence, Italy, and look at the city and the rocky, hilly country around it, you may think that all of this has changed very little since the great palaces and bridges were first built.[2]

There is little doubt that the first, which opens like a novel, is more effective in engaging the young reader's interest.
    Though a sample unit on biography is outlined later in this chapter, the direct "biography" unit is not the only vehicle for

[1] Nina Brown Baker, *Garibaldi* (New York: Vanguard, 1944), p. 11.
[2] Emily Hahn, *Leonardo da Vinci* (New York: Random House, 1956), p. 1.

teaching or introducing the genre. Often biographies and autobiographies can be included in thematic units that involve the various types of literature. Biographies of heroes in sports and other fields might be included in an eighth-grade unit on "Heroes Past and Present"; a tenth-grade unit on "To Dare Greatly" might be organized with autobiographical or biographical accounts of mountain climbing, undersea exploration, aviation, and so forth; and "Men of Destiny" in the twelfth grade might include drama and fiction as well as mature biography.

Skills in Reading Biography

No matter what the plan of organization for introducing and teaching biography, however, one responsibility is clear: students need to be taught how to read the form, just as they must be taught how to read the other genres of literature. Mature reading of biography demands two major skills: skill in following various patterns of organization, and skill in critical evaluation.

Biographies may be either narrative or expository in organization. In the junior high school, of course, narrative biography will be the staple, forming the natural bridge from fiction. Senior high school students, though, should be introduced to biographies that are organized in a variety of expository patterns. For example, the biographer may choose to interpret the character and assess the stature of his subject through analysis of a number of key episodes in his life. This is true, for instance, of Benjamin Thomas' fine one-volume biography of Lincoln.[3] Or the biographer may analyze the various influences on the life and work of the subject. This is often done in biographies of literary figures. A familiarity with various expository forms of organization in biography is especially important for the able student in the senior high school.

Critical evaluation in reading biography, of course, as in reading other forms of literature, is vital. One useful method is for the teacher and the class to draw up a check list that can be used for critically judging biography, whether read individually or by the class in common. Such a check list might be based on two major points.

[3] Benjamin Thomas, *Abraham Lincoln* (New York: Knopf, 1952).

AUTHENTICITY. It is often hard, without doing research on the subject, to make a judgment about the authenticity of a biography when the subject is relatively obscure or the events are remote. A first distinction that students need to make, with the help of the teacher, is that between biography and biographical fiction, such as the popular stories of Presidents' wives written by Irving Stone or the novels based on biography. Usually, simple examination of the book makes this clear, and permits one to expect that a writer assumed the responsibilities of either the biographer or the novelist.

Having determined that he is dealing with biography, how can the student arrive at some conclusions about authenticity? First, he can look to see whether any bibliography, or list of sources, is given. One or the other often appears even in the better junior biography. He can then consider the adequacy of those sources. Thus, he might be suspicious of one biography of the great Filipino, Carlos Romulo, that is based almost entirely on the speeches and writings of Romulo himself.

One difficulty in trying to assess authenticity is that even in the best of biography certain techniques of fiction might be used. Dialogue may be manufactured, events guessed at, and sequence occasionally based on hypothesis. Lytton Strachey, who is represented frequently in high school anthologies, and who was the most influential biographer in the world during the early twentieth century, introduced the school of readable biography that "broke away from documentation and the rigid bonds of fact,"[4] and paved the way for other biographers to exploit its innovations to the fullest. John Garraty writes:

> Some of them ventured daringly beyond the sources; they invented dialogue, described minute actions that *might* have occurred, and presumed to record the thoughts as well as the words and deeds of their subjects. Of course this practice was as old as biography itself—Xenophon could never have remembered Socrates' conversations in the detail with which he recorded them in the *Memorabilia*. Plutarch was a master of this technique as of most others, and even the conscientious Boswell was not above elaborating on his notes.[5]

---

[4] John A. Garraty, *The Nature of Biography* (New York: Knopf, 1957), p. 122.
[5] *Ibid.*, pp. 126–127.

However, even in the junior high school the pupils can begin to practice identifying obviously fictitious incidents and conversations in biography and those that might have been based on actual documentation. For example, in Garst's *Sitting Bull* there are some things that could have been verified by United States government records, others that could have come from no source but the imagination of the author.

BIOGRAPHER'S RELATIONSHIP TO THE SUBJECT. The significance and worth of a biography may depend much on the relationship of the biographer to his subject, and appraisal of this relationship is important to discriminating reading of the work. Most good biographies grow out of a biographer's natural affinity for his subject—not true of the authors of the potboilers relatively prevalent among junior biographies. Many junior (and adult) biographies are produced to fill a gap in the market, and the adolescent, after some experience in reading the form, can usually tell when a book "is the product of a harmonious mixture of writer, subject, and surrounding circumstance"[6]—and when it is not.

Garraty complains that "too many biographers drift to their subjects haphazardly, depending upon chance alone for a happy combination. They have not weighed their interests and capabilities against the requirements of their selected tasks." Furthermore, Garraty points out that "Many biographies are the result of mutual interest. A specialist in some field, whose work has made him aware of the contribution of one of his predecessors, decides to expand his knowledge and ends in writing a biography."[7] The high school reader of biography, then, can ask, "What qualifications does this biographer have for writing this biography?"

An intimate knowledge of the subject does not necessarily ensure good biography, of course. Quite frequently, the biographer may be a member of the subject's family—a wife or husband, son or daughter. Usually, when that is true, the work is designed as a monument, and the reader needs to separate this from the more objective type of biography. On the other hand, the high school reader should become familiar, too, with the "debunking" tradition in biography. Again, the biographer's background almost

[6] *Ibid.*, p. 155.
[7] *Ibid.*

always will furnish the clues to this information; and one may guess, for example, that the lifelong conservative is not likely to write anything but a debunking biography of Franklin Delano Roosevelt.

The biographer, then, will be criticized on the grounds of his use of and access to authentic information about his subject, his relationship to the subject and his qualifications for writing the biography, and his literary artistry. The perfect combination of these will result in the biography that presents with vividness a human being and the significance of his achievement.

OUTLINE OF SEQUENCE FOR A UNIT ON BIOGRAPHY (NINTH GRADE)

People in Print[8]

 I. The teacher leads a discussion of well-known contemporary persons who, in the class members' opinions, are leading interesting lives. Then the discussion switches to which well-known, contemporary people are making the greatest contribution to the welfare of the country or civilization as a whole.

 II. A teacher-prepared quiz is given in which the students are asked to identify a number of famous people in various areas—sports and entertainment, military, general adventure, science, education, the arts, politics, and so on. (Invariably, the students are able to identify more people in the sports-entertainment area than in any other. The teacher may do a bit of good-natured baiting at this point!)

 III. The teacher leads a discussion of biographies and autobiographies that class members have already read, jotting various titles on the board. Discussion includes which ones were liked or disliked and why; then proceeds to the purposes and values of reading biography and autobiography.

 IV. The teacher distributes a list, appropriate to the range of ability and interest in the class, of biographies and autobiographies available in the school or public library or

---

[8] This unit was taught by the author in classes at East High School, Superior, Wisconsin, and at University High School, Minneapolis, Minnesota.

locally in paperback form. The assignment is that each student must read one book.

V. The teacher and class draw up a check list for judging and evaluating biographies. (The teacher has this mimeographed, and distributes it to the class.)

VI. For two or three days, while the class members are choosing books and beginning reading, the class as a whole reads and discusses the several short selections of biography and auto-biography included in the class anthology. Reference is made to the check list drawn up earlier.

VII. While the individual reading is progressing, the class studies a series of poems about people, character sketches in verse, which are included in the class anthology, or which the teacher reads aloud or has mimeographed from other sources.

VIII. Several subgroups are formed within the class, according to the types of biographies being read. For example, there may be groups of students reading about scientists, sports figures, adventurers, political figures, and so forth.

Assignments of group and individual reports are made:

A. Group report: Each group prepares a report of a type such as the following:

   1. A panel discussion on the field (science, politics, or others), its opportunities and obstacles, as revealed in the books read in the group.

   2. A "This Is Your Life" program based on the career of one of the people read about in the group.

   3. A series of interviews in which group members play the roles of people read about.

   4. A "Guess Who" quiz in which a series of clues are given until someone in the class can guess each of the subjects of the biographies read.

B. Individual reports: All students must write an evaluation of their books, using the check list drawn up earlier.

C. For extra credit, individual students may:

   1. Read another biography of the same person and compare the two treatments.

   2. Do library research on the person, using factual sources, and discuss the biography in view of this research.

IX. While individual reading is being completed and group reports are being prepared, the class members write character sketches of people they admire in real life. Class time is given to criticism and correction of the papers, as with any set of themes.

X. Group and individual reports are made.

Junior Biography

Paralleling the rise of the junior novel is that of the junior biography. The history of the two forms has been similar. Both became distinct genres in the 1930's and have developed rapidly since. Both are popular with the adolescent audience. Achievement in each genre ranges from the completely patterned potboiler to the truly and distinctively artistic work. Didacticism, the passion to teach, has hamstrung junior biography even more than it has the junior novel. Many of the juvenile biographies are sketches of the lives of the great, held up as examples ("Lives of great men all remind us . . ."). Hero worship is, of course, rife in the junior biography. Often, too, junior biography has been excessively preoccupied with "human interest," with the "color angle," to the detriment of character interpretation and evaluation of deeds. Despite such inherently crippling tendencies, however, there are some remarkable achievements in the field of junior biography.

Athletes and Adventurers

The themes of sports and adventure are as popular in biography as in fiction. Leading the list in this category for years has been Doris Shannon Garst with her fictionalized biographies of frontier heroes, Indian and white—Sitting Bull, Crazy Horse, Buffalo Bill, Kit Carson, and others. Using the techniques of the adventure novel, Garst's books stress action and spectacle and the capacity of the superhero for surpassing deeds. Few early adolescent readers can distinguish between fiction and the biographies by Garst, and there is little need that they should.

Biographies of sports figures are almost as plentiful as novels about sports; in each case, distinguished books are few. Gene Schoor has risen above the run of the mill with his biographies of Jim Thorpe, the great Indian athlete, and of Casey Stengel, the baseball manager. Frank Graham's biography, *Lou Gehrig, A Quiet Hero,* tells with extraordinary skill the thrilling and poignant story of a great baseball player, and makes a real attempt to re-create a personality. Highly successful, too, though more for its subject than for its technique, is Bill Roeder's *Jackie Robinson,* an account of the career of the first Negro to enter big-league baseball.

A truly masterful junior biography, which towers above most of the others in the field, is Geoffrey Trease's *Sir Walter Raleigh.* Of course, the colorful Raleigh furnishes a natural subject for an exciting biography, and Trease takes full advantage of the intrigue-surrounded, up-by-the-bootstraps career of this great Elizabethan. Raleigh's struggle for success despite humble origins and his historic rivalry with Essex are both themes with great appeal to the adolescent. The authentic background of Queen Elizabeth's court and the passing references to literary figures of the time are bonuses in this biography, which reads like a superior romantic novel.

Nina Brown Baker, one of the leaders and pioneers in junior biography, also usually chooses colorful political figures as her subjects. Her biographies, though relatively mature, employ techniques of fiction that make them highly readable, and many students have come to know such figures as Garibaldi and Juárez more vividly through her books than through their study of history. More than most junior biographers, Nina Baker stresses the significance of her subjects' endeavors.

Scientists and Nurses

There have always been adolescents, especially boys, who have found their major literary experiences in biographies of scientists. This age of science no doubt will swell their ranks, and even the standard anthologies surely will give increasing amounts of space to the lives of scientists. The junior biographies of scientists have suffered from the problem of having to explain difficult material, of interpreting the subject in an abstruse context. Yet courageous, and in some cases successful, attempts have been made. One of the most notable of these is Rachel Baker's *Sigmund Freud*. Most adolescents—and adults, too—who have heard of Freud connect him vaguely with sex dreams; Baker boldly presents the famous psychiatrist in a thoroughly acceptable way. Though the book is eminently readable, explaining in elementary terms the basis of Freud's theories, a curious poetic strain runs through the pages, exemplified in a line like: "Now the green years of growing come upon the boy. . . ."

Outstanding, too, is the achievement of Elma E. Levinger in her biographies of Galileo and Leonardo da Vinci. The story of Galileo is cast in dramatic fictional form as it builds up to the trial scene in which the suspense is acute. Unlike many junior biographies, it does not ignore earthy aspects of the subject's life—Galileo's refusal to marry his mistress, for example. Levinger's dialogue, though rather lavish in the Galileo biography, is patently unreal, even for a Renaissance life; it is markedly better in her book on Da Vinci. Levinger is one of the few writers who have conquered the problem of making intellectual and artistic adventure interesting reading for adolescents.

J. Alvin Kugelmass assumed a formidable task in his biography, *J. Robert Oppenheimer and the Atomic Story*. Though, like Rachel Baker, Kugelmass is able to put in elementary terms some difficult principles of science, he never really brings his subject—a genius—to life, and the final effect of the work is awe rather than understanding. Kugelmass is far more successful in his biographies of Louis Braille, Ralph Bunche, and Roald Amundsen, whose careers, of course, lend themselves more readily to junior biography. The great Albert Schweitzer inspires awe, too, and a number of junior biographies of him have been attempted. The most successful is Joseph Gollomb's readable *Genius of the Jungle*. The famous Negro scientist, George Washington Carver, has also inspired a number of junior, as well as adult, biographers. The best biography of Carver for the senior high school reader is undoubtedly that by Rackham Holt.

Nursing, too, has been as popular a theme in biography as in the junior novel and, from a literary point of view, several of the biographies of nurses are far superior to most of the junior novels about nursing. Of course, the two most famous nurses of the world are Florence Nightingale and Clara Barton. Jeannette Nolan, a well-known name in juvenile biography, has written books on both. These books feature the technique of the novelist, particularly in the lavish use of dialogue. Though *Florence Nightingale* evidences a good sense of scene and handling of incident, it is less mature in organization and style than *The Story of Clara Barton*. Among the best of the many junior biographies of Florence Nightingale is that by Cecil Woodham-Smith, a rewritten version of his adult piece. Clara Barton receives her best treatment, perhaps, in the work by Mildred Pace.

An extremely moving biography of a nurse is that by Juliette Elkon, *Edith Cavell, Heroic Nurse,* the story of the English nurse who was put to death by the Germans for her underground activities in Belgium during World War I. Like most successful junior biographies, this one is cast solidly in the pattern of the novel, with skillful use of dialogue and detail. The tragic ending is dramatic without being melodramatic. As in other good junior biographies, a bibliography of sources is appended. Striking, too, is Rachel Baker's *Angel of Mercy,* the biography of "America's Florence Nightingale," Dorothea Lynde Dix. However, this book is not so well written as most of the others by Rachel Baker, and is not so popular as her earlier *The First Woman Doctor,* concerning Elizabeth Blackwell.

Literary and Artistic Figures

Biographies of people renowned in literature and the arts usually are not widely read, either in the adult or the adolescent field. However, in the senior high school, especially, such biographies can be helpful in enriching the study of literature and in meeting highly individual interests. For the latter purpose, the biographies of musicians by Madeleine Goss and those of figures in drama and dance by Gladys Malvern, for example, are especially appropriate. One of the most unusual biographies in the field of the arts is that of Louis Armstrong, the great jazz musician, by Jeannette Eaton —*Trumpeter's Tale.* Although the book gives little insight into the nature of jazz, it is an unforgettable story of a true rags-to-riches career of the Negro boy born in the New Orleans slums, who learned to play his horn in a reform school and later played before the crowned heads of Europe and in the concert halls and entertainment centers of America.

Of literary biographies, Cornelia Meigs's *Invincible Louisa* is easily the most popular. Its appeal, of course, lies mainly in its engaging picture of the family life of Louisa May Alcott rather than in the story of her writing career. No other junior biographies of literary figures, and there are not many, have found more than a handful of readers. May Lamberton Becker, in her *Presenting Miss Jane Austen,* has written the kind of biography that teachers wish adolescents would read! Actually, some of the more mature and literate girls do read it, and for them it is rewarding. It is more in the tradition of scholarly adult biography than in the typical novel pattern of junior biography. To the girl who reads it, it furnishes considerable insight into the major novels of Jane Austen. In the field of general literary biography, Marchette Chute, with her books on Shakespeare, Chaucer, and Ben Jonson, is a leader. These are useful reference works for senior high school classes studying English literature.

Varied Fields

One of the most publicized books in recent times is the *Diary of a Young Girl* by Anne Frank. This autobiography, of the Jewish girl who hid from the Nazis with her family in an Amsterdam retreat during World War II, was ultimately captured, and died in a concentration camp, is dated in its setting and events, but its amazing insight into the personality of an adolescent girl and the traumatic impact of its story will undoubtedly make its popularity endure.

Prolific Jeannette Eaton, already mentioned as the author of a junior biography of Louis Armstrong, has contributed some excellent biographies of people famous in public life. Among her best is *Gandhi, Fighter without a Sword,* the story of the great Indian patriot and pacifist. Many girls will find her biography of Eleanor Roosevelt interesting also.

Shirley Graham has taken biographies of outstanding Negroes as her field, and from this effort has come one of the best junior biographies of Booker T. Washington, as well as some of lesser-known Negroes. Elizabeth Yates's Newbery Prize winning book on a Negro slave who purchased his freedom, *Amos Fortune, Free Man,* is appealing to pupils in the early junior high school, and her biography, *Prudence Crandall, Woman of Courage,* of a teacher who fought for the right of all to be educated, is of interest to older girls. Though Clara Ingram Judson's fine biographies are more appropriate for elementary school children than for adolescents, some of her books, for instance *City Neighbor,* the story of Jane Addams, also are appropriate for the junior high school.

The Essay

The essential difficulty today in dealing with the teaching of the essay lies in defining "essay." The student in the junior and senior high school assuredly should deal with a wide range of nonfictional prose, other than the biography. But how much of this can be labeled "essay"? For example, are magazine articles essays? And what about editorials or letters? These things—articles, editorials, informative and argumentative prose generally —are the province of all teachers, not merely English teachers, just as the development of general reading ability is an all-school rather than an English-class responsibility. However, many English teachers have organized units on the magazine and newspaper in which both survey and criticism is likely to be stressed.[9]

Examination of courses of study in literature and commonly used textbook anthologies shows that the essay is a vaguely defined literary genre but that it enjoys a secure place in the school program. One popular textbook anthology for the ninth grade, for example, includes eight different essays and articles, ranging from a humorous sketch by James Thurber to a deductively organized discussion of the habits and characteristic of Britons. Ex-

[9] See, for example, *A Guide for Instruction in the Language Arts* (St. Paul: Minnesota Department of Education, 1956).

perienced teachers are aware, though, of the general unpopularity of essays of the formal type. Of course, the major reason for this unpopularity is the inherent difficulty of the formal essay. In his very early book on the teaching of high school English, Charles Swain Thomas recognized this difficulty:

Our taste for story is innate, melody and rhyme delight us in our juvenile years, we are early won by the concreteness of the drama; but a liking for the essay has, in most cases, to be carefully developed. This is particularly true if a writer deals primarily with abstract subjects.[10]

Reed Smith has pointed out that the formal essay, such as that written by Bacon, Emerson, Macaulay, Huxley, or Newman, "is the product of an adult mind, written for other adult, trained minds."[11] Of course, even the much anthologized informal or personal essays of Addison, Lamb, and Stevenson, for example, are adult and urbane reflections and meditations.

Many students do enjoy such light, humorous essays as those by James Thurber, Stephen Leacock, and Robert Benchley. The skills required in reading such essays are essentially the same as the skills required in reading fiction. Indeed, it is difficult to draw the line, for instance, between a Thurber essay and a Thurber short story.

The skills necessary to read the formal essay are the same as those needed to read general formal or analytical discourse—textbooks, for example. Many of the essays commonly included in anthologies for the eleventh and twelfth grades are extremely difficult and abstract. Naturally, it is all to the good for the able student to tackle Bacon or Emerson or Huxley. But it is futile to expect students of less than average ability to read essays by these writers. Essentially, the reading problem, of course, is one of organization. Reed Smith suggested in his book of thirty years ago that teachers furnish the students with outlines of difficult essays. Yet perhaps the process is too often reversed; the teacher

---

[10] Charles S. Thomas, *The Teaching of English in the Secondary School* (Boston: Houghton Mifflin, 1917).

[11] Reed Smith, *The Teaching of Literature in the High School* (New York: American Book, 1935).

asks students to outline essays they are not ready to read. Reading the formal essay requires logical thinking and recognition of patterns of organization in expository discourse. Improvement in these abilities is as gradual as other aspects of literary education. Though essay reading should not be the vehicle for grueling exercises in outlining, it may be extremely valuable as a springboard for student writing. This is true especially of the personal essay that deals with the seeming trivialities, the small awarenesses of living. Currently, this form of writing is largely relegated to newspaper and magazine columns and "departments." It is the mark of the immature adolescent to think that he has nothing worth writing about unless he has undergone harrowing adventure. His reading of informal essays may cause him to reflect, and thus to be prepared to write, on the everyday details of his own existence. And in this lies one pathway to maturity.

The Case for the Essay

Jerome Carlin, head of the English Department in the Fort Hamilton High School of Brooklyn, presents a lively case for the teaching of the modern essay. A portion of Dr. Carlin's article follows:

The case against the essay includes these charges: (1) It's dull. There's no story line. Kids won't be interested. (2) It's difficult. Since nothing *happens* and since so much is on an abstract level, those lower-I.Q. boys and girls especially won't stay afloat in an essay unit. (3) It's archaic. Addison and Steele haven't much to say to the generation of Lerner and Loewe. (4) Its form is hard to analyze. Plot, setting, climax, blank verse, rhyme scheme—terms like those, which are such handy labels in lessons on other works, are not so readily available for the essay. Let's look at these charges.

Appeal of the Essay

Dull, is it? Young people do take interest in dating, automobiles, flying, sports, comics, money, parents, vacation, college, and even high school. These are the topics of essays in today's textbooks.

"Malinda didn't look as though she knew I was alive after we arrived at the dance. . . . She didn't speak to me except to talk about other boys. . . . I found out among other things that she liked 'muscle goons.' I am definitely not athletic. . . . I ended up by walking home alone on my first date." One would be ashamed to accept his monthly check if he failed to draw fire from a class with those lines in the story essay "My Last Date." Written by a fourteen-year-old high school freshman, Philip Thompson, and published originally in *Boy's Life,* the essay appears in a recently published textbook. There is no need to analyze its fascination.

There is no need to puzzle, either, over the appeal of a story essay which appears at the beginning of another textbook collection, the essay "Father Opens My Mail" by Clarence Day. The rights and responsibilities of children and parents give rise to fighting talk even in a drowsy nine o'clock class. A few staunch supporters of respect for parents are bound to speak for patience and filial submission to Father's foibles. Some others will argue, perhaps with careful impersonality, "Yes, many parents are like that—but shouldn't be." With that lead the man behind the desk has a chance to say, "When you become a parent, how will you avoid the failings that you find in Father in this essay?"

For shock effect bring a class face to face with Art Buchwald's statement in "Don't Be a Pal to Your Son": ". . . we should give American children something they desperately need and crave for—brutality. We must make them feel neglected, insecure, unwanted and unloved. . . . They'll be so eager to be wanted that they'll do everything in the world to please us." Come on in, kids. The water is cold—but bracing.

Another kind of interest is aroused by Ruth Sawyer's poignant essay "Crippled: An Appeal to Motorists." "John Paul," says Mrs. Sawyer, "is four years old. He will never get up again—that is, never as a whole, free, exultant little boy. He will never throw back the covers of his cot, shoot across his room and ours, and drop like a plummet, stomach down, on our bed, shouting, "Here I come—Daddy and Mum!" Farther along, the author describes the youth who had been driving a borrowed car without a license, who still doesn't know what he has done—the boy who is restless, nervous, shallow; the boy who says "straightforwardly to the police: 'I was going fifty—late for a date.'" When he visits the hospital and learns that the crippled child is out of danger, this boy is "relieved of all responsibility. Gee, I'm glad. If he'd died now—I'd felt awful.'" Even if a student has never sat behind the wheel of a moving car, he is a potential driver. Many a one is eagerly awaiting the day when Dad and the law will allow him to unhitch the Chevrolet and gallop gallantly down the road. Once when I asked a wholesome class of average juniors—no intellectuals—what makes drivers like the one described in the essay so dangerous, I heard wonderful talk of the reckless use of the motor car as a prop to the weak ego, as a display of powers that the driver relates to himself, and as a status symbol of maturity falsely assumed by the immature.

Once drawn in by the lure of essays with such direct appeal to youthful interests, boys and girls won't flinch at tackling subjects of greater depth. In no other type of literature are the opportunities so great to deal directly with values. By the time a student has reached sixteen, the beginning of the middle age of youth, he is ripe for a look at Big Questions. If the groundwork is properly laid, he will react seriously and searchingly to the excerpt from Thoreau's *Walden* "Where I Lived, and What I Lived For." He will read critically Fosdick's "Six Ways to Tell Right from Wrong," and he will single out those of the six which seem most useful in everyday moral decisions. He will come to grips with problems of human relationships and justice in Neuberger's "Their Brothers' Keepers"; of economic relationships in Johnston's "A Warning to Labor and Management"; of governmental and political relationships in Russell's "How to Beat Communism."

So much of the time, the English teacher is a poor Don Quixote leveling his spindly red pencil against errors. If there were a Hippocratic Oath for those entering the profession of English teaching, surely it would declare, "You will exercise your art for the spiritual enrichment of your charges, and you will not spend all of your powers in the cure or prevention of material ills alone." The splendor of literature teaching is its illumination of life. With the essay, particularly, teacher and student can probe at the ideas about life and society that thoughtful writers have deliberately exposed to view. Other literary forms may have other aims. There is no ambiguity about the serious essayist's intention to put ideas before the reader.

What Is the Essay?

Some of the titles already mentioned provide evidence that the essay is a flourishing part of contemporary literature. What has become almost archaic in commercial usage is only the word *essay* itself. The form is as up-to-date as this morning's newspaper or this week's magazine. The current issue (when this was written) of the *Saturday Evening Post* includes in its contents: an article on social attitudes toward the physically disabled, "They Think We Have the Evil Eye," by Bentz Plagemann; a discussion of "Why I Deprive My Children" by Katharine Britton Mishler; and an analysis of economic thinking, pro and con, in "The Great Tariff Battle" by Joe Alex Morris. The current *Harper's* parallels the *Post* with articles on subjects attuned to the interests of its own readers: attitudes of the public toward contemporary art, proposals for a better way to teach deaf children, and the pros and cons of foreign policy regarding Africa, Asia, and the Western Alliance. Examples from local newspapers of the past week include an analysis of the problem of twin children whose capacities are not equal, an exposé and a slashing attack on abuses of mental hospitals, and a dance critique concluding that, in Jacques d'Amboise, America has at last produced a great male ballet dancer. If any of these examples seem too elevated for average readers in or out of high school, a few glances through the pages of teen and movie magazines will reveal the equivalents on another level. There is something for every taste and interest in the modern essay, which in newspaper and magazine goes by the name of article, feature, department, or column.

By the same token every level of reading difficulty exists among essays in commercial publications and has its counterpart in high school textbooks. Where your students tend to take their stand on the normal curve of reading ability should determine your choice of essays for their study. Whether you depend on the essay section of a general anthology or whether you have at hand a textbook collection solely devoted to the essay, you can command materials with a level of reading difficulty ranging from that of *Boys' Life* to that of *Atlantic*.

Neither from the student's point of view nor from the teacher's, need the essay be the psychological hazard that it sometimes becomes. True, if our teaching approach stresses form more than substance, it will prove to be bad magic, drying up that sea of hands around us.

Matters of form need not, should not, be overlooked. Labels enough are ready for application: formal, informal, personal, familiar, descriptive, reflective, philosophic, critical, abstract, factual. But these are mechanical matters of classification—too much like cataloguing books in a library instead of taking them home to read and enjoy.

Keep that shiny enthusiasm undulled. Bring the reader to any essays with the promise that it will reveal something worth considering about a live topic. "What do you think of the practice followed by many colleges in giving valuable scholarships to inferior students who are good athletes?" . . . "How do *you* decide whether a particular action is right or wrong?" By such questions arouse interest in the topic; then study the essay for what it has to say on that subject; and only afterwards turn to the matter of form. "Now that we've considered what the author has to say, let's see *how* he said it. . . . How did he organize his ideas? . . . What are the characteristics of his style? . . . What examples can you find of statements that are especially appealing or forceful in style? . . . What does this author do that you can put into practice in your own writing?" For the student there is much more excitement, as well as much more to be gained, in first dealing with the substance and in then briefly studying the technical processes by which that content is conveyed.[12]

How to use the essay as a vehicle for teaching thinking, writing, reading furnishes the subject matter for a very helpful pamphlet that suggests specific ways of approaching a number of essays.[13] Since today, as this pamphlet states, the essay offers "an endless variety of appealing material close to the everyday experiences of young people at every level of development," it can add an important ingredient to the literature program.

POSSIBILITIES FOR STUDENT READING

(Biographies discussed in the preceding chapter are marked with an asterisk [*]. Titles are annotated only if the nature of the content was not made clear in the chapter. A indicates adult biographies; E, especially easy ones.)

*Baker, Louise, *Out on a Limb*, McGraw-Hill. (A)
A girl who loses a leg early in life learns to dance and swim and becomes a reporter.

12 Jerome Carlin, "This I Believe—about the Essay," *English Journal*, LI (September 1962), 403–411.
13 Metropolitan School Study Council, *Using the Essay to Teach Reading, Writing, Thinking* (New York: Bureau of Publications, Teachers College, 1957).

*Baker, Nina Brown, *Garibaldi*, Vanguard.
Well-written story of the great Italian patriot. (Also, *Juárez, Hero of Mexico*.)

*Baker, Rachel, *The First Woman Doctor*, Messner.
Elizabeth Blackwell overcame prejudice to enter the medical profession a century ago.

————, *Sigmund Freud*, Messner.
(Also *Angel of Mercy, about Dorothea Lynde Dix.)

*Becker, May Lamberton, *Presenting Miss Jane Austen*. Dodd, Mead. (A)

*Boynick, David, *Champions by Setback*, Crowell. (A)
Inspiring short accounts of the careers of athletes who overcame serious physical handicaps to become champions.

Chevigny, Hector, *My Eyes Have a Cold Nose*, Yale University Press. (A)
Autobiographical account of conquering blindness with the help of a seeing-eye dog.

Curie, Eve, *Madame Curie*, Doubleday. (A)
The amazing story of the discoverer of radium told by her daughter.

Daugherty, James, *Daniel Boone*, Viking. (E)
Beautifully written story of the great frontier hero.

*Eaton, Jeannette, *Trumpeter's Tale*, Morrow.
(Also *Gandhi, Fighter without a Sword*.)

*Elkon, Juliette, *Edith Cavell, Heroic Nurse*, Messner.

*Frank, Anne, *Diary of a Young Girl*, Doubleday.

*Galt, Tom, *Peter Zenger, Fighter for Freedom*, Crowell.

*Garst, Doris Shannon, *Sitting Bull*, Messner. (E)
Exciting fictionalized story of the great Sioux chief. (Also *Buffalo Bill and *Kit Carson.)

*Gollomb, Joseph, *Albert Schweitzer, Genius of the Jungle*, Vanguard.

Goss, Madeleine, *Beethoven, Master Musician*, Doubleday.
The strange childhood and life of the great composer.

*Graham, Frank, *Lou Gehrig, A Quiet Hero*, Putnam.

*Graham, Shirley, and George Lipscomb, *Dr. George Washington Carver, Scientist*, Messner.

*Holt, Rackham, *George Washington Carver*, Doubleday. (A)

*Judson, Clara I., *City Neighbor*, Scribner.

*Keller, Helen, *Story of My Life*, Doubleday. (A)
Famous story of Helen Keller and her teacher, Anne Sullivan Macy.

*Kugelmass, J. Alvin, *Roald Amundsen*, Messner.
(Also *Ralph J. Bunche: Fighter for Peace* and *Louis Braille*.)

*Levinger, Elma E., *Galileo*, Messner.
(Also *Leonardo da Vinci*.)

Malvern, Gladys, *Curtain Going Up!* Messner.
The career of Katherine Cornell to 1943.

*Meigs, Cornelia, *Invincible Louisa*, Little, Brown.

Miller, Floyd, *The Electrical Genius of Liberty Hall: Charles Steinmetz*, McGraw-Hill. (E)
A readable treatment of Steinmetz' human and intellectual qualities.

*Pace, Mildred, *Clara Barton*, Scribner.

Strachey, Lytton, *Elizabeth and Essex: A Tragic History*, Harcourt.
The dramatic story of Elizabeth I and Essex.

Syme, Ronald, *African Traveler: The Story of Mary Kingsley*, Morrow.
Miss Kingsley's unusual adventures in exploring Africa.

*Trease, Geoffrey, *Sir Walter Raleigh*, Vanguard.

Warner, Oliver, *Nelson and the Age of Fighting Sail*, American Heritage.
A well-documented and readable narrative of the great British sea captain.

*Woodham-Smith, Cecil, *Lonely Crusader* (Florence Nightingale), McGraw-Hill.

*Yates, Elizabeth, *Prudence Crandall, Woman of Courage*, Dutton.

USEFUL COLLECTIONS OF ESSAYS

Chamberlain, Essie (Ed.), *Essays Old and New* (3d ed.; New York: Harcourt, 1955).

Cross, E. A., and Neal M. Cross (Eds.), *Types of Literature* (Rev. ed.; New York: Macmillan, 1945).

Gehlmann, John (Ed.), *The Challenge of Ideas: An Essay Reader* (New York: Odyssey Press, 1950).

Greene, Jay (Ed.), *Essays for Modern Youth* (New York: Globe Book, 1961).

McClay, Harriet L., and Helen Judson (Eds.), *Story Essays* (New York: Holt, Rinehart and Winston, 1947).

Mead, Douglass (Ed.), *Great English and American Essays* (New York: Holt, Rinehart and Winston, 1957).

Peterson, Houston (Ed.), *Great Essays* (New York: Pocket Books, 1954).

Satin, Joseph (Ed.), *Ideas in Context* (New York: Houghton Mifflin, 1958).

THE
TEACHING
OF
POETRY[1]

Most teachers of high school English seem to agree tacitly that the study of poetry should occupy an important place in the English curriculum. At least, English teachers spend long, and often unrewarding, hours at the task of "covering" with their students the poems included in the anthologies to which so many of them are bound. Whether this practice stems from the training and convictions of the English teacher or simply from the whims of the anthology publishers, the instinct that causes special emphasis to fall on the study of poetry is very sound. There are excellent reasons for regarding poetry as the vital heart and center of a good English program.

Yet, in spite of the time and attention given to this aspect of the subject called English, the results are often unimpressive. Widespread is the complaint among secondary school English teachers that adolescent boys and (less often) girls simply do not like poetry. Young or inexperienced teachers, particularly, are prone to frustration in their efforts to "sell" their charges on a literary construct that, they maintain, seems artificial to the teenager and totally alien to his culture. In fact, this frustration has

[1] This chapter was prepared by John A. Myers, Jr., The Hun School, Princeton, New Jersey.

been projected into an almost mythic belief that there is something in the teen-age mentality or emotional make-up that is inherently opposed to the poetic experience.

The odds against which most such teachers continue to struggle, however, are largely of their own making. The fact is that adolescents can and will respond more excitedly to poetry than to any other form of literature—if the approach to the teaching of poetry is sound, if the teacher knows what he is doing and why he is doing it. And whether or not the student continues to read poetry after leaving high school or college, he can derive more lasting benefits from his brief love affair with poetry than he can from any other aspect of the English program. For this reason it is important that some of the more common and pernicious fallacies in the teaching of poetry be identified.

Fallacies in Teaching Poetry

It has been maintained that too much of the literature in the secondary school curriculum has been selected by women for girls. Girls, the argument goes, tend to like whatever is presented anyway and that therefore we should select poetry with boys in mind. This argument, of course, is unsound. In the first place, poems are not so much *selected* as they are *found* in "omnibus" anthologies, and it would be hard to prove that the editors of these works are predominantly females. In the second place, poems cannot be identified by their sexual characteristics, and there is no essential difference between the male way of responding to a poem and the female way. If a poem has been well taught and if the whole approach to poetry has been sound, boys and girls will respond with equal enthusiasm to a wide range of English and American poetry dealing with every conceivable subject from love to war. In considering the value of poetry, one of the first things to keep in mind is that it springs from a basic human impulse and fulfills a basic human interest.

But the argument based on a difference in response according to sex does suggest an important truth, often ignored by English teachers, that may be the source of much of their frustration. It may be true, that is, that girls will often respond to bad poems for the same reason that boys will reject poetry altogether. When this happens, it usually means that the teacher has made the mistake of sentimentalizing poetry in his whole approach to the subject. It is not so much poetry—or poems—that boys are suspicious of as it is what they come to conceive of as "the poetic." Possibly because of the scientific and practical orientation of the culture in which they function, many English teachers protest too much that poetry embodies the good, the true, and the beautiful. Somehow the notion gets abroad that poetry deals exclusively "with sunsets, flowers, butterflies, love, and God" or that "poetry is a precious affair, the enjoyment only of delicate souls, removed from the heat and sweat of ordinary life."[2]

Rather than being taken as a cause for despair, the instinct among adolescents that rejects this notion of the poetic should be recognized as an opportunity, an opportunity to show the toughness and excitement of poetic language, the wide variety and virility of the subject matter of poetry. One might, for instance, introduce a class of ninth- or tenth-graders to Wilfred Owen's "Dulce et Decorum Est" with its "ugly" lines,

> If in some smothering dreams, you too could pace
> Behind the wagon that we flung him in,
> And watch the white eyes writhing in his face,
> His hanging face, like a devil's sick of sin;
> If you could hear, at every jolt, the blood
> Come gargling from the froth-corrupted lungs,
> Bitter as the cud
> Of vile, incurable sores on innocent tongues,
> My friend, you would not tell with such high zest
> To children ardent for some desperate glory,
> The old Lie: Dulce et decorum est
> Pro patria mori.[3]

[2] Laurence Perrine, *Sound and Sense: An Introduction to Poetry* (New York: Harcourt, 1956), pp. 7–8.

[3] Wilfred Owen, "Dulce et Decorum Est," *The Poems of Wilfred Owen* (Rev. ed.; New York: New Directions, 1959). By permission of the puplishers and Chatto & Windus, London.

It may come as a healthy surprise to both boys and girls that such "unattractive" subject matter as the physical effects on soldiers of a gas attack in World War I can be the legitimate material for a poem. More important will be their realization (if it is clarified by the teacher) that when they respond with pleasure to such lines, they are responding to something infinitely more subtle and complex than the subject matter. What they are responding to, of course, is the *language* of the poem and the way in which the poet has *ordered* the various resources of language so as to give us a pleasing *esthetic* whole. The teacher can show that by his art the poet has resolved individually ugly items in the poem into an *experience of the poem* that is anything but ugly, an experience that gives not only pleasure but a kind of knowledge.

Intellectual and Emotional Response

By a skillful reading of the poem and then by careful questioning, the teacher can make the student aware that his response to the poem was both emotional and intellectual. Emotionally the student will have responded, albeit unconsciously, to such sound effects as the combination of alliteration and assonance in "watch the white eyes writhing" and "devil's sick of sin." Nor does the teacher have to use these technical terms to point out the onomatopoetic effect of such words as "gargling" and "froth-corrupted."

Intellectually, as well as emotionally, the student can be made to respond to the "drama" of these lines, to the bitter irony with which the speaker regards Horace's "old Lie"—"It is sweet and becoming to die for one's country," an irony that is emphasized by the rhyming of *glory* and *mori, zest* and *est*. It can be pointed out that even the most innocent tongues, deceived by dreams of glory, can be corrupted in war and that both *innocent* and *corrupted* have double meanings here. The teacher might ask if there is a connection between the "devil" simile and the idea of "froth-*corrupted* lungs." Students love word play, and they can easily be made to understand that the poet has dramatized—through his imagery, his sound effects, his tonal irony—how really *desperate* such glory can become.

Finally, young students can learn from this poem (there are three other stanzas) that it is the legitimate business of poets to use descriptive details, sometimes with no direct commentary on these details, to convey a deeply felt *attitude* toward some institution such as war.

It is, of course, enough if an attitude has been dramatized, captured, conveyed—a certain feeling on the poet's part. There need be no moral or message, no high truth that the poet has managed to decorate a bit or, as many students believe, obscure or hide beneath the "flowery" language. This tendency to go message hunting, indeed, is one of the other great fallacies that teachers have somehow managed to foster among their students. In Owen's poem it might be instructive for the teacher to point out that the poet is much more interested in the irony, *for its own dramatic sake,* that is caught in the discrepancy between the horrible details of the gas attack and the noble words of Horace, than he is in saying "War is evil." It is precisely here, of course, that the teacher has a perfect opportunity to show *what* poetry is and *why* poetry is, for he can easily demonstrate the difference between the *poem,* as an *experience* of an attitude, and any *statement* that can be abstracted from the poem—any statement of its theme or paraphrase of its "meaning." Teachers should never cease in their efforts to make students aware of the enormous and crucial difference between the paraphrase of the poem and the poem itself.

It has, of course, been taken for granted here that high school students *will* respond to the language, the poetry, of a poem like "Dulce et Decorum Est" (and, by implication, many other poems on different subjects) even without the teacher's help. It has also been implied that the teacher's main task is to make the student more aware of what he is responding to, thereby increasing and deepening his capacity to respond to this and other poems. Some educators will protest that this assumes too much. They will maintain that there is a natural decline of the elementary school child's zest for poetry to a growing negativism toward it on the part of the adolescent. Poetry appeals largely to the emotions, and some teachers feel that as the child grows older, the emotions retreat further and further below the surface, and hence that adolescence is a time of inhibition. This theory, insofar as it applies to the teaching of poetry, should be examined closely.

There is, of course, abundant evidence that poetry, or something very close to it, plays a significant role in the life of the young child. We all recognize his love of nursery rhymes, his use of song and rhyme and incantation in games, his unconscious use of rhythm in his play. The use of and response to such elements of poetry is inherent in the human make-up. That this power or this sensitivity declines in adolescence, however, is not supported by the evidence. Do not adolescents respond to mottoes, slogans, proverbs? Are they not titillated, as much as any other age group, by the jingles and other forms of word play used in commercials and advertisements? Are they not themselves given to slang and colorful language and even a kind of rudimentary irony in their own speech?

As for their emotions retreating below the surface, their being inhibited, how do we explain their emotional enthusiasm at rallies and athletic contests? their love of cheers? their exuberance at parties? A good speaker at a school assembly or even a good sermon can stir them to their roots. No, any decline in adolescent enthusiasm for poetry will have to be explained by reference to some specific misconception about poetry derived from their experience with poetry in the classroom.

The Basic Appeal of Poetry

The truth is that high school students are capable of becoming—indeed, are inclined to become—just as interested in poetry as they are in any other form of literature—the novel, the play, the short story. In fact, poetry is really only a kind of intensification of the language of literature, and every satisfactory literary experience that the student undergoes can be thought of as a kind of preparation for the appreciation and enjoyment of poetry. Teachers, therefore, must keep in mind that every literary experience is essentially a *verbal* or *language* experience that approaches to some degree the condition of a poetic experience. Enjoyment of poetry is very closely associated with verbal awareness, the ability to read sensitively. Every time a class examines carefully a passage of prose—in novel, essay, short story, or drama—it is performing essentially the same kind of operation it performs on a poem, but in poetry the elements are arranged much more carefully or formally and are much more highly concentrated. The difference is not one of kind but of degree. The poetic experience is simply more intense because the poem makes more precise, more organized, more self-conscious use of all the devices by means of which language makes its gestures and suggestions and achieves its more powerful effects: figurative language, the sense image, sound, rhythm, repetition, and tone.

The Challenge of Poetry

Because of this problem and this paradox—that poetry is at once both similar to and different from other literary uses of language—the teacher has the double task of engaging the student's interest and trust in literature *as such* and at the same time preparing him to accept the more rigorous demands that poetry makes upon the reader. One should not be afraid to admit that in many ways poetry *is* more difficult than other forms of literature and demands more attention and more intellectual discipline. But before the teacher can ask his students to make such an effort, he must gain their confidence in literature, provide them with a series of real literary experiences. Usually this is best achieved through the study of novels, short stories, and plays. And although some teachers feel that poetry should be interspersed with other kinds of literature throughout the year, that young students are incapable of sustaining their interest in poetry studied in a prolonged unit, there are good reasons for saving the study of poetry until toward the end of each year (the spring somehow seems appropriate for poetry), and dealing with it very deliberately for a month or two—with perhaps a novel or a play thrown in halfway through this unit, to break the monotony and remind the student that poetry and prose are at least kissing cousins.

Nor should it be forgotten that many of the themes and ideas encountered in poetry in concentrated form will have already been explored by the student in his other reading. The joy of recognition can provide a student with one of his most intense intellectual delights; the power to synthesize, to perceive thematic connections, to encounter important ideas and concerns in different works and literary types can be his most profitable intellectual experience.

Formal Study

Since, however, poetry does embody certain formal characteristics that distinguish it from other forms of literature and that figure prominently in its discussion and analysis, sooner or later the student will have to become familiar with certain technical terms used to identify these characteristics. Just as the study of grammar, usage, and rhetoric provides the teacher and the student with a common vocabulary for discussing writing problems, so poetry has its own "grammar," which can help to expedite and sharpen any discussion of a poem. Much as we desire the student's experience of the poem to be a felt synthesis of all its elements, we cannot teach a poem without being able to converse intelligently about its separable parts: its diction, its imagery, its figures of speech, its controlling metaphors, its sound effects, its tone, its dramatic structure, its rhythmical movement, even its punctuation and its grammar. The terms used to identify and describe these elements and their functioning should be kept to the very barest minimum, at least until the tenth grade; but there is no reason why the average student, in the upper two or three grades, should not be able to recognize and use such concepts as connotation and denotation, imagery, metaphor, symbol, and allusion. On the other hand, much more important than being able to distinguish between metaphor, simile, metonymy, synecdoche, and personification is the understanding of the *principle* of metaphor in its broadest sense, which is the analogical or comparative principle fundamental to poetry. As one writer reminds us, metaphor in its largest sense "is not, as we were taught at school, a figure of speech. In language it is the means by which we extend our awareness of experience into new realms. Poetry is a part of this process of giving apparent order to the flux of experience."[4]

As the student matures and gains more experience with language analysis, he should be able to recognize and manipulate the more intellectual terms related to *tone* in poetry: irony, understatement, overstatement, paradox. He should gradually become acquainted with the terms by means of which we describe the *sounds* of poetry: alliteration, assonance, consonance, onomatopoeia, and rhyme schemes. He should be encouraged to read poetry aloud and develop an ear not only for its sounds and rhythms but for its syntactic structures. He should know when a line is end-stopped and when it is a run-on line. He should develop an eye for the phrase, the clause, and the sentence and learn to attend to the *natural* pause, pitch, and stress patterns, leaving the meter to take care of itself rather than allowing it to dominate his reading and produce a monotonous singsong effect.

Most difficult and perhaps least important in the student's equipment for reading poetry is the whole area of prosody and the various line and stanza forms. There is nothing instrinsically difficult about learning and recognizing the five basic feet in English poetry (iambic, trochaic, anapestic, dactylic, and spondaic) and the names for the number of feet per line (tetrameter, pentameter, and so on), and there is no particular reason for avoiding these terms; but nothing is more futile than having the student indulge in scansion *for its own sake*. If advanced students can be taught to relate meter and metrical variation (along with various sound effects) to the *sense* of the poem, if they can learn to view these things functionally and see their contribution to the *total meaning* of the poem, there is no reason for the teacher to hold back on these things. But this is a subtle business, difficult for even the most experienced English teachers, and more time has probably been wasted in the classroom on prosody than on any other aspect of the teaching of poetry.

[4] David Holbrook, *English for Maturity* (New York: Cambridge, 1961), p. 69.

Of course, none of the technical aspects of poetry, from metaphor to meter, should be thought of or taught as ends in themselves. One of the other great fallacies in the teaching of poetry, often indulged in by the brightest and most energetic teachers, is what might be called the scientific or academic fallacy. Some teachers, that is, place so much emphasis on the terminology of poetic analysis that they lose sight of what they are teaching and the student loses sight of the poem. These teachers use the poem as a vehicle for teaching the oxymoron or the hyperbole or the paradox instead of using these concepts, unobtrusively and often without calling them by name, to help the student to an understanding of the poem. Poetry analysis can be an exciting and enormously profitable intellectual experience for young students, but the teacher must remember that analysis should always be followed by synthesis or there has been no real response to the *whole* poem, which is always greater than and different from the sum of its parts. The terminology of poetry can easily become abstract and meaningless for the student, and a teacher's preoccupation with it can leave a student feeling that poetry is nothing more than an elaborate and boring system of jargon.

Proven Paths in Teaching

If, however, there are many traps for the teacher to avoid in teaching poetry, there are a number of tried and proven paths by which he can safely lead the student into the poem. It is not within the scope of this chapter to describe in detail the process of poetic analysis. Besides, there are so many excellent critical anthologies available today in inexpensive editions, and so many exegeses of individual poems, that no English teacher need remain uninstructed in these techniques. But it may be helpful to list the questions some or all of which teachers can ask, and train their students to ask, about any poem. The order in which these questions are asked and the emphasis that different questions receive will depend upon the individual poem.

Who is the *speaker* of the poem (for all poems have a speaker, who is either a projection of one of the "selves" of the poet or a

character created by the poet for a particular occasion and purpose) and what can you tell about him from his diction and his
tone of voice? Whom is the speaker *addressing* and what is the
occasion for this particular utterance? What is the *setting* in time
and place? What is the purpose of the poem? What is its *theme* or
underlying idea or main concern? Can you paraphrase the poem?
How does the poem's *diction* and *imagery* contribute to its *tone?*
What examples of figurative language do you find in the poem
and what do these contribute to the over-all effect? Do they seem
appropriate? Is there a *pattern* to the imagery? the figures of
speech? What evidence is there of *progression* in the *structure* of
the poem? Are all the steps in the "logic" of the poem provided? Does the poem contain any words that can be regarded as
symbols? Can the whole poem be regarded as an allegory? If so,
what is the allegorical meaning? Are there any *allusions* and why
has the poet used them? Do you find examples of *understatement,
overstatement, irony, paradox?* What is their function? What
striking devices of *sound* and *meter* do you find? How is the
sound "an echo to the sense"? Do you understand the *syntactical
structure* of each of the poem's sentences?

Teaching Individual Poems

It should be apparent that there is more than enough to teach
about poetry, about individual poems, simply by looking at them
steadily as individual works of art with the power to move us or
delight us or to give us some new awareness. At the high school
level teachers should not feel bound to teach a particular body of
poetry or to teach it in the framework of a survey of American
or British literary history, with all the distractions of biographical
and historical detail. Biography and history should enter the classroom discussion of poetry only when they can help to shed light
on the total meaning of the particular poem. Some teachers like
to group the poems they teach according to theme or subject matter, but such order as is achieved by this process is more often
than not artificial and illusory. Even attempts to group and study

poems according to type (narrative, descriptive, lyric, dramatic, those emphasizing tone as opposed to imagery or idea) do not serve any very useful purpose because every poem is a unique construct and provides a unique experience; and what all poems have in common is more important than how they differ. The categories we set up have a tendency to slip and slide and blend into one another.

In this chapter little attempt has been made to suggest specific poems that should be taught or the appropriate grade level for particular poems. Such matters are best left to the teacher's discrimination and taste and his judgment of his students' abilities. If it is felt that this places too great a responsibility upon the individual teacher, we should realize that that is the only pedagogically safe place for such a responsibility. The teaching of poetry is a curiously private affair, and no teacher will have much success with a poem unless it is a poem he or she cares something about and for the teaching of which he has worked out some approach of his own. David Holbrook reminds us forcefully of this truth:

Teaching poetry is at the centre of English, and yet it is something you cannot do unless you find joy in it. A teacher can only teach the poems he or she likes: there is no joy or purpose in teaching a poem you loathe out of a sense of duty because you are told it is a "classic." Whatever those excellent people who believe in disciplines of learning say, you cannot teach a poem under such circumstances. You will be doing something, certainly, maybe something of value, such as giving children the experience of how dull and exasperating adults can be at times. But you will not be giving them the disciplines of enjoying poetry.[5]

How Important Is Poetry?

How, finally, *do* we justify the claims we have made for the importance of poetry? Why, after all, do we say that poetry, particularly the intensive reading of poetry, is very near the center

[5] *Ibid.*, p. 63.

of the English program and central to the student's training in English? There are at least three reasons. First of all, poetry can provide intense enjoyment, can add a rich dimension of delight in the language that is our heritage, can make us more responsive to the verbal world in which we do so much of our living. And because of this increased verbal awareness, students can find much more in and take much more from all their other reading, all their other experiences with language.

Second, the close reading of poetry provides us with a kind of verbal or semantic safeguard and censor. It makes us more discriminating in our own use of language and more exacting in the standards of verbal honesty and precision we demand from others. It makes us less willing to abide language that is cheap and slovenly and fraudulent, less likely to fall victims to those who would manipulate us to their own ends, be they the political or merely the commercial persuaders. It is poetry, after all, that keeps the language alive and vital, that saves it from the ravages of time and hard use.

Finally, poetry extends the territory of our perceptions, enlarges and deepens and refines our emotional sensibilities, our capacity to feel—and by so doing makes us into more sensitive, more responsive, more sympathetic human beings. This, indeed, may be its most important contribution to our lives. For it may well be that the crucial danger of our times is the terrible separation of thought and *feeling,* and the attendant atrophy of the imagination. Archibald MacLeish reminds us powerfully of this last and greatest contribution of poetry:

Great poems are instruments of knowledge—a knowledge carried alive into the heart by passion . . . knowledge without feeling is not knowledge and can lead to public irresponsibility and indifference, and conceivably to ruin. . . . We are deluged with facts, but we have lost, or are losing, our human ability to feel them. . . . Slavery begins when men give up the human need to know *with the whole heart.* . . . The real defense of freedom is imagination, that *feeling* life of the mind which actually knows because it involves itself in its knowing, puts itself in the place where its thought goes, walks in the body of the little Negro girl who feels the spittle dribbling on her cheek. . . . The man who knows with his heart knows himself to be a man, feels as himself, cannot be silenced.[6]

SELECTED REFERENCES

Critical Anthologies

Brooks, Cleanth, and Robert Penn Warren, *Understanding Poetry* 3d ed., (New York: Holt, Rinehart and Winston, 1960).
Primarily for the teacher, this is a seminal book whose first edition helped to revolutionize the teaching of poetry. Can be used as a text with advanced high school seniors. Fine analyses of individual poems.

Engle, Paul, and Warren Carrier, *Reading Modern Poetry* (Chicago: Scott, Foresman, 1955).
An excellent critical anthology of modern poetry, with many fine analyses of key modern poems.

Main, C. F., and Peter J. Seng, *Poems* (Belmont, Calif.: Wadsworth Publishing Company, 1961).
Another fine critical anthology with an interesting collection of poems and excellent study aids.

Perrine, Laurence, *Sound and Sense: An Introduction to Poetry* (2d ed., New York: Harcourt, 1962).
An excellent text for the upper grades in high school. The elements of poetry are treated systematically chapter by chapter. A fine collection of poems with excellent study questions and teaching aids.

Reid, James M., John Ciardi, and Laurence Perrine, *Poetry: A Closer Look* (New York: Harcourt, 1963).
A new text with detailed programmed instruction on two poems and an excellent small selection of poems for further analysis. May be an excellent text for introducing the close reading of poems in the lower high school grades.

Books on the Subject of Poetry

Kreuzer, James R., *Elements of Poetry* (New York: Macmillan, 1955).

[6] Archibald MacLeish, "The Poet and the Press," *Atlantic,* CCIII (March 1959), 44–46, *passim.*

For further study by the teacher. Mostly text but some poems included and some excellent analyses of poems. If used as a textbook, would have to be supplemented by additional poems.

Stauffer, Donald A., *The Nature of Poetry* (New York: Norton, 1946).
Excellent additional reading for the teacher. Has a fine feel for poetry.

Books on the Teaching of English with Excellent Chapters on Poetry

Holbrook, David, *English for Maturity* (New York: Cambridge, 1961).

Sauer, Edwin H., *English in the Secondary School* (New York: Holt, Rinehart and Winston, 1961).

Anthologies—Noncritical

Swallow, Alan (Ed.), *The Rinehart Book of Verse* (Rinehart Editions; New York: Holt, Rinehart and Winston, 1958).
An excellent, inexpensive (paperback), highly selective anthology of British and American poetry.

Ward, Herman M. (Ed.), *Poems for Pleasure* (New York: Hill & Wang, 1963).
A fine collection of the favorite poems selected by high school students.

Williams, Oscar (Ed.), *Immortal Poems of the English Language* (New York: Pocket Books, 1957).
With 447 British and American poems by 150 poets, this is one of the best inexpensive (50 cents) collections covering the whole range of British and American poetry.

Special

End-of-Year Examinations in English for College-Bound Students: Grades 9–12. A Project-Report by the Commission on English, College Entrance Examination Board (Box 592, Princeton, N.J., or Box 27,896, Los Angeles 27, Calif.), 1963.
An invaluable collection of examination questions, many of them on poetry, with sample responses by students and evaluations of these responses.

DRAMA
IN THE
ENGLISH
CLASSROOM[1]

10 ✤

It is not surprising that many students acquire the impression that drama flowered—and died—in the sixteenth century; for drama, unfortunately, has prevailingly been treated as the Cinderella of the English classroom, glorified briefly for the annual unit on Shakespeare, then sidelined for the rest of the year. In too many schools, drama means only Shakespeare, and the other rich resources of our dramatic heritage remain largely untapped. Maynard Mack has asserted that "if drama appears at all in our scholastic English programs outside of the college preparatory course, it runs a poor third or fourth to novels, short stories, poems, and discursive prose."[2] How necessary it becomes, then, to reaffirm drama's rightful position in the English curriculum. What place it should hold, however, can be determined only through a careful examination of why it should be taught, what should be taught, and how.

[1] This chapter was prepared by Gladys Veidemanis, Nicolet High School, Milwaukee, Wisconsin.

[2] Maynard Mack, "Teaching Drama: *Julius Caesar*," in Edward J. Gordon and Edward S. Noyes (Eds.), *Essays on the Teaching of English* (New York: Appleton, 1960), p. 320.

Drama—A Mirror of Life and Ourselves

Why teach drama? Perhaps the most important reason is to discover more about what it is to be a human being, for man, in all his complexity and conflicts, constitutes the central subject matter of drama. Not only does drama mirror the environment, but helps us to surmount it, to grow in sympathy, imagination, and understanding. The very root of the term "drama"—the Greek *dràu*, to act, to do—suggests its possibilities: it is perhaps our most effective and direct means for depicting and working out social conflicts, moral dilemmas, and personal problems without suffering the specific consequences of our actions. The dramatist compels us to empathize with the play's protagonist, to feel his emotions, and to experience his conflicts, yet spares us the actual suffering or indignity his characters must endure. Through tragedy, for example, we are enabled with little pain to learn what life could so painfully teach and are provided a vision of man's endurance and nobility to admire and emulate. Through comedy we can enjoy the purging of laughter, the revelation of "human beings for what they are in contrast to what they profess to be."[3] Well-wrought melodrama, fantasy, or farce can dispel our skepticism, enlarge our imaginations, and take us temporarily out of ourselves. It is not surprising, therefore, that drama has become a recognized tool for therapy. Psychiatrists, for example, have discovered they can use psychodrama as an effective means of enabling patients to gain insight into their past experiences and to prepare them in advance for "roles" they will have to resume in normal life. Sociodramas have been found to perform a similar function for small groups, enabling participants to assume fictional identities while working out conflicts that face them in family and community living.

Drama, then, must be viewed as an essential humanizer, a spur to imagination, to insight, to reflection, and, hopefully, to self-knowledge. Appraising the importance of the dramatic arts, busi-

---

[3] Louis Kronenberger, "Some Prefatory Words on Comedy," in Marvin Felheim (Ed.), *Comedy: Plays, Theory, and Criticism* (New York: Harcourt, 1962), p. 195

ness executive Fletcher B. Coleman, speaking at the dedication of the new dramatic arts building at Illinois Wesleyan University, so eloquently commented:

Are the dramatic arts important? Do they serve the welfare of a free society? I think they do for these reasons.

They hold up the mirror in which society can see itself. They give life, impact, form and substance to the printed word. They stimulate popular support for noble goals; they prick pomposity. They bring light and color and sound and movement to great ideas. They resurrect history and remind us of its lessons.

The dramatic arts rephrase and refreshen a society's ideals and aspirations and remind it of its failure. They help man see himself in an infinite variety of contexts. They bring to life experiences and situations remote in time or distance—they let us share the cultures of other peoples and give us new insight into the many worlds in which we live. They can probe as no other medium can into man's mind, his societies, his institutions. . . .

Yes, we are in a race with Russia, but we are locked in a larger combat . . . This is man's unending war with himself, his higher nature against the base animal, his age-old wavering choice between the bright stars and the black abyss, between his visions and venality.

From Aristophanes and Sophocles to O'Neill and Williams, this is the battle to which the dramatic arts have always been committed.[4]

So committed, the dramatic arts justify, indeed demand, our thoughtful attention.

Drama Redefined for the Twentieth Century

What drama should we teach? To limit our definition of drama to works performed on the legitimate stage is to ignore the revolution in mass media that has permanently altered the character of our lives and introduced "new languages" for us to assimilate.[5] To think only of television and movies as the theater of our day,

---

[4] As cited in *The Milwaukee Journal* (November 5, 1962), p. 22.
[5] See the interesting interpretation of mass media as "new languages" in William D. Boutwell (Ed.), *Using Mass Media in the Schools* (New York: Appleton, 1962).

however, is also to betray an overly limited horizon. We need, therefore, to accept a broadened definition of drama that encompasses its various contemporary manifestations—the theater, television, and motion pictures—and to regard each as fulfilling valuable and complementary functions. That these media compete for attention is surely true, but that one need eclipse another, as some critics have asserted, is to overlook the distinctive features of each. Their very differences suggest a starting point for the teacher of English, who must convey to students the rich possibilities inherent in each medium.

We might discuss, for example, what happens to *Cyrano de Bergerac* or *The Caine Mutiny* when transfered from the stage to the movie lot, from there to the television studio. Father John Culkin has suggested that the emphasis in *The Caine Mutiny* was shifted in every medium in which it was conveyed.[6] In the novel, Willy Keith, the immature sailor who advances to self-knowledge, is clearly the hero. In the film version, with its vaster sets and sweeping camera eye, the United States Navy comes to dominate. In *The Caine Mutiny Court Martial* stage production, Greenwald, the intellectual, emerges as the commanding figure, while in the television performance and for a different kind of audience, Captain Queeg appears in ascendancy. Other works, too, could be similarly analyzed. For example, what happens to a *Pygmalion* when transformed into *My Fair Lady,* and an *Advise and Consent* that moves from the massive novel to the stage to film? By tracing this kind of metamorphosis, we can lead students to see that one medium need not replace or imitate another but rather enhance, complement, and extend.

In widening our definition of drama to include television and film, we must also emphasize the need for attention to drama of all periods. Without in any way undermining the value and appropriateness of those Shakespearean perennials—*Julius Caesar, Macbeth,* and *Hamlet*—we would have to argue that such one-sided attention to a few plays from a single historical period does injustice to the tradition from which they arose and helped to perpetuate. Students need to experience not only tragedy, but also the comedy of manners, farce, melodrama, fantasy, and to discern

[6] Father John M. Culkin, S.J., "Of Media Study and Male Alligators," speech presented at NCTE Convention, Miami, Florida, November 24, 1962.

for themselves the recurring themes, dilemmas, and human needs reflected in drama of every age. They should have the opportunity to discover that an Antigone joins hands across the centuries with a John Proctor of *The Crucible,* choosing personal integrity to a life of dishonor; that a Medea shares the agony of jealousy with a passionately tormented Othello; that a fervid Lavinia in O'Neill's *Mourning Becomes Electra* emulates the vindictiveness and persuasiveness of her Greek counterpart. Neither can we afford to neglect drama of the modern period, even though we must weed out some works too adult in content and appeal. Children of the *Status Seekers* and *Pyramid Climbers,* our students could particularly benefit from evaluating the decisions and characters of Odets' *Golden Boy,* Miller's Willy Loman and Joe Keller, Hellman's Regina of *The Little Foxes,* all of whom place material concerns above ethical ideals. They need, also, to recognize through such plays as *Journey's End, The Diary of Anne Frank,* or *Home of the Brave* the inhumanity man can inflict—and also endure. Indeed, we owe our students the critical and enlightening view of their own world that contemporary drama can uniquely provide.

Objectives for Drama Teaching

How should drama be taught? Having broadened the definition of drama and affirmed its values in the English program, we need to formulate specific objectives that can, in turn, determine the nature and amount of drama emphasis at a particular level. These objectives, to be sure, should be shaped within the larger context of the overall goals for the course and should include emphasis on the development of those skills of thinking and communication for which the total English program assumes major responsibility. Since the concentrated study of drama is best commenced in the ninth grade, the following set of objectives suggests goals that could be reasonably attempted in a four-year high school drama program:

DEVELOP PLEASURE AND SKILL IN READING AND INTERPRETING DRAMA, AND ACQUAINT STUDENTS WITH SOME SIGNIFICANT DRAMATIC WORKS

AND LISTS OF PLAYS FOR FUTURE READING. On the whole, the difficulties entailed in reading plays have probably been overstressed. Most of us can testify that students genuinely enjoy reading plays; and while they have to learn to interpret stage directions and to visualize scenes for themselves, they are rewarded by getting a lot in a short time, by fewer vocabulary problems than often face them in novels or short stories, and by peaks of action in every act. We would have to agree with Dr. Mack that "drama is by far the easiest of all the literary forms to make exciting in the classroom . . . and it is also the most effective introduction to the pleasure of reading literature and the skills involved in enjoying it."[7] We would also have to agree that unless a person learns to enjoy *reading* plays, he will never discover most of the great dramatic works of the past, which are so rarely, if ever, performed in our theaters. For that matter, he will know very little about contemporary drama, since only "smash hits" stay on Broadway and most community theaters limit their production choices to a few well-known works.

ACQUAINT STUDENTS WITH THE DRAMATIC TRADITION, THE ROLE OF DRAMA IN THE HISTORY OF MAN. Since drama is so integral a part of our literary and cultural heritage, the study of its rich and varied history is warranted for its own sake as well as for its value as background against which to appraise the theater of our own day. The program of study, however, should concentrate less on the surface history of drama, more on the causes for the emergence of particular dramatic forms and theaters during different historical periods. For example, students better perceive the intentions of tragedy once they realize that it has been the product not of disillusioned, depressed cultures, but of societies, like those during the times of Sophocles and Shakespeare, that most prized individual resourcefulness, personal freedom, and human happiness. Indeed, as William Van O'Connor suggests, "The Greeks' joyful consciousness of life sharpened their awareness of death. . . . When life lost its zest for the Greeks the tragic muse departed."[8] Similarly the comedy of manners or satirical drama should be seen in the

---

[7] Mack, *loc. cit.*, p. 321.

[8] William Van O'Connor, *Climates of Tragedy* (Baton Rouge: Louisiana State University Press, 1943), pp. 21–22.

context of the Restoration Period, broken loose from a decade of Puritan austerity, or of the eighteenth century, with its surface proprieties, material concerns, and inflexible class distinctions inviting the playwright's mocking or witty scrutiny.

Students should also be led to analyze the ways in which audience expectation and the actual shape of the theater building have affected the form and content of drama. Recent developments in the American theater are illustrative: the present movement away from realism is being accompanied by a parallel movement away from formal staging, confining sets, explicit stage directions. According to Alan Schneider, the Broadway director, probably the most significant—and precedent-setting—dramatic event of our century has been the erection of the Stratford, Ontario, theater building, which discards the proscenium arch and the box seat, with their rigid frame around life, and brings the audience back again into more immediate contact with the play.[9]

In appraising twentieth-century drama, we must also assure students that even though Broadway continues to have both financial and artistic problems, the theater in America is not "dead"! Regional theater groups are developing at an unprecedented rate, as in such communities as Dallas, Houston, San Francisco, and Minneapolis, and our national capital also has its own local theater at last. In 1962, in a major move to strengthen repertory theater in the United States, the Ford Foundation alone dispensed grants totaling $6.1 million to nine theater companies in several regions of the country. Indeed, students should be motivated to share in this widening endeavor to make theater a more vital part of American culture.

DEVELOP CRITICAL STANDARDS AND TASTE IN DRAMA, FILM, TELEVISION. In an outspoken editorial in the *Saturday Review* for November 21, 1959, Norman Cousins accused television of perpetrating a massive fraud—not that publicized by the quiz show scandals, but the incessant exploitation of crime and the glamorizing of violence.[10] He condemned, in particular, the excessive brutality on

---

[9] Alan Schneider, "The Theater in Transition," lecture presented at the University of Wisconsin–Milwaukee Fine Arts Festival, July 1961.

[10] Norman Cousins, "The Real Fraud," *Saturday Review* (November 21, 1959), p. 27.

many programs, their obvious indifference to the fragility and value of human life. His comments could as well apply to many films and stage plays, whose "adult entertainment" formulas or persistent glorification of artificial values make them increasingly undesirable for an immature audience. Our consequent responsibility is clear: to introduce students to publications that discuss and evaluate the arts and to plan assignments that will help to sharpen their critical judgment and taste in drama in all its forms.

One of our first tasks is to make students more articulate about the films and plays they see, to lead them beyond a monosyllabic or cliché reaction. They should therefore be taught to evaluate drama both as an art and as a craft, to perceive it as a medium demanding integrity, self-control, significance of theme and language, discipline of body and voice, fusion of spectacle, technique, and idea. They should further learn to distinguish the artistic and original production from the tawdry or imitative and to recognize the hidden persuaders, the stereotypes, the false view of American life frequently presented. Surely a major directive for our teaching should be that advocated by Gilbert Seldes in his essay "Radio, TV, and the Common Man":[11] to make students realize that more discriminating audiences are needed, and that the American public isn't necessarily getting what it wants, but often what it is too passive to reject.

ENCOURAGE INTEREST IN PLAYGOING AND THE SUPPORT OF COMMUNITY VENTURES IN DRAMA. Playwright Marc Connelly has commented that the United States is the only country that seems not to recognize the importance of theater to "national health."[12] He was, of course, implying a need for subsidies to the arts, especially in these times when production costs have become so prohibitive. His remarks remind us, however, that unless the school stimulates interest in playgoing, both through planned theater trips and regular publicizing of worthwhile community productions, the majority of our students will probably never shift from exclusive patronage of motion pictures and television, the less expensive and

[11] Gilbert Seldes, "Radio, TV, and the Common Man," *Saturday Review Reader No. 3* (New York: 1954), pp. 20–27.
[12] Marc Connelly, lecture at the University of Wisconsin–Milwaukee, July 23, 1962.

more accessible media. In addition, we must do more to encourage young people to support not only the tested and established drama, but the new—and on faith. Professor Ronald Mitchell advises:

> Let us be theatregoers, but not just "fashionable" theatregoers, seeing only those plays "everyone sees." This type of person is proud to wait for his tickets, pay double, and lord it over the person who is still waiting. Everyone then having seen the same thing—there is nothing to talk about![13]

We need to educate students to determine hits for themselves and to resist the blinding power of the critic, whose judgment is surely fallible!

INCREASE STUDENTS' UNDERSTANDING OF THE IMPORTANCE OF DRAMA AS A SOURCE OF INSIGHT INTO PERSONAL AND SOCIAL PROBLEMS. As their tastes refine, young people should also grow in understanding of others and of themselves through the study of drama. George Jean Nathan has well said that great drama speaks to man "in solitude and in crowds"—and we know what he means. We have all been lonely; and thus we can understand Frankie when she says in *Member of the Wedding,* "All people belong to a 'we' except me." And we know that feeling of inadequacy that Biff in *Death of a Salesman* suggests when he exclaims, "I'm a dime a dozen!" Or reading such plays as Elmer Rice's *Adding Machine* or Capek's *R.U.R.* or seeing such films as *On the Beach* and *Judgment at Nuremberg,* we can recognize the forces in our own society that threaten to destroy individuality, thwart creativity, induce disaster. Clearly, the experience of drama compels us to penetrating self-examination, to enlargement of sympathy and tolerance, to awareness of what it is to be a human being.

A Sequential Four-Year Plan for the Teaching of Drama

If these objectives are to be realized, drama must find its place in the total curriculum and be planned for and structured so that skills can be developed in sequence and constant overlapping

[13] Ronald Mitchell, "Learn by Theatregoing," lecture at the Winter Workshop of the English Association of Greater Milwaukee, February 10, 1962.

avoided. One common shortcoming of our present procedures is that we often end up doing practically the same things with a dramatic work on every level and ignoring what the student has done before. There is surely room in our curriculum for handling drama by several methods—as a type or within thematic or chronological units—but surely it should not be handled as a type on all four levels, nor should the history of drama or the Shakespearean theater be discussed in detail every time students start a drama unit. By whatever method of organization, drama should be taught both as literature and as theater, not exclusively as one or the other. A play is language, rhythm, spectacle; and we do it injustice to act as though it were either permanently entombed on its pages or just as ephemeral as the life of a single production.

The study of drama, of course, must directly contribute to the development of the basic communication skills with which the English program is most concerned. The following outline of a four-year program attempts to take into account the kinds of skills needed to read and evaluate drama and to suggest kinds of assignments that simultaneously meet the objectives of the drama program as well as those of the over-all course. (Starred [*] activities are recommended for fast groups primarily or as optional assignments.)

I. English 9 and 10—Introduction to the play as a literary type
   and as a work for the stage
   A. English 9
      1. Type: One-act plays primarily; three-act with capable groups
      2. Skills to be developed
         a. Visualizing setting, character
         b. Interpreting characters from dialogue, action
         c. Detecting foreshadowing, plot unfolding, climax
         d. Identifying theme
         e. Supplying missing segments
         f. Recognizing stage directions
         g. Demonstrating clear, meaningful oral reading
         h. Distinguishing differences in methods of TV, film, theatrical presentations
         i. Applying criteria for evaluating effective TV programs

3. Concepts
   a. Understanding why the author chose the dramatic form
   b. Being aware that plays reflect human life and experience
   c. Recognizing that a play can provide reading pleasure
   d. Being aware that playgoing is both enjoyable and worthwhile
4. Suggested activities
   a. Discussion
      1) Give out a sheet of selected dialogue passages and have students infer from these character traits, problems, social class, and so on. Such an exercise well illustrates what dialogue is used to reveal in a play.
      2) Take a short story and discuss what changes would have to be made to transform it into a play. Emphasize the importance of dialogue to convey characterization and conflict. Identify ways of creating mood by means other than author description.
      3) Inductively arrive at criteria for evaluating TV programs by starting with the question, "What is there to say about a TV program besides 'I liked it' or 'It bored me' "? Try to lead students to an awareness of the three "I's" with which to view and evaluate:

      Determine: *I*ntention —purpose, theme (if any)
      *I*nvention—originality of plot treatment, quality of dialogue, use of setting, special effects
      *I*mpact   —power to move, convince, apply to our own lives

      4) Plan varied experiences to develop skills in oral reading by having students undertake such activities as these:
         a) Select passages to read that introduce a major character and reveal his dominant traits.
         b) Pick out and read only the climax scene and

state why you consider it the turning point of the play.

c) Pick out the *funniest* passage of a play and justify your choice by getting the class to laugh.

d) Choose passages that appeal to a specific emotion—grief, terror, hate, jealousy, and so forth —and try to convey that emotion through skillful reading.

b. Composition

1) Assign various topics for expository writing, 1 to 3 paragraphs in length:

   a) Why I *didn't* like a specific TV program

   b) Reaction to a school play or dramatic assembly

   c) The purpose for a minor character

   *d) Proving why a specific judgment of a character is or is not false (In advance, distribute a sheet of quotations appraising a dramatic character. Have students find proof in the play to support the particular stand they are defending.)

   e) Tracing clues that give away the ending (requires recognition of foreshadowing)

2) Encourage occasional narrative/descriptive writing:

   *a) Dramatize a short ballad or one scene from a longer narrative poem.

   b) Describe the most memorable movie "minute" in your film-viewing experience.

   c) Describe an episode in your life that could well provide the basis for a dramatization.

*c. Individual/Small-group projects

1) Do a collage that suggests the different moods of a play you have read or seen.

2) Read additional one-act plays to discuss individually with the teacher. Possibly prepare an interesting report on one you would like to persuade others in the class to read.

3) Report on a community play you have seen and that you considered particularly effective.

4) Actually dramatize a short episode out of your own life or that of a person you have known closely.

B. English 10

1. Type: Three-act plays primarily; introduction to Shakespeare

2. Skills to be developed
   a. Review of skills from English 9
   b. Identifying mood and tone
   c. Reading a Shakespearean play
      1) Reading blank verse
      2) Adjusting to Elizabethan theater conventions: soliloquies, asides, absence of stage directions, archaic expressions, allusions, metaphor
   d. Discussing criteria for evaluating effective films
   e. Evaluating view of life given in some current TV or movie productions (especially view of family)

3. Concepts
   a. Review of concepts from English 9
   b. Awareness of historical development of drama from Age of Sophocles to Age of Elizabeth
   c. Discovering universality of Shakespeare, pertinence of ideas to our own lives

4. Suggested activities
   a. Discussion
      1) Provide and discuss a list of vocabulary words that suggest character traits—diabolical, furtive, pert, impudent, and so on.
      Then apply to various characters, having students justify their judgments with textual proofs. A list of verbs could be used similarly and applied to character actions.
      2) Do occasional paraphrasing to check on meaning of selected passages—and not only from Shakespearean plays.
      3) Discuss popular "family," western, or nature programs on TV. Identify common characteristics in these programs and evaluate to what extent they represent realistic life situations.[14]

[14] See Neil Postman, *Television and the Teaching of English* (New York: Appleton, 1961), pp. 105–107.

4) Present Shakespeare within the context of his times. Find out what students already know and work from there. Discuss ways in which the stage and audience would affect the kind of play that could be presented. Identify some major differences in English language usage in Shakespeare's time and ours and different theatrical conventions. Discuss the term "Renaissance" and how Shakespeare fits into the movement.

5) Drawing particularly from *Julius Caesar*, identify ideas that continue to have pertinence for our time, such as the difficulty of balancing personal and public loyalties, feeling and reason, practical goals with ideals.[15]

b. Composition
1) Have students describe an idea for a TV show that they think would attract a large audience, but that, to their knowledge, has never been tried.

2) Analyze:
a) Nature of conflict in a play—inward, outward
b) What the play has to say to us today
*c) Effect of a particular theater building and audience expectation on dramatic structure and content

3) Compare two characters within the same play, emphasizing a dominant trait they share in common. Use proofs from the text to support your comparison.

*4) Creative writing:
a) Write dialogues revealing character traits or attitudes (for example, arrogance, uncertainty, jealousy). Punctuate and paragraph conversation accurately and work for creating convincing and natural dialogue.
b) Rewrite the ending of a play to fit another logical interpretation.
c) Dramatize an episode that will arouse our indignation.

---

[15] See Mack, *loc. cit.,* pp. 320–336, and Robert Ornstein, *Shakespeare in the Classroom* (Urbana, Illinois: Educational Illustrators, 1960).

         d) Write stage directions for a play that lacks them (especially Shakespearean).

*c. Individual/Small-group projects

    1) Prepare bulletin boards on such subjects as these: drama of different periods; worthwhile current movies and TV productions; ideas suggested by *Scholastic* or *Literary Cavalcade* material, on personalities that have dominated the stage, and so on.

    2) Prepare tape recordings of significant episodes from plays studied.

    3) Design a model set or prepare a series of set sketches for a play studied in class or read individually. Adhere closely to directions given in the play and try to capture the essential mood and period.

    4) Present original oral topics on aspects of dramatic history, A Visit to the Annual Festival of Dionysus, The Revival of Drama in the Middle Ages, The Debate over Shakespeare's Identity. Avoid the flat encyclopedia recital!

II. English 11 and 12—Evaluation and extended reading of drama

A. English 11

    1. Type: Three-act plays primarily: American drama, Shakespearean

    2. Skills to be developed

        a. Understanding irony, symbolism, and implication

        b. justification of outcomes

        c. Independent interpretation of plays

        d. Relating drama to larger themes, Puritanism, individualism, and so forth

        e. Applying criteria to the evaluation of a play, movie, or TV production

        f. Revealing drama as an exposition of significant ideas

    3. Concepts

        a. Insight about the place of drama in American life and literature

        b. Familiarity with major American playwrights and significant developments in American drama

        c. Introduction to idea of tragedy

    d. Evaluation of the view of American life commonly represented on TV and in films

    e. Developing empathy with characters

4. Suggested activities

    a. Discussion

       1) Acquaint students with major American dramatists, both by studying them individually and by using reading lists. Have students as a class compile their own annotated list of recommended plays.

       2) Discuss the impression that American films and TV convey to others, especially people abroad. To what extent is this view of American life convincing, real, precise? Identify productions that have given a valid or a deceptive view.

       3) Try role playing, in which students assume the roles of characters in a play and speak in justification of some action or conduct in the play.

       4) Have students select a TV program, film, or play and discuss how creative thinking could give it more richness, meaning, significance.

       5) Discuss how ideas in drama apply to contemporary situations. Explore such issues, for example, as what *Inherit the Wind* has to say about freedom of thought in a democracy, how *The Crucible* reflects on twentieth-century "witch-hunting," what *Point of No Return* suggests about the role of the individual in big business, and so on.

       6) Debate the responsibility of the protagonist for his actions: Is Macbeth a free agent or merely a pawn of fate? Is Captain de Vere justified in applying the death penalty to Billy Budd? Is Joe Keller of *All My Sons* to be condemned for thinking first of his family's well-being?

       7) Do oral paraphrases of difficult or especially significant passages.

    b. Composition

       1) Analysis:

          a) Consistency and logic of ending, fate of protagonist

          b) Characters as types, representations

c) Playwright's method of developing his theme

d) Some aspect of style: symbolism, irony, and so forth.

e) Critical analysis of play read independently

2) Evaluate a movie, play, or TV production according to given criteria.

3) Compare handling of theme, character, or conflict in two different plays.

*4) Creative writing:

   a) Dramatize a short story or scene from a novel or biography.

   b) Attempt a parody of a selected scene. Study the style of the original carefully.

   c) Attempt an original scene suggested by a play and in the style of the original.

*c. Individual/Small-group activities

1) Present a well-planned floor talk on a major American play.

2) Organize a panel discussion on a significant TV production, such as a Hallmark Theater special.

3) Attend special after-school sessions to hear special play recordings or tapes which cannot be fitted into the regular class program.

B. English 12

1. Type: Three-act plays primarily: Greek, Shakespearean, modern

2. Skills to be developed

   a. Review of techniques for evaluating plays, movies, TV productions

   b. Evaluating reviews of mass media in periodicals; distinguishing responsible and irresponsible reviewing

  *c. Recognizing specific dramatic genres—comedy of manners, tragedy, melodrama, satire

  *d. Comparing drama of different historical periods, for example, Greek, Shakespearean, modern tragedy

3. Concepts

   a. Acquaintance with some key theatrical personalities of past and present times

   b. Awareness of major English and world dramatists to explore for future reading

   c. Enlightenment on recent developments in drama in the local community

*d. Insight into the place of drama, TV, film in contemporary life and recent developments in each media

*e. Deepened insight into the concept of tragedy, its origins and development to modern times

*f. Knowledge of key periodicals dealing with evaluation, discussion of mass media, theater

4. Suggested activities

  a. Discussion

    1) Hold round-table talks on plays that students have individually read. These could be structured around a theme, for example, "Facing Reality"— or else each student could be asked to discuss a play he has most enjoyed, pointedly commenting on (a) the play's central conflict, (b) theme(s) the author has directly expressed or suggested, (c) key characters and the change in them throughout the play, (d) a key scene, in which the central character most reveals himself, (e) an estimate of whether the play provides a significant dramatic experience.

    2) Have occasional preplanned ten to fifteen-minute discussions on "What's New on Broadway." Encourage students to bring in newspaper and magazine articles on dramatic personalities and writers. Also use "What's New in TV, in Films."

    3) Discuss characteristics of effective reviews as well as of irresponsible, destructive reviewing. Encourage comparison of reviews from several sources as well as confidence in one's own judgment.

    4) Discuss imaginative and unimaginative TV productions. Encourage a discussion about whether TV, movies, or theater is living up to its public responsibility. Stimulate thinking about the problems of the script writer today and the sponsor's potentially stifling power.

    5) Use various essays and articles that discuss modern drama and mass media. Identify some of the problems faced by drama today—the plight of Broadway, the subsidiary position of drama in American culture.

    6) Have panel presentations on important books on

theatrical personalities or historical developments, *Act One, Prince of Players, Gertrude Lawrence as Mrs. A,* and so on.

b. Composition

 1) Analyze:

  a) Use of minor characters as foils, contrast, "lenses"

  b) Moral dilemmas or themes, integrity, love, social protest, illusion/reality

  c) Play's significance for revealing the values and norms of an age

  d) The contributions of an individual to the theater—or price of success as revealed in a significant biography

  e) The role of drama in our own community, in American life

 2) Compare/contrast:

  a) Author's handling of the same theme in two different plays

  b) Dramatic techniques and conventions of different periods

  *c) Play "Twins," for example, *Electra, Mourning Becomes Electra; Hamlet, Winterset*

  *d) Play with its film or TV counterpart

  *e) Various reviews of the same play

 3) Evaluate:

  a) A play's unity, integrity, effectiveness

  b) A play as dramatic experience: staging, impact, actors' response to challenge of the role

  *c) Extent to which a particular play fulfills intentions of its type: satire, tragedy, comedy, and so on

 *4) Creative writing

  a) Write an original scene suggested by a play, Ophelia's soliloquy, Saint Joan in prison, and so forth, in style of original

  b) Write a dramatic sketch suggested by a news story, choosing one with definite conflict

c. Individual/Small-group projects

 1) Keep journals of individual play-reading, especially noting theme and resolution of conflict.

2) Report on major theatrical personalities, books revealing them.

*3) Explore some developments in the *avant-garde* or European theater, the theater of the "absurd," Bertolt Brecht Company in East Germany.

III. Activities for all levels

A. Encourage attendance at and follow-up discussion of school plays.

B. Plan occasional field trips to community plays. Publicize and discuss plays that students could get to; take advantage of the many opportunities for student rates.

C. Expand filmstrip library, such as those on the Shakespearean theater. Allocate important films to various levels and keep a departmental file on worthwhile films, records, filmstrips, tapes.

D. Use recorded scenes of plays not directly studied, but which illustrate emphasized concepts.

E. Try to have at least one drama-oriented bulletin board display during the year.

Special Problems in Drama Teaching

Unless a teacher plans wisely, drama study can easily become overextended and tedious. Nothing can be more depressing, for example, for both teacher and students than belaboring a play week after week until it has lost all vitality or appeal. Avoidance of both superficiality and surfeit thus requires a skillful varying of approaches and emphases. Although more experimentation is surely needed to illuminate the best approaches for teaching drama, a few persisting problems must be resolved by drawing on common sense and experience.

Method of Discussion

Should a play be discussed in its entirety or piece by piece? Perhaps the best answer is a compromise: suit the method to the play. A Shakespearean drama, by virtue of length and complexity, usually requires a section-by-section approach. Students first starting to read three-act plays probably also need to be assigned individual scenes or acts at a time. Yet in both instances the sections must ultimately be put together more meaningfully to illuminate the whole. Students in the junior and senior years, when studying non-Shakespearean plays, should more and more be required to have read the entire work prior to initial discussion, then to go back for a second and, hopefully, a third rereading and careful analysis of selected sections. This method has the advantage of putting greater responsibility on the student for drawing his own conclusions and seeing the play as an artistic unit and avoids the problem of holding all students to specific page limits. Rather than straining to make a single play yield all of its riches, the high school teacher is perhaps wiser to distribute emphasis, letting one play reveal the possibilities of dialogue, another the force of ideas, yet another the use of irony, contrast, or symbolism. Ultimately the skills emphasized in one should transfer to and illuminate the reading of other plays. Above all, students must be encouraged to read widely, even at the expense of some detail, if teachers are to expect them to acquire an interest and skill in an area in which they usually have far too few experiences.

Oral Reading or Dramatizing of Play Scenes

We all know what happens when parts are assigned and dead-pan Jane runs monotone through every passage, despite prepreparation. We also know that students are occasionally forced to hear a scene they have carefully read on their own massacred by poor classroom readers, then played on record, and finally dissected endlessly in class until it has lost all freshness. Again a compromise must be made so that students have opportunities to cultivate skills in oral reading without killing all pleasure for the others in the class. The best solution, perhaps, is to make very specific assignments in oral reading: students select and read key scenes, passages revealing character, or moments of climax—all of which require careful planning, yet which are brief enough to retain classroom interest. Also, rather than stressing the same scenes again and again, teachers should use recordings for plays beyond the difficulty of student readers but not duplicate what has already been sufficiently handled.

The Best Use of Audio-Visual Aids

Audio-visual aids should fulfill the promise of their name—to serve as aids and enrichment rather than replacements for the original work. Too often records and films totally supplant rather than supplement the dramatic experience. More use, then, should be made of films and records to motivate study, to suggest an approach for reading, possibly to present a different interpretation. In addition, we should make more use of records of plays that have not been directly studied, so that students learn to listen more carefully, to transfer skills acquired in the study of one work to the interpretation of another. More time should also be given to evaluating film and record interpretations—in appraising characterization, ensemble work, total effectiveness. Too often we use records or films just to fill up time or merely entertain, obviating their educational values. If students consider visual aids as recreation alone, we know we need to re-evaluate the use we are making of them.

Special Techniques in Teaching a Shakespearean Play

Enobarbus' words in praise of Cleopatra—"Age cannot wither her, nor custom stale her infinite variety"—apply to Shakespeare's works as well. W. H. Auden has noted that every one of Shakespeare's works is unique so that the reader must experience them all to get a proper idea of the Shakespearean world. However, he also comments that "no one is less a writer for the young, for persons, that is, under the age of thirty."[16] Difficult, mature, demanding—Shakespearean drama calls upon the full resources of a teacher's creativity, persuasiveness, and careful planning. In particular, the classroom teacher must overcome the problems of attention, of verse, of emphasis.

THE PROBLEM OF ATTENTION. While Shakespeare fills his plays with considerable attractions for the "groundlings"—murders, quarrels, suicides, duelings, insanity, slapstick comedy, patriotic fervor, and spectacle—his essential appeal is to the ear, to the mind, to refined

16 W. H. Auden, "Three Memoranda on the New Arden Shakespeare," *The Mid-Century*, No. 21 (January 1961), 3.

perception. The problem of attention, then, is basically that of luring students to come to grips with a literature requiring mature thought, concentration, and insight. "Well digested in the scenes, set down with as much modesty as cunning," his plays call for an ear attuned to subtlety, paradox, ambiguity. In the first place, students must learn that a play can be enjoyable even when the plot is know in advance. Like more sophisticated members of the Greek or Elizabethan audience, they must learn to anticipate and enjoy the unique treatment of a previously worked subject and to let language more than spectacle and action work upon their imaginations and emotions. Robert Ornstein has well observed that "the relatively bare Elizabethan stage was perfectly suited to the drama of great personalities which Shakespeare created," for his heroic characters dwarfed their background and shaped their worlds and their own destinies.[17] The focus of attention must thus be upon the inner conflicts with which his characters struggle and the consequences of their actions—and especially upon the language they use to define these conflicts. Thus viewed, Shakespeare's characters take on universal significance, for they wrestle with and clarify problems men of all periods have struggled to resolve.

THE PROBLEM OF VERSE. Besides demonstrating maturity and sensitivity, students reading Shakespeare must develop specific skills for handling poetic drama. T. S. Eliot, in "The Three Voices of Poetry," well reminds us that the poetic line in drama bears the weight of three responsibilities: conveying plot and character while retaining its poetic form.[18] Students must thus acquire a series of reading skills that work together. First they must learn to read blank verse without halting at the end of each line or being trapped by occasional archaic expressions or extended figures of speech. Then they must learn to see how specific passages reflect the character traits of the speaker. For example, they should come to detect how Polonius' mishandling of language reflects his mismanagement of human affairs, or how Laertes betrays a strain of superficiality by indulging in florid bombast. They should also become skilled enough to discern how Hamlet's shifts from introspection and depression to passionate anger with himself and the world

[17] Ornstein, *op cit.*, pp. 5–6.
[18] T. S. Eliot, *On Poetry and Poets* (New York: Farrar, Straus, 1957), pp. 96–112.

are precisely reflected by the variety of his speech, the flavor of his rhetoric. Unless they see language as mirroring essential character traits, they will miss much of the impact of the Shakespearean line. Students must also discover how richly Shakespeare uses imagery to enforce mood and idea. For example, how repeatedly throughout the history plays he apostrophizes sleep and thereby emphasizes the wearying responsibility of a king upon whose head "uneasy" lies the crown. Using the images of disease, plague, disruption, insanity, and revolt in *Julius Caesar, Macbeth, Hamlet,* and *Lear,* Shakespeare succeeds in conveying the very atmosphere of states whose social organization has suffered violent change and upheaval. John Ciardi also reminds us that Shakespeare's verse needs to be studied for its own sake as poetry, particularly for its precise word choice, skillfully suggestive overtones, unified construction.[19] Rather than wearying every line with exhausting interpretation, however, we need to vary discussion procedures, letting one passage, for example, serve as a reflection of an inner state of mind, another as revealing specific character traits, yet another to show contrast and irony. Often it may be necessary to concentrate on plot events alone, for verse analysis must never become so laborious that students feel they are making no headway in the play.

THE PROBLEM OF EMPHASIS. Those who have taught Shakespeare over a period of years recognize how rewarding recurrent experiences have proven to be, for each rereading with different classes brings new insights and values. On the other hand, how dangerous it is to assume that every student will gain as much from a first contact! The solution, then, is to suggest, not exhaust, the possibilities of a Shakespearean play, to make it rewarding enough that a student will want of his own accord to return to it for rereading or to go out of his way to attend an actual performance. Most teachers spend perhaps too much time on a single play and do too much for the students, who thus fail to acquire the skills necessary for independent exploration in other Shakespearean works. Three to four weeks are ample time for most works used in high school and is actually all that can be reasonably afforded in the already overcrowded English program. However, since the major themes of

[19] John Ciardi, *How Does a Poem Mean?* (Boston: Houghton Mifflin, 1959), p. 785.

Shakespeare's plays recur in literature of all periods, the teacher has the opportunity frequently to refer back to the works studied earlier and thus revive their significance and applicability. Not without warrant has it been said Shakespeare's plays were "for all time."

Integrating Drama in a Thematic Unit

Perhaps one of the reasons for the persistent neglect of drama has been that it has been treated too exclusively as a literary type rather than worked into thematic units throughout the year. The following unit, "Facing Reality," which draws upon novels, drama, poetry, and essays, is illustrative of the kind of thematic unit in which drama can be particularly well incorporated and thereby linked more closely to other literary forms. However, while the theme is valuable for providing a method of organization and a center for discussion, it must never be used to force an unnatural interpretation on a piece of literature or restrain the class from experiencing other values in a particular work.

FACING REALITY

Unit for Grade 12, Time: About 6 weeks

I. Rationale

 One of the essential characteristics of the mature man should be the capacity to appraise realistically his own strengths and shortcomings and to shape his goals in the light of that knowledge. This unit therefore focuses on literature (especially short stories and plays) in which the contrast can be drawn between individuals who realistically resolve their conflicts and those who resort instead to illusion, cruelty, violence, or revenge rather than face up to the truth about themselves or a specific situation. To be sure, a major objective must be to teach students to avoid applying automatic black-and-white judgments to people's behavior. Indeed, few of us "face reality" all the time nor is it always actually desirable. In addition, the fact that an individual recognizes the realities of a particular situation doesn't necessarily mean that he can therefore go ahead successfully to solve an existing problem or that a satisfactory solution is even possible. The major value of the unit therefore lies in its emphasis on the importance of acquiring self-knowledge as well as sympathetic tolerance for the plight of those incapable of relying solely on their own inner strength.

II. Objectives
   A. To illuminate how difficult it is for any of us to "face reality" all the time and to identify the major methods and reasons for avoiding reality.
   B. To widen contact with and to sharpen skills in reading and evaluating short stories, poems, plays.
   C. To encourage self-analysis, especially of one's own patterns of thinking and rationalizing.

III. Suggested activities
   A. Use such essays as Robinson's "Four Kinds of Thinking" or Bettelheim's "The Ignored Lesson of Anne Frank," or a play such as Miller's *All My Sons* or Williams' *The Glass Menagerie* to launch the unit. Discuss the expression "facing reality," making clear how difficult "facing reality" can be, especially when alternatives are equally unpleasant.
   B. Identify ways in which people use language to conceal unpleasant conditions or undesirable status designations— euphemisms, big words, exaggerations, etc. Also illustrate ways in which language is used as a cover-up, a front, for the person's real feelings or character. Readings on semantics, such as Hayakawa's "How Words Change Our Lives," could well be incorporated here.
   C. Use a series of selections that illustrate admirable resolution of problems or realistic adjustments to adverse situations: Conrad's "The Secret Sharer," Faulkner's "Barn Burning," Tennyson's "Ulysses," Lizette Reese's "Tears," Byron's "Prisoner of Chillon," Walsh's "The Quiet Man."
   D. Use selections that build students' tolerance for others despite their shortcomings. Stress that failure to face reality should not brand a character as totally weak or unadmirable. Examples: Robert in O'Neill's *Beyond the Horizon*, Warburton in Maugham's "The Outstation," Molly in Steinbeck's "Molly Morgan." Indeed, the maintenance of an illusion very often enables some individuals to act more surely and nobly.

E. Illuminate some of the great moral dilemmas of life revealed in literature, dilemmas that force the protagonist to decisions where the alternatives are almost equally unacceptable: the dilemmas of tragic characters, such as Oedipus and Antigone; the choice between conformity or death of Nunez in H. G. Wells's "Country of the Blind"; discovering that it may be wrong to tell the truth, as in Ibsen's *The Wild Duck.*

F. Discuss forms of evasion or inflexibility that prove destructive or inhuman, as in such selections as Cather's "Paul's Case," Miller's *All My Sons* or *Death of a Salesman,* Boulle's *The Bridge over the River Kwai,* Browning's "My Last Duchess," Lanier's "The Revenge of Hamish."

G. Give out a reading list and ask students to do extended reading of plays and short stories, keeping journal annotations that show they have caught the theme, major conflicts, and resolutions—and have also done some personal reflecting. Keep sets of *Literary Cavalcade* and play anthologies in the room, and provide occasional periods for reading and individual conferences.

H. Have students write an essay that requires self-analysis, such as the following:
1. Often we say we have "good" reasons for holding an attitude or behaving in some way. Actually we are rationalizing or making excuses instead. Discuss an attitude or opinion you hold and compare your "good" with your "real" reasons for thinking as you do.
2. Discuss "The Necessity for White Lies"—or "All Men Need Illusions."
3. Present an experience of your own in which you show a change of attitude: to girls or to dancing; to a subject you feared; to a vacation in the country; to a specific relative or acquaintance.
4. Everyone has those famous "pet peeves." Write down your own. Then select one and discuss how you could intelligently overcome it or reduce its irritating effects.

I. Assign writing which calls for analysis of the way characters in literature or mass media productions "face reality":
1. Select and analyze a recent film, play, or TV production that illustrated either the effective or the ineffective handling of a problem in human relations or that re-

vealed that a central character was—or was not—capable of facing reality. Although you must give an overview of the action spend little time on plot telling.

2. Compare two or three characters who evade reality by depending on illusion. Explain the progress of the illusion, whether it gets destroyed, and the effects of the destruction or maintenance of this illusion.

J. Have round-table talks on plays that students have read. Have students comment briefly on a play they have most enjoyed reading on their own. They should bring out (1) the play's central conflict, (2) key characters and their way of handling the conflict, (3) theme(s), which the author has directly expressed or suggested, and (4) an estimate of the play's over-all impact and significance.

K. Hold a "key scene" reading session, in which students work in small groups to identify a major scene, prepare it for interpretive reading, and present it to the rest of the class. These scenes should be taken from plays read individually rather than studied by the entire group. Each presentation should occupy no more than fifteen minutes of a class period.

L. Possibly lead from this unit into two or three weeks' work on narrative and descriptive writing, drawing on knowledge of techniques illustrated especially in the short-story readings.

IV. Evaluation

A. Use essay questions on topics such as these:

1. Drawing upon examples from at least three selections we have studied, discuss some *values* of illusions—what they contribute to the beauty, security, or motivation of individuals.

2. Discuss how overemphasis on material wealth or social class leads to inhuman behavior by a character in a story, a poem, and a play we have read.

3. How would you answer a person who condemned Robert Mayo of *Beyond the Horizon* as a weak, lazy man who should have settled down to being a competent farmer?

B. Check journal annotations, especially for depth of observation and choice of selections for extended reading.

C. Have students prepare an annotated list of recommended plays for future classes.

Restoring Drama to the Center of the Stage

The responsibility for developing a rich and meaningful drama program falls, of course, on already overburdened English teachers, who may also have to overcome the handicap of poor background preparation. Taking more courses in drama is surely only a partial solution, for the love of drama can be transmitted only by teachers who genuinely value reading plays, regularly attending theatrical productions, reading periodicals dealing with the dramatic arts, seeing effective TV and film productions, and following the development of drama in all its forms within our American culture and in other countries of the world. Only through such enthusiastic and dedicated persons can drama be withdrawn from the wings and restored to the center of the classroom stage, to share a leading role with the other dominant forms of our literary tradition.

SELECTED REFERENCES (*Outstanding)

Bentley, Eric, *In Search of Theater* (New York: Vintage Books, 1954).

———, *The Playwright as Thinker* (New York: Meridian, 1955).

Bradley, A. C., *Shakespearean Tragedy* (New York: St. Martin's, 1904).

Brustein, Robert, "Repertory Fever," *Harper's*, December 1960, pp. 44–51.

Downer, Alan S., *Fifty Years of American Drama* (Chicago: Regnery, 1951).

*Esslin, Martin, *The Theatre of the Absurd* (New York: Doubleday Anchor Books, 1961).

Fergusson, Francis, *The Idea of a Theater* (New York: Doubleday Anchor Books, 1955).

Freedley, George, and John A. Reeves, *A History of the Theatre* (New York: Crown, 1943).

Gassner, John, *Producing the Play* (New York: Holt, Rinehart and Winston, 1942).

*Granville-Barker, Harley, *Prefaces to Shakespeare* (2 vols.; Princeton, N.J.: Princeton University Press, 1927–1946).

Harbage, Alfred, *Shakespeare's Audience* (New York: Columbia University Press, 1941).

Harbrace Drama Sourcebooks:

Felheim, Marvin (Ed.), *Comedy: Plays, Theory, and Criticism,* 1961.

Harrison, G. B., *Julius Caesar in Shakespeare, Shaw and the Ancients,* 1961.

Kernan, Alvin B., *Modern Satire,* 1962.

Levin, Richard (Ed.), *Tragedy: Plays, Theory, and Criticism,* 1961.

Knight, Arthur, *The Liveliest Art: A Panoramic History of the Movies* (New York: Macmillan, 1957).

*Lerner, Max, "The Arts and Popular Culture" in *America as a Civilization* (New York: Simon and Schuster, 1957), Chap. 11.

*McCarthy, Mary, "Realism in the American Theater," *Harper's,* July 1961, pp. 45–52.

———, "General MacBeth," *Harper's,* June 1962, pp. 35–39.

*MacIver, R. M. (Ed.) *Great Moral Dilemmas in Literature: Past and Present* (New York: Harper & Row, 1956).

Roberts, Vera Mowry, *On Stage: A History of Theater* (New York: Harper & Row, 1962).

Schramm, Wilbur, *et al.,* *Television in the Lives of Our Children* (Stanford, Calif.: Stanford University Press, 1961).

Seldes, Gilbert, *The Public Arts* (New York: Simon and Schuster, 1956).

*Sewall, Richard B., *The Vision of Tragedy* (New Haven, Conn.: Yale University Press, 1959).

Simonson, Lee, *The Stage Is Set* (New York: Dover, 1946).

Wilson, John Dover, *Life in Shakespeare's England* (Baltimore: Penguin, 1959).

Sources Pertaining to Teaching of Drama

Aggertt, Otis J., and Elbert R. Bowen, *Communicative Reading* (New York: Macmillan, 1956).

Boutwell, William D., *Using Mass Media in the Schools* (New York: Appleton, 1962).

College English, Volume XXIII, April 1962. Entire issue on drama.

Loban, Walter, Margaret Ryan, James R. Squire, "Literature: Drama and Poetry," in *Teaching Language and Literature* (New York: Harcourt, 1961), Chap. 7.

*Mack, Maynard, "Teaching Drama: *Julius Caesar*," in Edward J. Gordon and Edward S. Noyes (Eds.), *Essays on the Teaching of English* (New York: Appleton, 1960), Chap. 17.

Mersand, Joseph, *et al.*, *Guide to Play Selection* (2d ed.; Appleton, 1958). NCTE publication.

NCTE Studies in the Mass Media, 508 South Sixth St., Champaign, Ill. Eight issues a year.

Ong, Walter J., "Wired for Sound: Teaching, Communications, and Technological Culture," *College English*, Vol. XXI, No. 5, February 1960, 245–251.

*Ornstein, Robert, *Shakespeare in the Classroom* (Urbana, Ill.: Educational Illustrators, 1960). NCTE publication.

Postman, Neil, *Television and the Teaching of English* (New York: Appleton, 1961). NCTE publication.

SELECTED MODERN PLAYS FOR CLASS USE

Grade 9

One-act plays

The Valiant, Holworthy Hall and Robert Middlemas
A Shipment of Mute Fate, Les Crutchfield
Trifles, Susan Glaspell
The Devil and Daniel Webster, Stephen Vincent Benét
The Will, James M. Barrie
Two Crooks and a Lady, Eugene Pillot
Beauty and the Jacobin, Booth Tarkington
Exchange, Althea Thurston
The Stolen Prince, Don Totherch
The Brink of Silence, Esther Galbraith
Spreading the News, Lady Gregory

TV and radio plays

The Weans, Robert Nathan
Invasion from Mars, H. G. Wells

Visit from a Small Planet, Gore Vidal
Out of Control, William Bruckner

Three-act plays

I Remember Mama, John Van Druten
The Barretts of Wimpole Street, Rudolf Besier
Life with Father, Howard Lindsay and Russell Crouse
The King and I, Richard Rodgers and Oscar Hammerstein II
The Hasty Heart, John Patrick
Abe Lincoln in Illinois, Robert Sherwood

Grade 10

The Miracle Worker, William Gibson
Desperate Hours, Joseph Hayes
Yellow Jack, Sidney Howard
The Admirable Crichton, James M. Barrie
Journey's End, R. C. Sherriff
The Winslow Boy, Terence Rattigan
Ah, Wilderness!, Eugene O'Neill
Teahouse of the August Moon, John Patrick and Vern Sneider
Ten Little Indians, Agatha Christie
A Majority of One, Leonard Spigelgass
Watch on the Rhine, Lillian Hellman
Justice, John Galsworthy
Romanov and Juliet, Peter Ustinov

Grade 11

The Emperor Jones, Eugene O'Neill
The Adding Machine, Street Scene, Elmer Rice
Inherit the Wind, Lawrence and Lee
The Glass Menagerie, Tennessee Williams
The Green Pastures, Marc Connelly
The Little Foxes, Lillian Hellman
Point of No Return, J. P. Marquand
A Raisin in the Sun, Lorraine Hansberry
The Silver Cord, Sidney Howard
Death Takes a Holiday, Walter Ferris
A Bell for Adano, Paul Osborn
Our Town, Thornton Wilder
All My Sons, The Crucible, Arthur Miller

Of Mice and Men, John Steinbeck
The Time of Your Life, William Saroyan
What Price Glory?, Maxwell Anderson and Laurence Stallings
State of the Union, Howard Lindsay and Russell Crouse
Time Limit, Harry Denker and Ralph Berkey
Billy Budd, Louis Coxe and Robert Chapman
The Andersonville Trial, Saul Levitt
The Caine Mutiny Court Martial, Herman Wouk
High Tor, Both Your Houses, Maxwell Anderson

Grade 12

Victoria Regina, Laurence Housman
Cyrano de Bergerac, Edmond Rostand
A Doll's House, The Wild Duck, An Enemy of the People, Henrik
    Ibsen
Pygmalion, Caesar and Cleopatra, Saint Joan, Major Barbara,
    G. B. Shaw
The Cherry Orchard, Anton Chekhov
The Corn Is Green, Emlyn Williams
Death of a Salesman, Arthur Miller
Medea, Robinson Jeffers
Darkness at Noon, Sidney Kingsley
The Member of the Wedding, Carson McCullers
Winterset, Elizabeth the Queen, Mary of Scotland, Maxwell Ander-
    son
A Man for All Seasons, Robert Bolt
The Skin of Our Teeth, Thornton Wilder
The Mad Woman of Chaillot, Jean Giraudoux
The Importance of Being Earnest, Oscar Wilde
R. U. R., Karel Capek
Murder in the Cathedral, T. S. Eliot
Blood Wedding, Federico Garcia Lorca
Beyond the Horizon, The Hairy Ape, Mourning Becomes Electra,
    Eugene O'Neill
The Second Mrs. Tanqueray, Arthur W. Pinero
The Circle, Somerset Maugham
J. B., Archibald MacLeish
The Visit, Friedrich Duerrenmatt
Dear Brutus, J. M. Barrie

ORGANIZING
THE PROGRAM
IN
LITERATURE

THE PROBLEM OF organizing instruction is a major one, especially for the new teacher. Having prepared and taught one unit, perhaps, or having taught for a few weeks under the guidance of the directing teacher during a term of student teaching, the beginning teacher that first September faces the rather terrifying prospect of preparing five or six fifty or fifty-five minute classes every day, five days a week, for some forty weeks! Of course, the problem is not only the beginning teacher's. For years, conferences and workshops of English teachers have resounded with arguments about whether or not to teach certain "classics," about whether to organize the literature program by types, by themes or topics, or by chronological survey. There is no magic inherent in any plan of organization; none can offer a sixty-day guaranty of success. The important outcomes discussed in the first chapter of this book can be sought quite successfully through various plans of organization, and the most successful junior and senior high school literature programs probably are eclectic in their basis. On the Day of Judgment, no doubt, teachers of literature will be adjudged the quick and the dull without regard to their scheme of organization. Each of the major plans has advantages and disadvantages; these are discussed in the remainder of this section.

Ways of Organizing the Literature Program

Following an Anthology

Organizing the literature program according to an anthology may seem too obvious to list, but any honest analysis of classroom practice must place this method of organization first in frequency. In many English classrooms, the literature anthology *is* the program in literature. It would be easy to grow cynical about this, and to place the blame for unimpressive results in the high school literature program on unimaginative plodding through anthologies. Some blame may be justified. There are those teachers who use the anthology as a convenient excuse for not doing any of their own planning or organizing. Yet in some schools the crowded curriculum in English and the excessive teacher loads make any other course of action virtually impossible. Quite possibly, too, the teacher who "teaches" an anthology well may be achieving much more important results than the teacher whose program is completely haphazard, or permits only on Fridays periods of "free reading" or unguided browsing in the library.

Though there seems little justification for uncritical use of anthologies or for making them the complete curriculum in literature, still they are valuable, and indeed indispensable, aids in teaching literature—no matter what the basic scheme of organization may be. The anthology, after all, brings together a collection of selections, many of which would not be available otherwise. Many of these are good, appropriate choices for the particular grade level. Most high school graduates can remember from their anthologies at least some selections they keenly enjoyed. Furthermore, many teachers find the study questions, suggested activities, and other editorial material valuable. To many, the anthology represents secure, respectable, comfortable routine.

Yet there is an inherent crippling if the anthology becomes the complete teaching program—as may be the practice in some schools. The limitations of any anthology or series of anthologies should be considered. First, many selections will be inappropriate for any given class. Anthologies are designed for use on a national basis and thus are geared to theoretical grade levels; the anthology that is good for one tenth grade may not be for another. Second, selections often are included merely by tradition—they have always been in anthologies and have become trademarks. There has been, for example, a tradition among publishers—no longer invariably followed—that a tenth-grade anthology that does not include *Julius Caesar* cannot be sold. Selections for eleventh- and twelfth-grade anthologies, especially, are often chosen because they "represent" a certain writer or fit into the chronological development of English or American literature, no matter what their literary merit or appeal for teen-agers. Also, selections taken from long works are likely to be garbled and of little value out of their complete context, and limitations of space in the anthology usually prohibit inclusion of novels or full-length biographies or nonfiction pieces in the upper-year books. Thus the anthology gives the student little or no training in reading these forms.

Another important drawback of overdependence upon an anthology is that opportunities for any adjustment to the range of ability, sensitivity, and interest in the typical class are seriously curtailed. Of course, even in a program based solely on the anthology, the teacher can make some adjustment to this range by assigning different selections to different groups of students within the class, and by differentiating the discussion questions or the activities that follow reading. Yet such differentiation is not typical of anthology-limited programs, for the teacher who sees the need for such differentiation would not, in most cases, be committed to such a program in the first place. For a combination of reasons, anthologies tend to be too difficult for the grade levels for which they are designed. Often, a given anthology is appropriate principally for the upper 50 percent of a heterogeneous class.

Most teachers are aware of these various limitations, and even many of those who gear their programs closely to the anthology recognize the need for broad individual reading outside the anthology and the general need to enrich and supplement it. Some teachers use several sets of anthologies in the same class, rather than insisting that all students use the same one.

Organization through a Set of Specified Selections

A plan of organization popular thirty years ago was based on certain selections. Then one might have seen very commonly, in senior high school classes at least, sets of thin volumes of individual books, from *The Courtship of Miles Standish* to *The House of the Seven Gables* and *A Tale of Two Cities.* Certain selections were allocated to each grade level, and entire classes studied them in common. However, this neat and uniform, and rather deadly, method of organizing the year's literature program disappeared, largely because of the appearance of the "omnibus" anthology for each grade, and the majority of teachers turned to the anthology plan just discussed. Certain standard selections, or "classics," however, became attached to the various grades, and tradition has tended to keep them there: *Snowbound, Evangeline,* and *The Courtship of Miles Standish* for seventh and eighth; *Ivanhoe, The Lady of the Lake, Silas Marner, Julius Caesar,* and *A Tale of Two Cities* for ninth and tenth; *Macbeth, Hamlet, The Return of the Native, Our Town* in eleventh and twelfth. A number of these selections have been perpetuated for various grade levels by the anthologies.

The wide distribution of paperbound books has brought a revival of the use of sets of novels, biographies, plays, and books of nonfiction. Many junior high school teachers, especially, have taken advantage of the facilities of the Teen Age Book Club,[1] which offers a convenient monthly plan for buying paperbound books. Some teachers in both junior and senior high school have used sets of paperbound books both for common reading by entire classes and for reading in small groups. Paperbacks have been widely used, too, as the basis for classroom libraries. A number of publishers have made available inexpensive editions of full-length works with study guides and teaching aids. Outstanding among these is Houghton Mifflin's Riverside Literature Series edited by Kenneth S. Lynn and Arno Jewett.

The absence of an over-all pattern for the literature program may indicate in some schools that literature study is haphazard and aimless, with no meaningful context, a series of assignments

[1] 50 West 44th Street, New York 36, N.Y.

or lessons that add up to nothing in the mind of the student. Some teachers, on the other hand, maintain that an overall pattern of themes, topics, or chronology is unduly restricting and distorting, that each selection of literature should be approached as a thing in itself, an individual work of art. Organization by individual selections is probably most effective in advanced senior high school classes in which the students already have developed rich backgrounds and sophisticated insights and are ready to progress through a series of major works.

Organization by Types

One of the oldest and best-known ways of organizing the literature program is through study of the types of literature—novel, short story, poetry, drama, biography, and essay. This plan is especially prevalent at the ninth- and tenth-grade levels, and most of the anthologies for use in those grades are organized by literary types.

There are important advantages in this method. It is neat, orderly, easy to plan and administer, and easily understood by the students. Furthermore, it provides an obvious context in which to teach the skills necessary for reading the various forms of literature.

There are some serious drawbacks, however, in this plan of organization. First, it is easy for the teacher to become preoccupied with technique, with literary craftsmanship—with verse forms and meter, plot construction, dramatic structure, and so forth. Of course, these things have importance, but they should not be stressed at the expense of interest and broader interpretation. Naturally, skillful teachers can avoid this pitfall in the types plan of organization as they can in any other.

Then, too, some of the literary genres do not lend themselves readily to the types approach. This is true of the longer forms—novel, epic, drama, and biography. It is virtually impossible for a class to read more than one of these types during one unit of work. Therefore, the comparing and contrasting essential in the types approach cannot be done except over a long period of time. Teachers—and anthologies—often resort to excerpts from long works, although as material for types study excerpts have obvious failings, since they do not represent artistic wholes. Another drawback is that poetry does not fit well into the types approach. A diet of po-

etry, sustained over several weeks, is too concentrated for many high
school students. Even the most mature readers rarely read poetry
that way.

Organization by Chronological Survey

The chronological survey of literature is ordinarily limited to
courses in the eleventh and twelfth grades, but there it is widespread. Tradition has placed American literature in the eleventh
grade, English literature in the twelfth. In recent years there has
been a trend toward other patterns of organization at these grade
levels, but probably the majority of eleventh- and twelfth-grade
teachers, and certainly the great majority of anthologies for the
two grades, still follow the chronological plan. The principal advantage of the chronological survey lies in the perspective it can
give to the origin and development of forms of literature and to
the growth of the literary tradition as it is related to the development of English and American culture in general. Again, this plan
is orderly, logical, and satisfying to the teacher who thinks it important to teach adolescents the historical development of literature.

A trenchant summary of the disadvantages of the chronological
survey was made by Robert C. Pooley, in an article published more
than two decades ago:

> The grave danger of chronology in literature is the tendency to teach
> the history of literature rather than the literature itself. Facts, dates,
> and details of biography are stressed. Often relatively unimportant
> literature is dragged in to complete the historical picture, or student
> interest is sacrificed to scholarly thoroughness. The early periods in
> English and American literature are difficult and rarely interesting to
> more than a few students, yet they come at the beginning of the course
> when interest is hard to arouse. Furthermore, the chronological plan
> is exceedingly difficult to tie up with the normal voluntary reading of
> students. Only exceptional students will read voluntarily literature
> prior to 1800 with genuine enjoyment and profit.[2]

What is done within the framework of the chronological survey
may differ greatly from teacher to teacher. There is no doubt that

[2] Robert C. Pooley, "Varied Patterns of Approach in the Teaching of Literature,"
English Journal, XXVIII (May 1939), 345.

in terms of student experiences, the chronological survey in many classrooms is "deadly." Many teachers are unable to avoid the "factual error" in teaching literature, as defined by Thomas Clark Pollock:

> . . . the history of a work of literature is not the work of literature. Facts about a poem are not the poem. They may help a student to understand the poem. To the degree that they do, they are important to the teacher; but it is the literary experience itself in which the teacher should be primarily interested. Our literary heritage lies in the *actual*, if in one sense vicarious, *experiences* which literature can communicate. It is still true that the letter killeth, while the spirit giveth life; and we cannot make our literary heritage real to the youth of America through the letter of factualism.[3]

Yet some teachers, even within the context of the chronological survey, are able to avoid this as well as other pitfalls. One description of an enlightened approach to the survey of English literature is given in an article by Dorothy Bratton.[4] Within recent years, many schools have experimented with modest modifications of the traditional surveys. For example, such American writers as Melville, Mark Twain, Thomas Wolfe, Hemingway, and Faulkner, are often studied in the twelfth grade. Many senior courses have also introduced "world literature," involving mainly selections from European writers but occasionally from Oriental, Latin American, or other literature. A few twelfth-grade teachers are even experimenting with chronology in reverse—starting with the present and working backward, rather than vice versa. Certainly, there is merit in this if the aim is to make literature of the past relevant to the concerns of youth today.

Organization by Themes or Topics

During the last several years the plan of organizing the literature program by themes in human experience has gained great impetus, and the "thematic" or "topical" unit has been much discussed in

---

[3] Thomas Clark Pollock, "Transmitting Our Literary Heritage," *English Journal,* XXXI (March 1942), 204.

[4] Dorothy Bratton, "English Literature for the Non-College-Bound," *English Journal,* XLV (February 1956), 84–91.

professional articles. Actually, thematic organization may refer to three different, though closely related, plans: study of a group of selections that have something to do with a broad topic; tracing a particular theme through a group of selections; integration of the language arts—study of literature as well as of writing, speaking, and listening—through a particular theme.

Simple arrangement of selections under a general topic has been common in anthologies, particularly for the junior high school grades, for several years. One recent junior high school anthology, for example, includes these topics: "Animal Kingdom," "Salty Tales," "World of Sports," "Time for Laughter," "Suspense." Another includes: "Animals," "Sports," "Danger and Daring," "Our Scientific World," "Interesting People." In this plan of organization, the topic provides a convenient way of dividing up the selections to be read. The main stress is still on the individual selections, with little concern for the topic itself.

In some units of teaching, the major stress is on a theme of significance to adolescents as it is illuminated by a series of selections. For example, a junior high school group studied as a theme "The Many Faces of Courage," reading to discover how different kinds of courage were exhibited in a group of selections of prose and poetry. A class of seniors studied attitudes toward nature, as expressed in literature, in a unit entitled "Every Common Sight." A series of themes may provide the framework for the year's program in literature, as the following series of five themes did for one ninth-grade class: The Many Faces of Courage; Seeing the Funny Side; Those Hours from Four to Twelve; The Profile of Success; Daring to Be Different.

Another concept of the thematic unit goes beyond the study of literature as such, making the theme the center for the integration of all phases of the language arts—reading, writing, speaking, and listening. This is the point of view expressed in *The English Language Arts in the Secondary School,* prepared by the Commission on the English Curriculum of the National Council of Teachers of English. The volume defines a "unit" as meaning

that varied activities in the language arts are developed around a central theme or purpose, clear and significant to the student. It must be sufficiently broad to involve in some measure all four of the language arts and to permit each individual (1) to work in cooperation with his class and (2) to pursue certain special interests in a wide range of material and experiences suited to his ability.[5]

The chapter on "Building Instructional Units" presents in detail an illustrative unit called "Back-Country America."

In discussing the thematic unit, Virginia Alwin argues:

> They [thematic or topical units] are common sense because they provide context, create a climate, offer a situation in which one can teach the four language arts in an interrelated manner, just as one uses these language arts in the world outside the classroom.[6]

The widely used Scholastic Literature Units,[7] for grades seven through ten, attempt to integrate various aspects of the language arts, with literature as the core, although each of these units is a separate entity and has not been developed as part of a planned sequence. Each unit progresses through three phases. In the first, the students read in common from the unit anthology and engage in related language activities. In the second, small-group reading and activity are featured. The final phase involves individual reading and language work.

One high school English department has developed a "thematic categories curriculum" that is explained as follows: ". . . our curriculum is based on a series of broad themes. These broad themes are handled at each grade level throughout the six-year program, each year increasing the maturity with which the theme is treated."[8] One of the thematic categories, for example, is Conflict, which has these units for the various grades:

---

[5] Commission on the English Curriculum, National Council of Teachers of English, *The English Language Arts in the Secondary School* (New York: Appleton, 1956), pp. 69–70.

[6] Virginia Alwin, "A Setting for the Interrelation of the Language Arts," *English Journal*, XLVII (February 1958), 77.

[7] Stephen Dunning, supervising editor, Scholastic Book Services, 50 West 44th Street, New York 36, N.Y.

[8] Stanley B. Kegler and Rodger Kemp, *A Thematic Categories Curriculum* (Minneapolis: University High School, University of Minnesota, 1962), p. 13.

7. Man's Struggles
8. Man and Nature
9. Man at Sea
10. Man and Society
11. Man and the State
    Americans Abroad
12. Dissent (Satire)
    War
    Alien Views

One great advantage of the thematic unit, no matter which of the three varieties of those just discussed it may represent, is that it permits the teacher to start with aspects of experience that students themselves recognize as important. There is an inherently better chance of interesting students by introducing a theme or topic—sportsmanship, qualities of success, attitudes toward love—than by announcing a unit on poetry or one on the next forty pages in the anthology. Most students are interested in ideas, and a skillfully chosen idea, stated as a theme for study, may serve as a real spark to student motivation.

A second major advantage is that thematic organization provides an excellent opportunity to adjust the necessarily group process of teaching to a room full of individuals often startlingly disparate in their potentialities for emotional and intellectual adventure. Unable to deal profitably with the same selection or series of authors, they still may deal on a feasible level with the same theme or problem.

There are pitfalls to be avoided in the thematic plan of organization, as in any other. The first of these may lie in the selection of the theme. Is the theme significant to the intellectual and esthetic development of the students at a given grade level? This is a key question. Many thematic units probably dwell on fulsome platitudes or on ideas that may be bewitching to the teacher but completely baffling to the students. Though the teacher may have proudly produced a term paper on "The *Carpe Diem* Theme in Elizabethan Lyrics" in one of his graduate courses, the subject may not be appropriate for high school classes. On the other hand, student interest is not a completely reliable criterion either. Hot rods may seem a vital subject to many adolescents but they will not provide a sound basis for a teaching unit.

Another pitfall lies in the selection of material to be read in a certain unit. Once the theme is selected, the teacher's next step is to choose selections of literature that are relevant in developing the theme and appropriate both to the students and to important aims in teaching literature. All these conditions are important; it is not enough that the selections represent a useful kind of propaganda—that they merely "have something to say" about the theme. They must fit into the teacher's broader purposes in teaching literature to a particular group of students.

Attempts to find selections that "fit" a certain theme have sometimes involved teachers in the ludicrous. Teaching Shelley's "To a Skylark" in a unit on "Living in an Air Age," as one teacher did, seems farfetched. The problem of finding material appropriate to the theme may sometimes lead teachers to settle for inferior selections that give no real chance to teach literature or to lead students to higher levels of awareness. Doggerel about going swimming, for example, may be relevant to a unit on sports, but may not be useful in achieving the purposes of teaching poetry to a group of junior high school students.

The thematic unit is rather easily prey, too, to aimlessness or lack of direction. The teacher has to work constantly to keep the program of reading heading somewhere. Younger students, especially, may quickly lose sight of the theme unless the teacher keeps it constantly before them. Discussion of literature in a unit in which not everyone has read the same selections may wander into a directionless, though possibly interesting, morass unless the teacher carefully prepares and structures the discussions. Some teachers have found it helpful to prepare for and assign a discussion a day before it is actually to be held, rather than launch into it impromptu. Some years ago Bertha Handlan wrote an article on guiding discussion of reading in a class where students had read different things, which remains the most helpful reference on the topic.[9]

---

[9] Bertha Handlan, "Group Discussion of Individual Reading," *English Journal*, XXXII (February 1943), 67–74.

Combinations of Approaches

Many experienced teachers combine patterns of organization, of course, and in many well-conceived units of teaching, patterns tend to merge. Frequently, one type—short stories, plays, or poems—may be studied in relation to a theme. Sometimes individual "classics" may be studied in connection with a theme—one tenth-grade class studied *Silas Marner* as the climax of a unit on "The Small Town in Literature." Similarly, it is quite possible to utilize chronological organization at some times in the eleventh or twelfth grade without casting the entire year's program in that mold. Senior English classes might study the classical or romantic period and then examine the contemporary influences of that period, and at other times study types units or thematic units. In some programs, thematic units are organized within the general chronological framework of American or British literature. These five themes furnish the basis for the eleventh-grade course at the Taylor Allderdice High School of Pittsburgh, Pennsylvania: The Puritan Man, Man's Desire to Get Ahead, the Optimistic Romantics, the Darker Romantics, and The Realistic Outlook.[10]

In arguing for an eclectic plan of organization, Walter Loban points out:

A sound program of literature for any semester or year of the secondary school could very well feature a multiple approach; several thematic units, some established classics, at least one modern great book or document, some study of types of literature, and a considerable amount of individual reading with teacher guidance. . . .

The benefits of all four approaches—thematic units, great works of literary art, literary types, and guided individual reading—will be gained. The problems of adolescents can be emphasized in topical or thematic units. The values a literary tradition offers can be highlighted in study devoted to great books. The flexibility of the literary types approach to short stories, essays, poetry, and drama can feature both content and form. Individual interests and abilities can be accom-

---

[10] See Lois Josephs, "Man's Relationship to Nature: A Sub-theme in American Literature," *English Journal*, LI (March 1962), 180–183.

modated with changing classroom libraries that range from *Lou Gehrig, A Quiet Hero* to *War and Peace*.[11]

Evidence that teachers are combining patterns of approach in teaching literature comes from recently published guides and courses of study in English. The eclectic approach is clearly illustrated, for example, in the units outlined in the English guide of Baltimore County, Maryland:[12]

> *Seventh Grade*
> A Laugh a Day
> Adventure Near and Far
> Making the Most of One's Self
> Animals
> Sports and Hobbies
> One-Act Plays
> Enjoying Television, Radio, and Motion Pictures
> *Eighth Grade*
> Man against Nature
> All Manner of People
> Reading Short Stories
> Everybody Loves a Mystery
> Laughing Matter
> Science and Inventions
> Reading Magazines
> *Ninth Grade*
> Frontiers of Courage
> Fun on Your Own
> Old Stories That Live Today
> Characters to Remember (biography)
> Enjoying Narrative Verse
> Enjoying Long Fiction
> (In the senior high school grades, literature and language units are developed separately. Only literature units are listed here.)

[11] Walter Loban, "Teaching Literature: a Multiple Approach," *English Journal,* XLV (February 1956), 78, 91.
[12] *A Curriculum Supplement: Language Arts, Grades 1–12* (Baltimore County Public Schools: 1959, mimeographed).

Tenth Grade
  Fiction
  Poetry
  Nonfiction
  Drama
Eleventh Grade
  America as Seen through the Eyes of Modern Writers
  America's Cornerstone (New England literature)
  The Emergence of the West and the Rise of Realism
  The New South
Twelfth Grade
  Backgrounds of Literature (myths, Bible, legends, epics)
  Masterpieces of British Poetry
  Recurrent Themes in Literature: Good and Evil
                                The Search for the Self
                                The Nature of Tragedy
                                Aspects of Love

The Extensive Phase of the Program

The literature program should include intensive experiences that
come from class study and analysis of selections of literature and
extensive experiences that come from individual reading. The in-
class literature program that does not lead to voluntary out-of-class
reading by many of the students may well be suspect. But the
choice of whether or not to carry on individual reading cannot be
left to the adolescent. Individual reading, as distinct from purely
recreational reading, should be a part of the required work in literature. Individual and extensive reading grows very naturally out of
the topical or thematic pattern in which students first consider together selections related to the topic or theme and then go individually, or in small groups, to other selections suited to their
tastes and abilities but still relevant to the topic or theme. Whatever
the plan of organization, however, individual reading is essential
in promoting reading interests and in providing for individual
tastes and capacities. The individual reading program cannot be
something separate, something divorced from the in-class study of
literature. The fairly widespread requirement of "outside" reading
—involving usually a written or oral book report every six or eight

weeks—profits little if the outside reading program is not planned and individualized. The Tuesday book report session and the mimeographed reporting forms are remembered with distaste by the majority of high school graduates.

The outside, individual reading phase should be as carefully planned as the in-class, intensive phase of the literature program. There are two general ways in which a planned out-of-class program may be set up. First, the teacher may outline several alternatives for independent reading in each of the literature units during the year. These alternatives would be appropriate, of course, to the range of interests and capacities in the class. Provision is made for oral or individual reporting of the reading for each of the units. Second, the teacher may set up with each student an individual reading design that will appropriately supplement and enrich the in-class literature study for the term. Each student's reading design will reflect his interests and his capacities. In this plan, the teacher may hold a conference early in the year with each student in order to plan the reading design most beneficial for him.

In any plan for individual reading some kind of reporting will be needed. Certainly the stereotyped book report on the standardized form is outmoded, and certainly the student should not be required to report formally on everything he reads. At times a general, informal class discussion on a certain category of books—current novels, for example—will serve in lieu of individual reports. The teacher-student conference, when feasible, may cover a great deal of ground. Yet the individual report will occasionally be needed. Jerome Carlin describes a number of possibilities for the book report:

Analysis by a man of the future. In a time capsule or in the ruins on the planet Earth some man of the future finds the book and writes a paper on what it reveals of life of the earlier time.

The diary of a major character. At least three crucial days in the life of the character are dealt with as if they were being summarized in that person's diary.

A letter written in the role of a book character.

Written analysis from a specific standpoint.

Formal book review. The superior student can clip a book review from

a newspaper and use it as a model for a review of the book which
he has read.

The scholarly critical paper. Honors classes may combine research on
"what the critics and authorities think of the author" with critical
opinion on "what I think about those of his books which I have
read." A separate section on the latter is a wise requirement, to
encourage original thinking.

Round-table discussion under a student chairman.

Conversation. Students are paired for conversation about a book.

Oral reading and discussion of brief excerpts.

Significant incident or anecdote. Each student is a speaker on a TV
program about good books. He must interest the audience by telling
only one incident or anecdote from his book—comic, tragic, suspenseful, or otherwise possessed of human interest.

Dramatization. A committee prepares and presents a scene in radio-
script fashion.

Group performance in the style of "This Is Your Life."

Reporter at the scene. While it's happening, a crucial scene from the
book is described on the spot by a TV or radio reporter.

The trial of a major character. Defendant, prosecuting attorney, defense attorney, and witnesses may participate in the case. The charge
should preferably be one of acting unethically, unfairly, or even
unwisely, rather than one of breaking a law.

Interview. A character in the book is interviewed by a reporter or by
a TV interviewer.

The author meets the critics. Three, four, or five students may form a
group. Thus Charles Dickens may defend his *A Tale of Two Cities*
against two critics, as they ask: "Why didn't you save Carton by
some plot twist, giving the book a happy ending? . . ."

Monologue or dialogue. A pupil takes the role of the major character
and in a process of "thinking out loud" talks about the critical situation or problem he is facing at the high point of the story. This
may be varied by using two students in a dialogue.

Sales talk. The student represents himself as a salesman endeavoring
to sell the book to the class by means of a talk on its good points.

Presentation to a publisher. The class is the selection committee for a
publisher or for one of the publishing book clubs. The student
presents his report on a book from the standpoint of whether it

should be published or of whether it should be offered to the book club membership.

Discussion of proposed production conducted by a "playwright" and a "producer."

Outline of a TV or motion-picture version.

Art and other creative work. Book jackets, advertising blurbs, maps, scenes from the story, pictures of characters, posters, and the like are generally useful as supplements, but they do not always serve the purpose of requiring thoughtful consideration of the book. An accompanying analytical talk or paper is desirable if the creative work is intended to serve as a book report.[13]

Of course, the teacher scarcely can expect the students to read extensively and to share reading in various kinds of reports if he himself does not show an enthusiasm for reading and for sharing his reading experiences with his classes. The teacher's comments on the books he is reading or has read are a rich source of motivation for students. Not only is the well-prepared teacher of literature thoroughly grounded in the literary tradition; he also makes an effort to keep abreast of the current scene through active reading of new books and of magazines such as the *Saturday Review,* which presents reviews and a coverage of the literary world.

Approaches to Ranges of Ability

It is not through careless repetition that this book has frequently referred to the problem of a roomful of students startlingly varied in their abilities to deal with literature. The teacher meets that problem at every turn and his first encounter with it, in the flesh, is likely to be a shock, even though "individual differences" was a common refrain in his courses in teaching. The American people, by and large, have decided that all youth should have an education through the high school. And this is a fact of life, though the teacher may occasionally wring his hands over it. Under the roofs of American high schools have gathered the genius and the near

13 Jerome Carlin, "Your Next Book Report . . . ," *English Journal,* L (January 1961), 16–22.

moron, the serenely adjusted and the emotionally upset, the dweller in the shack and the dweller in the mansion. The junior and senior high school English teacher meets all these in his classes, and, though he may sometimes rebel against the task in the healing silence of 4:30 P.M., he cannot quail in the face of the challenge to educate all of these adolescents in the way that is best for them, and therefore best for the commonwealth. In America's unique experiment in mass education through the high school lies a well-spring of this country's strength and greatness. The education of the heterogeneous mass of high school students is both the cultural challenge and the cultural achievement of our time.

For several decades the challenge of heterogeneity has prompted vigorous experimentation with grouping students according to ability and has resulted in recent years in a widespread and steady trend toward ability grouping in high school English classes. Actually, the demand for such grouping has been greater in English than in some other subjects because there is greater heterogeneity in English classes than in most others. Students do not ordinarily enter classes in physics or chemistry, or in advanced algebra, geometry, or trigonometry, unless they have shown some proficiency in earlier courses in mathematics or science. This is not the case in English—nor should it be. It would be a serious error to restrict enrollment in eleventh- and twelfth-grade English, for example, to the able students alone. However, the idealism that opposes such a restriction creates practical problems—those of heterogeneity. One approach to them in senior high school English has been homogeneous grouping or the use of a "track" system, in which, quite frequently, students within each grade are grouped on three or four levels of ability. There are conflicting reports of the results of such grouping, and many problems surround it. Teachers of high-ability groups are usually pleased with the plan; teachers of low-ability groups are much less enthusiastic and, in fact, are often in despair. Discipline problems tend to pile up in the low-ability groups, and such groups lack the inspiration or leavening influence the brighter students can give. In general, success with ability grouping in English seems to depend upon two conditions:

1. *The grouping is actually effective in separating students according to their ability in literature or in other aspects of the English course.* Sometimes, groups may be real only on paper. Problems

of scheduling individual students, carelessness, or lack of guidance may result in many students being out of place. Potential and actual achievement have to be balanced in grouping students. For example, a student with a very high IQ may be basically uninterested and unmotivated in English and may therefore not belong in the highest ability group. A combination of past achievement in English, IQ, and reading ability seems to be the most effective basis on which to group students for work in English.

2. *Once the students are efficiently grouped, the program must be differentiated in each group.* It seems the height of futility to group students at three or four levels and then to offer the same English program at each level. Yet that is what is done in many schools. This practice accounts for many of the problems, disciplinary and otherwise, in lower-ability sections.

However, homogeneous grouping in the English curriculum is not the only, nor necessarily the best, answer to the problem of a range of abilities. In fact, in some schools, particularly small high schools, "track" systems may not be feasible. The teaching of literature can be effectively adjusted to the range of abilities in the ordinary heterogeneous class through a combination of three basic methods:

1. *Differentiation in the discussion or in the activities based on a selection read in common.* Reading of the same selection by all the members of a class does not rule out possibilities of adjusting to different levels of ability. In setting up guide questions for the reading, or in phrasing questions for discussion following the reading, the teacher can keep in mind the various categories of students in his class. Some questions should be beamed to the lowest ability level, some to the highest, some in between.

In working out questions for writing about or discussing a piece of literature, Edward J. Gordon has identified five levels, from simplest to most difficult, according to the ability each level demands: to remember a fact; to prove a generalization that someone else has made; to make one's own generalization; to generalize from a book to its application in life; and to carry over the generalization into one's own behavior.[14]

[14] Edward J. Gordon, "Levels of Teaching and Testing," *English Journal*, XLIV (September 1955), 331.

2. *Grouping within the class.* For many years, teachers in the elementary school have grouped classes for work in reading and other phases of the program. Often, a high school English class, too, may be divided into several groups to read certain selections or sets of selections. This method is common to the Scholastic Literature Units, discussed earlier in this chapter, and the technique is described in detail in an article by James Squire.[15]

3. *Individualization of reading.* At times good programs in literature will feature complete individualization in selections assigned or read. It was pointed out earlier that the thematic or topical unit is especially helpful in providing a core of unity for widely differentiated individual reading.

Use of the last two methods, grouping within the class and complete individualization of reading, will demand, in addition to a supply of appropriate materials, that the teacher be able to assess the "difficulty" of selections. This is not easy, and there are no pat formulas that can be applied to do the job completely. Three major factors must be taken into account when the assessment of difficulty is made.

READING LEVEL. Most experienced teachers can estimate reading levels fairly accurately by skimming through selections. Here, at least, formulas *can* be used. There are many formulas that make it possible to assign reading-grade levels to selections on the basis mainly of vocabulary and sentence complexity. A widely used formula is that worked out by Edgar Dale and Jeanne Chall.[16]

AMOUNT OF INDIRECT EXPRESSION OF IDEAS. How dependent is the selection on symbolism, allegory, and so forth? Obviously, the teacher's own good perception is the only guide here.

AMOUNT OF EXPERIENCE REMOTE FROM THE EVERYDAY LIFE OF THE STUDENT AT A GIVEN GRADE LEVEL. A subjective estimate must be made that is based on assumptions about what "average, everyday experience" would be for adolescents at a certain grade. Naturally, the reader at any age can deal most easily with that which is most familiar.

---

[15] James Squire, "Individualizing the Teaching of Literature," *English Journal,* XLV (September 1956), 314–319.

[16] Described in *Educational Research Bulletin* (February 1948), pp. 37–54.

Literature for Superior Students

The American decision to educate all youth through the high school has brought a concomitant demand to provide properly for the superior students. There has been a common criticism that the needs of "remedial" students have been given undue attention in the public schools. The validity of this criticism can be judged only in terms of individual schools, but it is certain, at any rate, that recent years have brought sharply accelerated interest in the gifted, or superior, students. In literature, the needs of superior students have been met by various applications of the basic procedures for differentiating instruction just discussed. A survey of actual practices of various schools throughout the country shows that the following are the principal ways of providing for superior students in literature:

1. *Ability grouping.* The general trend is toward ability grouping; its attendant problems were just discussed. In English classes that enroll only the students of highest ability, teachers can go far beyond the familiar boundaries of the high school course. Yet in these classes, the plans of organization and methodology tend to be similar to those in the heterogeneous classes. The most successful programs for high-ability students seem to be marked by wide reading of works too mature and difficult for the general run of students, by close analysis of individual works, and by exploration of themes or topics too advanced for average students. In the Portland, Oregon, public schools, superior students are allowed to enroll in "seminars," which carry on the following kinds of projects:

A sophomore project in one school presented the literature of certain high points in the development of Western civilization. For the period of the Greeks, for example, students read *The Iliad,* Euripides' *Trojan Women,* Plato's *Apology,* and supplementary readings in Sophocles, Aeschylus, and Xenephon. . . . In a junior English seminar, students studied contrasts in the philosophies of American writers—for example, the pragmatic approach to life's problems as exemplified by Samuel Sewall and Benjamin Franklin in contrast with the theological approach of

Jonathan Edwards; and the idealism of Whitman and Emerson in contrast with the critical realism of Sinclair Lewis. A senior seminar, aiming to deepen understanding of certain English masterpieces, made a comparative study of similar genres from other periods or countries: for example in the study of *The Canterbury Tales,* students also read *Tristram and Iseult* and *Aucassin and Nicolette,* and even the *Connecticut Yankee in King Arthur's Court,* and in comparison with *Macbeth,* certain Greek tragedies, and plays by Ibsen, Molière, and George Bernard Shaw.[17]

Literature study for gifted students needs to be carefully planned to avoid two common pitfalls.

Superior students should certainly be concerned with structure and form, and they are able to deal with technique in a way impossible in the regular class. Yet they are not a breed apart so far as interests and rewards sought in reading are concerned. It is quite possible for bright students to present glib technical analyses of selections without necessarily developing any expanded interests or any really mature understanding of literature as reconstruction of experience.

There is another closely related danger. In some high-ability classes a number of classics may be "covered"—given a surface reading, without any real understanding or appreciation resulting. Depth rather than coverage should be the goal in classes for superior students.

2. *Elective courses.* In some schools elective courses such as world literature, Shakespeare, and modern literature are provided for able students. In some schools, these electives may be substituted for the regular English course in the eleventh or twelfth grades.

3. *Special group or individual projects within regular classes.* Some teachers have required special advanced work of superior students, either as a substitute for or in addition to the regular class work. Socrates Lagios describes a project in which four superior students in his senior class at the Concord, Massachusetts,

[17] Reported by Marian Zollinger, Supervisor of Language Arts, Portland Public Schools, in a talk at the convention of the National Council of Teachers of English, Minneapolis, Minnesota, November 29, 1957.

High School read eighteen novels, one a week, starting with *Moll Flanders* and ending with *The Old Man and the Sea*.[18] These students were excused from some of the regular class work.

4. *"Honors" work.* A few high schools have experimented with plans in which superior students are exempt from a part of the curriculum in order to work independently. The English teacher, of course, directs projects in literature.

5. *Literary clubs.* Well-guided clubs, functioning as extracurricular activities, have provided rich experiences for able and interested students in some schools.

What selections of literature *do* superior high school students read? A comprehensive answer to this question was offered in the *Illinois English Bulletin* of February 1957.[19] This report gave a composite list of the selections discussed by 315 students, from twenty-five schools, in answering one of two essay questions included in an examination administered by the School and College Study of Admission with Advanced Standing. The selections mentioned by ten or more students are listed below. The number of students discussing the selection is given in parentheses.

World Classics

Homer, *Odyssey.* (12)

American Fiction

Hawthorne, *The Scarlet Letter.* (60)
Wharton, *Ethan Frome.* (56)
Melville, *Moby Dick.* (42)
Howells, *The Rise of Silas Lapham.* (20)
Lewis, *Babbitt.* (19)
Rölvaag, *Giants in the Earth.* (19)
Wouk, *The Caine Mutiny.* (16)
Steinbeck, *East of Eden.* (16)
Steinbeck, *The Grapes of Wrath.* (16)
Wolfe, *Look Homeward, Angel.* (15)

[18] Socrates Lagios, "Challenging the Gifted," *English Journal*, XLVI (November 1957), 501–503.

[19] Albert B. Friedman and R. S. Peterson, "The Reading of Superior Students," *Illinois English Bulletin*, XLIV (February 1957), 1–20.

Fitzgerald, *The Great Gatsby*. (14)
Hemingway, *A Farewell to Arms*. (14)
James, *Portrait of a Lady*. (14)
Porter, K., "Noon Wine." (12)
Hemingway, *The Old Man and the Sea*. (10)

American Drama

Miller, *Death of a Salesman*. (61)
O'Neill, *Emperor Jones*. (20)
O'Neill, *Mourning Becomes Electra*. (18)
O'Neill, *Beyond the Horizon*. (17)
Anderson, M., *Winterset*. (17)
Williams, *The Glass Menagerie*. (12)

American Poetry

T. S. Eliot. (Mentioned by 35 students; 5 poems mentioned.)
Robert Frost. (Mentioned by 33 students; 9 poems mentioned.)
E. A. Robinson. (Mentioned by 10 students; 2 poems mentioned.)

English Fiction

Hardy, *The Return of the Native*. (87)
Galsworthy, *The Man of Property*. (Forsyte Saga) (59)
Austen, *Pride and Prejudice*. (43)
Conrad, *Lord Jim*. (43)
Butler, *The Way of All Flesh*. (32)
Conrad, *Heart of Darkness*. (23)
Hardy, *The Mayor of Casterbridge*. (21)
Huxley, *Brave New World*. (20)
Swift, *Gulliver's Travels*. (20)
Lawrence, *Sons and Lovers*. (17)
Reade, *The Cloister and the Hearth*. (16)
Conrad, *Nostromo*. (14)
Eliot, *The Mill on the Floss*. (14)
Koestler, *Darkness at Noon*. (13)
Brontë, E., *Wuthering Heights*. (12)
Conrad, *The Nigger of the Narcissus*. (11)
Webb, *Precious Bane*. (11)
Joyce, "*Clay*." (11)

Orwell, *1984*. (10)
Thackeray, *Henry Esmond*. (10)
Fielding, *Tom Jones*.

English Drama

Shakespeare, *Hamlet*. (182)
Shakespeare, *Macbeth*. (155)
Shakespeare, *Othello*. (36)
Shakespeare, *Romeo and Juliet*. (20)
Shakespeare, *Antony and Cleopatra*. (13)
Shaw. (Mentioned by 17 students; 8 plays mentioned.)

English Poetry

Browning, R. (Mentioned by 35 students; 8 poems; "My Last Duchess," 16 mentions.)
Pope. (Mentioned by 19 students; 3 poems; "The Rape of the Lock," 16 mentions.)
Tennyson. (Mentioned by 16 students; 6 poems; *Idylls of the King,* 10 mentions.)
Wordsworth. (Mentioned by 12 students; 6 poems.)
Donne. (Mentioned by 12 students; 4 poems.)
Keats, "Ode on a Grecian Urn." (11)
Chaucer, *The Canterbury Tales*. (10)

Greek Drama

Sophocles, *Oedipus Rex*. (102)
Sophocles, *Electra*. (17)
Sophocles, *Antigone*. (12)

French Literature

Flaubert, *Madame Bovary*. (28)
Rostand, *Cyrano de Bergerac*. (21)
Balzac, *Père Goriot*. (16)

Scandinavian Literature

Ibsen, *An Enemy of the People*. (30)
Ibsen, *Hedda Gabler*. (20)
Ibsen, *Ghosts*. (16)

Ibsen, *A Doll's House*. (14)
Undset, *Kristin Lavransdatter*. (13)

Russian Literature

Dostoevski, *Crime and Punishment*. (21)
Tolstoi, *War and Peace*. (15)
Tolstoi, *Anna Karenina*. (15)
Turgenev, *Fathers and Sons*. (10)

ILLUSTRATIVE COURSE IN WORLD LITERATURE. There is a growing trend toward broadening the scope of literature instruction in the senior high school years from American and British literature to world literature, especially that of Western culture. Because of the difficulty of the material, courses in world literature have been designed primarily for able students. The following is an outline of the course in world literature at the Jackson High School, Miami, Florida.

UNIT I: ORIENTATION[20]

I. Objectives
    A. To introduce students to the importance of the study of world literature
    B. To acquaint students with materials and aids to be used in the study of world literature
    C. To acquaint students with class policies and requirements

II. Activities
    A. Class examination of Edward Steichen's *The Family of Man*, with an introduction by Carl Sandburg
    B. Class reading of Albert Einstein's "What I Believe"
    C. Lecture given by librarian on materials available in connection with world literature
    D. Class writing of paragraph expressing reasons for taking the course and conceptions of the importance of its study

---

[20] Designed by Jan Dougherty. Outline used by permission of Miss Dougherty and Barbara A. Goleman, chairman of the Department of English.

UNIT II: THE LITERARY HERO

I. Objectives
- A. To lead students to understand various personal and abstract qualities embodied in heroes of epic literature
- B. To help students to note changes in the attitude toward the hero through the centuries
- C. To identify the tragic hero as an archetype, comparing the tragic hero and the epic hero

II. Activities
- A. Epic hero
  - 1. Speaking and listening
    - a. Class discussion aiming at reviewing previous experiences with mythical and folk heroes
    - b. Panel discussions on the major national epics such as the *Odyssey, Aeneid, Song of Roland, El Cid,* students being divided into groups for such discussions
    - c. Evaluation of panel discussions, comparing panel's ideas with student's own
  - 2. Reading
    - a. Class reading as a whole of the *Iliad*
    - b. Individual reading of national epics in preparation for panel discussions
  - 3. Writing
    - a. Theme on the student's conception of a hero at beginning of unit
    - b. Class notes to be taken on panel discussions and kept in student's world literature notebook
- B. Tragic hero
  - 1. Speaking and listening
    - a. Class discussion of tragic hero; comparison with the epic hero
    - b. Individual oral reports on additional Greek, alternate Shakespearean, or modern tragedy
    - c. Listening to recordings of Euripides' *Medea,* Shakespeare's *Hamlet,* and Arthur Miller's *Death of a Salesman* as examples of the development of the tragic hero and heroine
  - 2. Reading
    - a. Outside reading in preparation for oral report

  b. Class reading of Sophocles' *Antigone*, relating it to
     the Oedipus myth
3. Writing
  a. Class notes on individual play reports
  b. Paper on play read outside class
  c. Theme written during class on topics from *Hamlet* or
     Death of a Salesman

III. Materials
   A. Suggested plays for reports
      1. Aeschylus, *Agamemnon, Seven against Thebes, Prometheus Bound*
      2. Euripides, *Orestes*
      3. Sophocles, *Oedipus Rex, Oedipus at Colonus*
      4. Shakespeare, *King Lear, Othello*
      5. O'Neill, *The Hairy Ape, Mourning Becomes Electra*
      6. Williams, *The Glass Menagerie*
   B. References
      1. Hamilton, Edith, *The Greek Way, The Roman Way*
      2. Wendell, Barrett, *Traditions of European Literature from
         Homer to Dante*
      3. Hook, Sidney, *The Hero in History*
      4. Sewall, Richard B., *The Vision of Tragedy*

UNIT III: THE MIDDLE AGES

 I. Objectives
   A. To provide students with an appreciation of the vast
      changes occurring in the literature of this time
   B. To introduce the class to Dante and Chaucer as two great
      transition writers
   C. To lead the students to an appreciation of symbolic writing
      such as the allegory

II. Activities
   A. Speaking and listening
      1. Listening to Ciardi's recording of Dante's *Inferno*,
         Cantos I–VIII
      2. Listening to segment of Chaucer's *Prologue* in Middle
         English
   B. Reading
      1. Reading in common of Dante's *Inferno* (translation by
         John Ciardi)

2. Reading for reports on one of the *Canterbury Tales*
3. Reading of selection from Adams' *Mont Saint Michel and Chartres*, pictures of two cathedrals to be shown

C. Writing
1. Notes on background discussion of Middle Ages
2. Written report on:
   a. One of *Canterbury Tales*
   b. Architecture of the Middle Ages
   c. The Scholastics—Roger Bacon, St. Thomas Aquinas

UNIT IV: SATIRE AND MAN'S SEARCH FOR UTOPIA

I. Objectives
   A. To introduce class to general characteristics of satire
   B. To define the term "utopia," its implications in man's literature, and its relation to satire in literature
   C. To help the students analyze critically similar themes that reappear through the ages

II. Activities
   A. Speaking and listening
      1. Listening to sections of Swift's *Gulliver's Travels* read by Alec Guinness
      2. Panel discussions on books read outside class on general topic of satire
   B. Reading
      1. Reading designed to trace man's search for the ideal society
         a. Selection from Plato's *Republic*
         b. Selection from Sir Thomas More's *Utopia*
         c. Selection from Rousseau's *The Social Contract*
      2. Reading in common of Voltaire's *Candide*
      3. Outside reading of books demonstrating techniques of satire and man's idea of a positive or negative utopia
         a. *Gulliver's Travels*, Jonathan Swift
         b. *Brave New World*, Aldous Huxley
         c. *1984*, George Orwell
         d. *Lord of the Flies*, William Golding
   C. Writing
      1. Note taking on panel discussions on above books
      2. Theme on one specific aspect of book read outside class

UNIT V: MAN LOOKS AT THE DEVIL

I. Objective:
   To lead the class in an investigation of the treatment of the Devil in various art forms

II. Activities
   A. Speaking and listening
      1. Discussion of student's previous acquaintance with the Devil in any art form
      2. Tracing of Faust legend in music by listening to sections of Gounod's opera *Faust* and Berlioz's *Damnation of Faust*
   B. Reading
      1. Reading in common of Goethe's *Faust*, Part One
      2. Outside reading of related selections
         a. *The Tragic History of Dr. Faustus*, Christopher Marlowe
         b. *Peer Gynt*, Henrik Ibsen
         c. *Devil's Disciple*, G. B. Shaw
         d. Short stories on the Devil—any three
         e. Devil in poetry
         f. *Doctor Faustus*, Thomas Mann
   C. Writing
      Theme on Goethe's philosophy as expressed in *Faust*

UNIT VI: THE DEVELOPMENT OF THE NOVEL

I. Objectives
   A. To help students appreciate the novel as an art form
   B. To lead students to an awareness of how national traits influence the style of the novelist
   C. To define for the students terms, styles, and trends in connection with their study of the novel as a literary form
   D. To foster a better understanding of the use of symbolism in the novel

II. Activities
   A. Reading
      1. Reading in common of modern short novels from *Six Great Modern Short Novels* (Dell Publishing Company,

paperback)—*The Dead* by James Joyce, *The Overcoat* by Nikolai Gogol, and *The Bear* by William Faulkner
2. Outside reading of a novel of the student's choice from the following list of authors
   a. English—Conrad, Hardy, Emily Brontë
   b. French—Balzac, Hugo, Flaubert, Dumas
   c. Russian—Tolstoi, Dostoevski, Chekhov

B. Writing
Report on novel, tracing author's central theme

UNIT VII: YOUTH—THE SEARCH FOR UNDERSTANDING

I. Objectives
   A. To examine the modern trend of writers to use adolescents to express the isolation, confusion, and searching of their adult counterparts
   B. To note the underlying philosophies of modern writers as expressed through their adolescent characters

II. Activities
   A. Reading
      1. Reading in common of John Knowles's *A Separate Peace*
      2. Reading outside of class of one of the following:
         a. *Huckleberry Finn*, Mark Twain
         b. *Cress Delahanty*, Jessamyn West
         c. *The Heart Is a Lonely Hunter*, Carson McCullers
         d. *To Kill a Mockingbird*, Harper Lee
         e. *Portrait of the Artist as a Young Man*, James Joyce
   B. Speaking
      Panel discussions on the above books, noting similarities in theme and stylistic approach

Literature for the Slow and Reluctant

The gifted student presents a challenge that deserves the best efforts of any teacher. Perhaps more conspicuous, however, as a problem in the everyday life of the teacher is the student at the opposite end of the spectrum. Certainly, he should not receive an undue amount of the teacher's attention. On the other hand, the poor student should not merely be tolerated or ignored as long as he is not a discipline problem—which he may be rather frequently. His literary education is important, too, though his literary achievement may never be very high.

The completely unresponsive students in the heterogeneous class, or those students who tend to congregate in the lower ability sections in homogeneous groups, may be of three types: the student who has a specific disability in reading—the "remedial" reader—whose problem may be solved if he gets the remedial help that he needs; it is not, however, within the scope of this volume (nor is it necessary, because a large amount of professional literature exists on the subject) to deal with the problems of the retarded reader; the "slow learner"—the student with low mental ability; and the "reluctant" or basically negative student—lack of mental ability may not be his problem; rather, he has decided that such things as literature (or anything else fitting into the category labeled "Culture") have no value or are for the haughty, or "hoity-toity," group to which he does not belong. These students often may come from families in the low socioeconomic category.

After a year of visiting schools throughout the country, made possible by a Ford Foundation grant, A. J. Beeler identified some principles that seem to underlie successful planning of work for slow-learning students. Several of these principles are applicable to the teaching of literature:

> activities as a whole must be simpler than those planned for average and above-average classes;
> plans should be clear and specific;
> the continuity of experience should be preserved; and
> demonstration and all "seeing" devices should be used extensively.[21]

In planning literature study for slow learners, teachers will have to ignore traditional patterns. Much of the difficulty teachers have with low-ability groups comes from the attempt to impose on them literature programs designed for average and above-average students. The problem of appropriate materials is a press-

---

[21] A. J. Beeler, *Providing for Individual Differences in English* (Champaign, Ill.: National Council of Teachers of English, 1957), p. 7. (Originally published in the *Kentucky English Bulletin*.)

ing one. Certainly, the standard anthologies are hardly useful with low-ability groups. Realizing this, some teachers have, in desperation, virtually given up altogether the teaching of literature to slow groups, stressing, instead, exercises in reading manuals and workbooks. Though this type of activity is important, literature study need not be abandoned in low-ability groups, but the teacher should realize that chronological study, reading of "classics," and analysis of types will be of little avail. Instead, short and very simple topical units—such as "Adventure at Sea" and "Brave People"—furnish the most fruitful approach. In such units, some of the junior novels and biographies can be used as well as such special series as the Landmark Books of Random House, the American Adventure Series of Harper & Row, or the Teen-Age Tales of D. C. Heath and Company.

A ninth-grade program in literature for less able students might be organized, for example, around the following units:

Stories People Talk About—retelling of famous myths, legends, American folk tales. Much use of recordings, films, pictures, and oral reading by the teacher and invited guests.

People Who Were Different—short, simple biography and nonfiction featuring individualism, idiosyncrasy, people who overcame handicaps.

The Smooth and the Not So Smooth—teen-age relations, school and social life, getting along—fiction and nonfiction.

Strange Things Happen—the weird and the grotesque in poetry, short stories, and nonfiction.

Western Days—reading of short selections nad common reading of Jack Schaefer's *Shane*.

Audio-visual aids, especially recorded readings of verse and fiction, have particular importance in classes of slow learners. Drama, especially one-act plays and television plays, is popular in slow classes. Paperback collections of TV plays may be very useful.

Traditional patterns in literature courses, especially those for the eleventh and twelfth grades, and the anthologies for those years, are geared largely to relatively able students and those planning to go to college. Planning literature study for general or vocational curriculums in these grades has been a major problem.

At the Senior High School of Elkhart, Indiana, Dorothy Kelly and Ada H. Sickels have designed a course in "Modern Literature" that is offered as an elective in the senior year to students not preparing for college. A brief outline of the course is given below:

MODERN LITERATURE; ELKHART, INDIANA, SENIOR HIGH SCHOOL

(Each student is charged a fee of $1.50 per semester for the purchase of books for a classroom library. These books are used in the classroom, on a sort of reading laboratory plan, and are not taken from the room except in unusual instances—following a student's long absence, for example.)

Unit I—Magazine Study (6 weeks)
  A. Each student studies twelve individual magazines, in various categories, and submits a written report on each, following criteria discussed and established in class.
  B. Small groups of students select one type of magazine for study. Each group makes an oral report to the rest of the class.
  C. Each student then selects one specific magazine for study, using a number of issues of the magazine. A written report is made, based on an outline furnished by the teacher.
  D. Written reports on ten short stories and five articles, read outside of class, are required.

Unit II—Novels (6 weeks)
  A. Carefully selected modern novels, from two to five copies of each, are available in the classroom library. Each student reads two novels during class time. Students reading the same book sit together at tables for easy conference as the reading proceeds, and all books are read by at least two students. Group oral reports, following an outline supplied by the teacher, are given on the second book each student reads.
  B. Each student is required to read two novels (approved by the teacher) outside class and to make written reports based on an outline supplied by the teacher.

Unit III—The Movies (6 weeks)
  A. A shelf of reference books supplies a variety of information concerning the moving-picture industry, the arts and crafts

that contribute to it, and the people who have been responsible for its growth. There are books on movie personalities and a good many clippings from magazines, including reviews of current movies.

B. Each student writes a critical review of a movie he has seen. An effort is made to have all students view the same movie so that the class members may discuss it together.

C. Chapters from reference books are assigned to individuals to report on orally.

D. The out-of-class assignment is the reading of a book from which a movie has been made and which movie the student has seen. He writes a comparative study of the two.

Unit IV—Biography (6 weeks)

A selection of biographies is available in the classroom library and the requirements and procedures are much the same as for the novel reading: two books read in class, and one read outside class. The students give group oral reports on the books read in class, and a written report on the biography read outside.

Unit V—Radio and Television (4 weeks)

A. Dictation and note taking from *Radio from Start to Finish* by Reck serves as a good introduction to the unit. Other books used are *TV and Radio in American Life*, Marx; *TV Story*, Floherty; *Introduction to Television*, Hylander and Harding.

B. Oral reports are given on parts of reference books and on interviews with local radio and TV officials.

C. The students write critical reviews of radio and television programs, and read professional reviews.

D. Several panel discussions are held on such special topics as "Pay TV."

E. The class visits local radio and TV stations.

Unit VI—Drama (5 weeks)

A. Several collections of modern plays, as well as singly bound plays, are in the classroom library.

B. The major requirement is the reading of four plays in class, with oral or written reports.

C. There is oral reading of significant scenes.

D. The school drama coach gives special lectures.

Unit VII—Newspapers (3 weeks)

A. Books on journalism and the newspaper are part of the classroom library. Essentials of a newspaper and its publication are studied.

B. Comparison is made of the handling of the same story by various newspapers. "News value" is discussed.

C. Feature material and advertising is studied, as well as news stories.

D. The class visits the local newspaper office and plant.

E. Several films are shown.

The course, as it is outlined here, no doubt includes some non-essential items and omits some valuable ones. It is offered as an example of recent attempts to make the senior high school literature program realistic and to incorporate in it the study of mass media of communication and entertainment.

The reluctant or negative student, whose problems may lie in attitude rather than ability, can be a greater vexation to the teacher than the student of low ability. There are no magic ways of making literature suddenly meaningful and enchanting to this type of student. One of the most perceptive discussions of the reluctant student is found in an article by Morris Finder,[22] who writes of his experiences in teaching English to high school students from the low socioeconomic group from which many of the "reluctant" students come. Finder points out, as many others have, that the high school curriculum tends to be oriented to the middle class and its values, often making the student who is not of the middle class feel that he is an outsider—not really involved in the class's work. Finder offers three criteria that may be helpful in planning literary experiences for the reluctant student:

First, the topic involves language and experiences that are common to all social-class cultures. Activities that call upon vocabulary and experiences involving golf, seashore vacations, Deepfreezes, and heirlooms are inappropriate. . . . But topics involving television, human relations, vocations, and current events are good choices. . . .

A second criterion is that the learning experiences are intrinsically interesting to the pupils. Since our lower-class child is conditioned to

[22] Morris Finder, "Teaching English to Slum-dwelling Pupils," *English Journal,* XLIV (April 1955), 199–204.

seek immediate satisfactions, we will not engage his interest unless the course work has what for him is on-the-spot interest.

A third criterion is that the pupil find immediate significance in his learning experience. Because he lives for today, his school work must have significance for today. Of course, immediate significance does not exclude universal significance. What "Stopping by Woods on a Snowy Evening" tells us about the conflict between our desires and our obligations is as true today as always.

The type of student Finder discusses may at times turn into the incorrigible hoodlum. But teachers need to avoid the human urge to give up on him too soon. Often he will respond to an unsentimental, relaxed approach to beauty and aspiration. Literature study may be for him one of the only places where this is possible.

APPENDIX
REFERENCES ON TEACHING LITERATURE IN
THE JUNIOR AND SENIOR HIGH SCHOOL

Criticism of Literature for Adolescents and of Commonly Taught Authors and Selections

Alm, Richard S., "The Glitter and the Gold," *English Journal,* XLIV (September 1955), 315–322, 350.
Evaluates junior novels that deal with the personal problems of adolescents.

Ballet, Arthur H., "In Our Living and in Our Dying," *English Journal,* XLV (May 1956), 243–249.
Explores the significance and appeal of Thornton Wilder's *Our Town.*

Beck, Warren, "Clouds upon Camelot," *English Journal,* XLV (November 1956), 447–454.
Reappraises *The Idylls of the King* and their place in the high school program.

Carlsen, G. Robert, "To Sail Beyond the Sunset," *English Journal,* XLII (September 1953), 297–302.
Critically examines adventure novels for adolescents.

Carpenter, Frederic I., "The Adolescent in American Fiction," *English Journal,* XLVI (September 1957), 313–319.
Analyzes adult novelists who write of adolescence—J. D. Salinger, Jessamyn West, Carson McCullers, Mark Twain, and others.

Chute, Marchette, "On the Pleasure of Meeting Chaucer," *English Journal,* XLV (October 1956), 373–380.
Explores affectionately the possibilities of the *Canterbury Tales* for reading in high school.

Cotter, Janet M., *"The Old Man and the Sea:* An 'Open' Literary Experience," *English Journal,* LI (October 1962), 459–463.
Offers a variety of suggestions in presenting the book and guiding the reading of it.

Crabbe, John K., "On the Playing Fields of Devon," *English Journal,* LII (February 1963), 109–111.

Reviews John Knowles's novel, *A Separate Peace,* and identifies problems of teaching it.

Cummings, Sherwood, "What's in *Huckleberry Finn?*" *English Journal,* L (January 1961), 1–8.

Dean, Leonard, *"Macbeth* and Modern Criticism," *English Journal,* XLVII (February 1958), 57–67.
Scholarly synthesis of recent criticism, furnishing fresh insights into the play.

———, *"Julius Caesar* and Modern Criticism," *English Journal,* L (October 1961), 451–456.

Edwards, Margaret A., "How Do I Love Thee?" *English Journal,* XLI (September 1952), 335–340.
Critical discussion of junior love stories.

———, "Let the Lower Lights Be Burning," *English Journal,* XLVI (November 1957), 461–469.
Discusses the functions of junior novels in the literature program.

Goldstone, Herbert, "The Question of Scott," *English Journal,* XLVI (April 1957), 187–195.
An analysis of Scott's method and an appraisal of *Ivanhoe* and *The Lady of the Lake.*

Gurko, Leo, "The Heroic Impulse in *The Old Man and the Sea,"* *English Journal,* XLIV (October 1955), 377–382.
A penetrating explication of Hemingway's Nobel Prize winner, giving insight into its levels of meaning.

Heilman, Robert, "Return to Raveloe: Thirty Years After," *English Journal,* XLVI (January 1957), 1–10.
A favorable analysis of the significance of *Silas Marner* and its place in the high school program.

Jennings, Frank G., "Literature for Adolescents—Pap or Protein?" *English Journal,* XLV (December 1956), 526–531.
A scathing examination of junior fiction; condemns the "over-innocuous" quality of teen-age literature.

Marcus, Fred H., *"The Scarlet Letter:* The Power of Ambiguity," *English Journal,* LI (October 1962), 449–458.
Generally treats the technique of the novel with specific discussion of structure and themes.

Owen, Charles A., Jr., "Structure in 'The Ancient Mariner,'" *College English,* XXIII (January 1962), 261–267.

Discusses three structural elements that develop significant inter-relationships that help to define the meaning of the poem.

Patterson, Emma L., "The Junior Novels and How They Grew," *English Journal*, XLV (October 1956), 381–387.
Traces the rise of the junior novel.

Petitt, Dorothy, "A Search for Self-Definition: The Picture of Life in the Novel for the Adolescent," *English Journal*, XLIX (December 1960), 616–626.
Identifies twenty-five popular novels offering valid assumptions about life, all having the common theme of the adolescent search for identity.

Stange, G. Robert, "Dickens and the Fiery Past: *A Tale of Two Cities* Reconsidered," *English Journal*, XLVI (October 1957), 79–89.
An incisive appraisal of a commonly taught novel.

Approaches in Teaching Literature

Bogart, Max, "Literature and the Humanities Ideal," *Educational Leadership*, XX (January 1963), 230–233.
Discusses literature as the vital link in preserving and communicating the humanistic tradition.

Bratton, Dorothy, "English Literature for the Non-College Bound," *English Journal*, XLV (February 1956), 84–91.
The "diary" of a twelfth-grade English teacher, showing how flexibility is possible within the chronological survey.

Broening, Angela M., "Development of Taste in Literature in the Senior High School," *English Journal*, LII (April 1963), 273–287.
An impressive review of the literature on the subject; includes factors, materials, and methods affecting taste.

Burton, Dwight L., "Literature in the Topical Unit," *English Journal*, XLII (December 1953), 497–501.
Some of the pitfalls and some of the possibilities in organizing literature study by topical or thematic units.

Carlin, Jerome, "This I Believe—about the Essay," *English Journal*, LI (September 1962), 403–411.
Offers specific suggestions for teaching the modern essay.

Ciardi, John, "Robert Frost: The Way to the Poem," *Saturday Review* (April 12, 1958), pp. 13–15, 65.

A meticulous explication of Frost's "Stopping by Woods on a Snowy Evening" and some excellent discussion of the use of symbols and metaphor in poetry.

Dunning, Stephen, "Toward Maturity in Judging Fiction," *English Journal*, XLIX (January 1960), 22–26.
Illustrates the discussion of the novel in a low-ability class with Jack Schaefer's *Shane*.

Early, Margaret J., "Stages of Growth in Literary Appreciation," *English Journal*, XLIX (March 1960), 161–167.
Discusses three major stages in literature appreciation and their implications for the teacher.

Evans, Dean H., "Individualized Reading—Myths and Facts," *Elementary English*, XXXIX (October 1962), 580–583.
Explains theory and practices of individualized reading supported by recent research data.

Finder, Morris, "Teaching English to Slum-Dwelling Students," *English Journal*, XLIV (April 1955), 199–204.
A realistic discussion of principles, as well as specific materials and procedures, of teaching English to those whose backgrounds tend to make them "reluctant" students.

Friedrich, Gerhard, "A Teaching Approach to Poetry," *English Journal*, XLIX (February 1960), 75–81.
Discusses and illustrates how a given form determines the poem's meaning.

Gordon, Edward J., "Levels of Teaching and Testing," *English Journal*, XLV (September 1955), 330–334.
Ways in which the teacher can structure class discussion of literature so as to stimulate students of various levels of ability.

————, "Teaching Students to Read Verse," *English Journal*, XXXIX (March 1950), 149–154.
Ways in which students can be taught an understanding of connotation of words, of imagery, and of metaphor—and of tempo, tone color, and inflection in oral interpretation.

Handlan, Bertha, "Group Discussion of Individual Reading," *English Journal*, XXXII (February 1943), 67–74.
Though not "recent," this is the best reference on guiding discussion when students have read many different selections.

Hook, J. N., *The Teaching of High School English* (New York: Ronald, 1950), Chaps. 5–7.

These chapters define six basic approaches in teaching literature and apply them to fiction, poetry, drama, and nonfiction.

Hunt, Kellogg W., "Getting into the Novel," *English Journal*, L (December 1961), 601–606.

Revitalizes the stock questions put to students in the discussion of novels. Makes particular reference to *Pride and Prejudice* and *The Return of the Native*.

Joll, Leonard W., "Developing Taste in Literature in the Junior High School," *Elementary English*, XL (February 1963), 183–188.

Discusses studies related to the development of literary taste in junior high school students and promising practices used to develop literary tastes at this level.

Loban, Walter, "Teaching Literature: A Multiple Approach," *English Journal*, XLV (February 1956), 75–78.

Presents a plan for organizing the term's work in literature on an eclectic basis.

————, Margaret Ryan, and James R. Squire, *Teaching Language and Literature* (New York: Harcourt, 1961), Chaps. 6, 7, 12.

Thorough discussions of the development of literary appreciation and of teaching approaches.

MacLeish, Archibald, "Why Do We Teach Poetry?" *Atlantic Monthly*, III CC (March 1956), 48–53.

A plea for vital teaching and reading of poetry, not teaching *about* poetry.

Ojala, William T., "Thematic Categories as an Approach to Sequence," *English Journal*, LII (March 1963), 178–185.

Illustrates the thematic-categories curriculum featuring thematic units based on literature with units presented in grades seven through twelve.

Perrine, Laurence, "The Nature of Proof in the Interpretation of Poetry," *English Journal*, LI (September 1962), 393–398.

Discusses the two major criteria used for judging any interpretation of a poem.

Reeves, Ruth, "The Gifted Student in the Literature Class," *English Journal*, XLV (November 1956), 462–469.

Discusses ways of helping able students in unselected classes through regular classwork, small-group work, and individual attention.

Rose, Elizabeth, "Teaching Poetry in the Junior High School," *English Journal*, XLVI (December 1957), 540–550.
A very specific discussion of principles, techniques, and materials.

Rosenblatt, Louise, "The Acid Test for Literature Teaching," *English Journal*, XLV (February 1956), 66–74.
Analyzes the "literary transaction" and suggests ways in which teachers can help students to truly experience a selection, not merely learn about it.

———, "Literature: The Reader's Role," *English Journal*, XLIX (May 1960), 304–310, 315.
Discusses literature as a social and personal kind of experience.

Ryan, Margaret, *Teaching the Novel in Paperback* (New York: Macmillan, 1963).
One of the books in the Macmillan paperback series; discusses plans for organizing study of the novel and presents study guides for several novels in paperback.

Shaffer, Virginia, "They Can Take It," *English Journal*, XLI (December 1952), 526–530.
A successful teacher identifies principles and describes techniques for teaching literature to low-ability students.

Sheridan, Marion C., "Teaching a Novel," *English Journal*, XLI (January 1952), 8–14.
Procedures in group reading of a novel, illustrated with *The Return of the Native*.

Squire, James, "Individualizing the Teaching of Literature," *English Journal*, XLV (September 1956), 314–319.
Discusses ways in which unity can be maintained and common reading carried on at the same time that adjustments are made to students of varying abilities.

INDEX